Small Dog Savvy

The Complete Training and Behavior Guide for Your Little Sidekick

Kate Naito, CDBC, CPDT-KA

Publishing

Wenatchee, Washington U.S.A.

Small Dog Savvy
The Complete Training and Behavior Guide for Your Little Sidekick
Kate Naito, CDBC, CPDT-KA

Dogwise Publishing
A Division of Direct Book Service, Inc.
403 South Mission Street, Wenatchee, Washington 98801
1-509-663-9115, 1-800-776-2665
www.dogwisepublishing.com / info@dogwisepublishing.com

Library of Congress Cataloging-in-Publication Data
Names: Naito, Kate author
Title: Small dog savvy : the complete training and behavior guide for your
    little sidekick / Kate Naito, CDBC, CPDT-KA.
Description: Wenatchee, Washington, U.S.A. : Dogwise Publishing, [2026] |
    Includes bibliographical references and index. | Summary: "Small dogs of
    any breed can be an unparalleled joy to live with, but only if you're
    small dog savvy. Once you understand what makes these little canines
    tick, as well as how to meet their mental and emotional needs, you can
    build a loving, lasting relationship unlike any other. Identifiers: LCCN 2025049058
(print) | LCCN 2025049059 (ebook) | ISBN
    9781617813016 paperback | ISBN 9781617813023 ebook
Subjects: LCSH: Dogs--Behavior--Popular works | Dogs--Training--Popular
    works | Toy dogs--Behavior--Popular works | Toy dogs--Training--Popular
    works | Terriers--Behavior--Popular works | Terriers--Training--Popular
    works
Classification: LCC SF433 .N35 2026 (print) | LCC SF433 (ebook)
LC record available at https://lccn.loc.gov/2025049058
LC ebook record available at https://lccn.loc.gov/2025049059

ISBN 9781617813016   Printed in the U.S.A.

Dedication

To Bonnie, Jim, and Jun for their unwavering
support of my Chihuahua addiction.

Table of Contents

More Praise for

Small Dog Savvy

Size Matters! Finally, small dogs get the love and attention that they deserve in *Small Dog Savvy,* by Kate Naito. There's so much good information here, but I especially love the sections that dispel the myths about little dogs, and help us understand what it's like to live in a world of giants. Well done!

Patricia McConnell, PhD, CAAB, author *of For the Love of a Dog* and a new novel, *Away To Me*

Small Dog Savvy is a book dog owners/guardians/trainers/consultants of dog of all sizes should read. As a "big" dog guardian myself and canine behavior consultant I am ashamed to admit I never really put much thought into making small dogs more comfortable with things like being picked up or putting harness on. Sure, I've stopped think about it from a puppy's' prospective that the world is a large place, but I am thankful for this book pointing out we can and should do more for our small dog friends. Having big or small dogs shouldn't change the most fundamentally important thing we can offer our dogs—agency. Just because a dog is 5lbs or even 15lbs does not mean that they shouldn't have more say in what happens to them through their day to day lives. *Small Dog Savvy* will help dog guardians and professionals working with all sizes and breeds do better by our furry best friends. After all if a large strange human picked me up without my content I would probably show my teeth too! Lets give our small dogs back that agency they so deserve.

Karen Chapdelaine CDBC, ADT, CPDT-KA, FFCP, DN-CET, owner of The Timeless Dog, LLC

I didn't expect to love *Small Dog Savvy* as much as I did. After all, I don't have a small dog. This book made me stop and rethink what it's actually like to be a small dog in a very big world. While the focus is on small dogs, the observations and strategies apply to all dogs—and to anyone who wants to be a better observer, handler, or advocate for them. I found myself learning new ways to notice what small dogs are communicating and how easily their needs can be overlooked. Kate Naito offers practical, thoughtful solutions to common challenges, with clear examples that feel realistic and doable. I also appreciated how the book is organized—it's easy to flip through when you're looking for something specific, and just as easy to sit down and really read. This is the kind of book you keep close at hand. I already know it's going to have a spot on my shelf—one at my veterinary hospital and another at my training facility. It's a book I didn't realize I was missing.

Linda Randall, DVM, KPA CTP, Tag Teach Level 3

A little book with BIG heart! Jam-packed with exercises, analogies, science and training tips, this is the book every well meaning guardian of a little dog needs.

Jenny Rossi, CPDT-KA, FDM

Introduction
Little Dog, Big Personality

I have a confession to make. Against my better judgment, despite the wishes of friends and family, and with complete disregard for my neighbors ... I am a Chihuahua collector.

I never meant for it to be this way. I'd long heard about the perils and pitfalls of little dogs. They bark, they bite, they spin in circles and bounce off the walls. Step on them and you'll break their toothpick toes, hug them and you'll flatten their brittle bodies. Not only that, but they also live forever, torturing their owners (as well as postal workers, neighbors, and visitors) for fifteen years *or more*. Wouldn't twelve years with a sturdy, smiling Lab be a better emotional investment?

But if you're reading this book, you've already realized that there is something uniquely fulfilling about life with little dogs. Watch a Papillon racing through an agility course, or a Toy Poodle doing tricks, and it's clear these gutsy little pups are special. Every time you fall asleep on the couch with a Maltese in the crook of your arm, all your problems seem to melt away. And when you come home to find your napping Dachshund peacefully nestled among the stuffing of a just-murdered pillow, you're more inclined to laugh (and grab that photo op) than yell.

Small dogs of any breed can be an unparalleled joy to live with, but only if you're small dog savvy. Once you understand what makes these little canines tick, as well as how to meet their mental and emotional needs, you can build a loving, lasting relationship unlike any other.

By following the guidelines in the following chapters, you will ensure that you're bringing out the absolute best in your canine companion. This is true whether your dog is an impressionable puppy or a grizzled senior; whether you're looking to prevent problem behaviors from day one, or you're already in over your head with behavior issues.

How this book is organized

The chapters are organized to be read one after the other. Although you may be able to skip certain sections that don't pertain to your dog, you'll find that the later chapters refer back to the foundational exercises in the earlier chapters. I recommend reading Chapters 1 to 7 in their entirety. This ensures that:

- You and your little one have a relationship built on mutual trust.

- You have strategies for both doggie and human politeness in your day-to-day life.

- Your dog has learned foundational skills such as recall, leash walking, and stay as they relate to your daily needs.

Chapter 8 takes a deep dive into behavioral issues. You may skip the sections of this chapter that don't relate to your dog. And then, let's not forget to have fun! Chapter 9 shows you some simple ways to keep your small dog's days enriched and active, using games and sport activities.

If you are a new puppy owner, consider the guidelines and activities in this book as a proactive prevention program to ensure that you and your little one will feel comfortable in all aspects of your daily life together. Even a puppy with a prestigious pedigree will have quirks, preferences, and challenges as he matures, so getting your puppy started with a foundation of trust and clear communication will set you up for lifelong success. As the months pass, you can gradually teach your little dog essential manners and nip any behavioral issues in the bud.

For the new adopter of an older puppy or dog, remember that no dog—or human, for that matter—is perfect. Your dog may have rough edges to smooth out, fears to overcome, or manners to learn. I have always adopted adult dogs, and even for me, the first month can be emotionally and financially draining, physically demanding ("She needs to go outside *again*?"), and disruptive to my lifestyle and routine. If you're feeling overwhelmed, it's fine to take this book one chapter at a time. Simply by working on the trust-building activities covered in the first three chapters, you will have a number of tools that will enable you to tackle Chapters 4 to 9 when you're ready.

For the guardian who has been dealing with little dog issues for a while: take a few deep breaths, as both you and your dog have probably been tense for quite some time. Your goal may be to jump into Chapter 8, Aggression and Reactivity in Small Dogs, but don't pass over the previous seven chapters. They will make the behavior modification possible. Behavior protocols take time, consistency, and patience to see results. It's a process that asks you to be compassionate toward your dog, but also toward yourself. Having adopted dogs with behavioral issues over the years, I've lived and worked through all of these protocols myself. I know from experience that success depends on following the steps methodically and patiently. However, training doesn't occur in an emotional vacuum. While you'll feel uplifted and optimistic to see your dog's progress, you may also feel frustrated or confused at times. This is normal.

Be kind to yourself as you navigate the training steps in this book. If you need to take a break, please do. If you are feeling at a dead end, reach out to a qualified professional for help. (More on how to locate one in Chapter 1.) Depending on the severity of your dog's issues, this book may provide you with all the tools you need to have a content, polite little dog. Or, it can lay a framework for understanding your dog and his behavior, and from there, you might benefit from the tailored assistance of a professional in your area or even online.

For the professional dog trainer or behavior consultant with small dog clients, this book is for you, too. The following chapters apply principles from several cooperative care and Fear Free® techniques, force-free training, body language assessment, and behavior modification procedures. The chapters are sprinkled with current research, as well as veterinarian input. As you read, note how the training and behavior modification techniques have been adapted to the unique needs of small dogs.

Throughout the book, you will see QR codes where steps are available via video. To access each video, follow the instructions below:

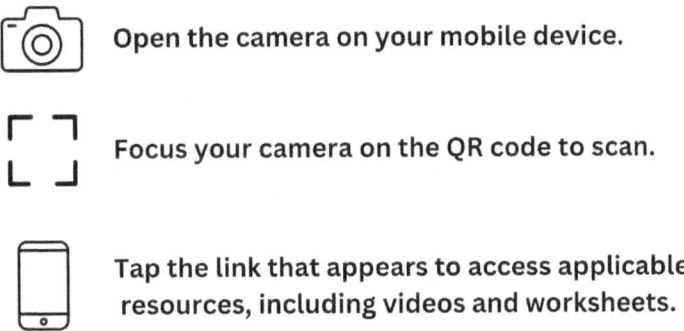

Open the camera on your mobile device.

Focus your camera on the QR code to scan.

Tap the link that appears to access applicable resources, including videos and worksheets.

https://www.bklnmanners.com/about.html

Chapter 1

Busting Small Dog Myths

Biting, alarm-barking, demanding, food-stealing, lap-guarding, peeing and pooping on the carpet … make it stop! But are these issues due solely to the dog's small stature? Is a small dog destined to be an untrainable terror? I would emphatically argue that the answer to both questions is "No!"

Yet, in my career as a certified dog behavior consultant (CDBC) and certified dog trainer (CPDT-KA), small dogs account for most of the barking, biting, and unwanted behavior that I've encountered. I have only been on the receiving end of two dog bites in my training career and both of those sets of teeth belonged to dogs in the 10-to-15-pound range. I am the guardian of a Chihuahua mix, Margaret, who had been rehomed numerous times before coming to us. Though we'll never know the specifics of Margaret's past, she had clearly learned to communicate with humans by using her razor-sharp canines with unnerving speed and precision.

What is a small dog, anyway?

There is no universally agreed upon definition of a little dog, but a few factors can point toward a dog being considered small. Given the wide variety of small dogs, your pup may only check one or two of the boxes below.

Height. Most little dogs are roughly 16 inches tall at the withers or less. For reference, a Yorkie may only be six inches tall, while an Italian Greyhound may reach 15 inches in height.

Weight. Small dogs can be as light as a three pound Chihuahua, as heavy as a 25 pound Boston Terrier, or anything in between. Essentially, if you can pick it up, it's probably a small dog.

Build. Not all short dogs would be considered small. Take a Basset Hound, a breed that may only measure 11 to 15 inches tall. But since Basset Hounds can weigh as much as 75 pounds, they are generally not considered small. On the flip side, I have seen some adorable Chihuahua mixes with supermodel-esque long legs; despite their height, these dogs may only weigh 15 pounds and therefore are still considered small.

American Kennel Club (or other registry) group classification. You'll find that most purebred small dogs are in the Toy group (Brussels Griffon, Toy Poodle, etc.) and the Terrier group (Cairn Terrier, Border Terrier, etc.), with some little-breed representation in the Non-Sporting group (French Bulldog, Bichon Frisé, etc.) as well. There is also an occasional outlier, such as the Dachshund, which is in the Hound group.

Minis. Mini Goldendoodles, Teacup Yorkies, and Mini or Toy Australian Shepherds are just a few of the shrunken versions of larger dogs. Some of these pint-sized pups are genetically similar to the full-sized breed, while others have been mixed with other breeds in their journey toward downsizing.

Behavior. Overall, the dogs discussed in this book tend to share many of the same behavior patterns. For example, many small dogs are enthusiastic barkers, whether they're happy, angry, scared, or seeking your attention. A lot of them will also jump, jump, jump until you give them that scrap of food. Additionally, many little dogs seem to be lap-addicts, which can lead to challenges with resource guarding of spaces and valued family members. The "Napoleon complex" stereotype has an ounce of truth, especially around larger dogs, as a lot of little ones believe the best defense is a good offense.

The role of genetics on small dog behavior

You may have heard the saying that "it's all how you raise them," meaning that a dog's behavior is made, not born. And while a dog is significantly shaped by life experiences, this belief is oversimplified and not entirely accurate. It is clear that genetics have at least some influences on a dog's behavior. Chihuahuas, generally speaking, are more wary of strangers than Golden Retrievers. If you hear incessant barking in the distance, I'd put my money on a Pomeranian before a Bulldog. A Dachshund tends to be less enthused about being restrained for a nail trim compared to a Bernese Mountain Dog. There is a reason why Old English Sheepdogs are called "nanny dogs" while Cairn Terriers are not. You get the idea.

This comes back to a small dog's original purpose. It's very likely your dog was originally bred for a job, particularly if you have a purebred dog. Many Toy breeds such as Shih Tzus and Chihuahuas were designed to be homebodies, with a built-in radar drawing them to the nearest warm lap. Pups bred to be little lap dogs are often sensitive souls; they bond strongly to their special people and may be wary of unknown humans, dogs, or environments.

Not all little canines are lap-obsessed, however. Particularly in the Non-Sporting group, you'll find small breeds with working or sporting origins, even though these days their primary purpose is companionship. For instance, Boston Terriers and

French Bulldogs were derived from bull-baiting Bully breeds before becoming cuddly apartment dwellers. Miniature Poodles are the smaller, handbag-sized version of the Standard Poodle, a reliable hunting breed.

Then are the Terriers. These spunky, spicy dogs were bred to hunt, catch, and sometimes kill vermin, and many of them still take this job very seriously. Breeds such as Russell Terriers, known for their high prey drive and independent thinking skills, are always looking for adventure regardless of the silly "Come" commands you are shouting at them.

Understanding your dog's genetic background allows you to have compassion for his quirks, as well as come up with activities that speak his love language, whether it's a passion for chillin' with mom or relentless toy murdering. For an in-depth discussion of types of small dogs, genetics and more, I recommend Kim Brophey's book, *Meet Your Dog*.

Choosing the small dog for you

If you're currently considering getting a small dog as you read this, here are some questions to ask yourself before you commit to a tiny new family member.

Kids. Are your kids old enough to treat a small dog with care? Many rescue organizations won't even let families with young children adopt a small dog, due to the risk of injury to the dog. If you have young kids, consider a sturdy lowrider, like a French Bulldog or a Terrier, rather than a more fragile Chihuahua or anything with "teacup" in the name.

Grooming needs. Those luxurious locks of a Shih Tzu or rolling curls of a Mini Goldendoodle come at a price. Are you prepared to take your dog to the groomer every six weeks, and maintain that silky coat with daily brushing? On the other hand, for dogs with fur that regularly sheds, expect to be doing a fair amount of brushing and bathing, whether at home or at a groomer. While small dogs leave fewer hairy tumbleweeds on your floors than a Golden Retriever, even tiny dogs seem to have an impressive amount of fur.

Medical needs. Some breeds are prone to certain allergies, diseases, and ailments. For instance, Miniature Schnauzers may experience anal gland issues, while French Bulldogs are known for their allergy and gastrointestinal problems. Many small breeds are prone to luxating patellas, which causes the kneecap to slip out of place. Budget accordingly and consider a pet insurance plan that covers the ailments to which your dog is predisposed.

Climate. If you live in a hot climate, you'll have to take extra care to keep your brachycephalic dog (think Pugs and Boston Terriers) from overheating due to breathing difficulties. If you live in the tundra, you'll be coming up with lots of indoor enrichment to keep your Italian Greyhound or hairless Chinese Crested from going stir crazy.

Home layout. If your home has lots of stairs, plan to use baby gates to prevent a short dog from falling. Make sure you can physically handle carrying your dog up and down the stairs as needed.

Activity level. Are you an avid hiker? A Jack Russell or Cairn Terrier might be just the companion for your adventures. On the other hand, a Pekingese or Cavalier King Charles might be more inclined to binge watch reality shows with you. Be realistic about what kind of activities you are willing to provide for your dog.

Apartment life. Small dogs tend to make great apartment pets, but if you have neighbors on all sides and paper-thin walls, consider the yappy factor that some breeds such as Pomeranians and Dachshunds are known for. Also consider the availability of exercise opportunities. If the nearest green space is thirty minutes away, do you have the time and resources to give your athletic Min Pin enough outlets for his energy?

Age. You said you wanted a puppy, but are you sure? Puppies are a joy if you can commit to their nearly constant needs. Otherwise, consider a small adult dog, millions of whom are sitting in shelters or foster homes, patiently waiting to be adopted.

How many of these breeds do you recognize? French Bulldogs, Chihuahuas, Cocka-poos, and Toy Manchester Terriers all have their unique characteristics and needs.

Chapter 2
Naughty by Nature? Not so Fast!

Your small dog's behavior is not determined only by his breed. Far from it! Even if your Toy Fox Terrier naturally loves the sound of his own voice, we shouldn't throw up our hands in defeat, dismissing his hours-long daily bark fests as hopeless. A small stature does not give your dog a free pass to act disruptively in your home or out in the world. Let's look at four of the main reasons why small dogs end up behaving in ways that we humans find inappropriate.

Reason 1: Owners having low expectations

Firstly, we tend not to hold little dogs to the same politeness standards to which we hold bigger dogs. We often allow small dogs to act inappropriately—for instance, jumping on your lap while you're eating dinner—because their behavior often falls under the category of "annoying" as opposed to "dangerous." Imagine a Rottweiler jumping into your lap during dinner. Dishware goes flying, you're launched out of your chair, and your meatloaf has become dog food in the blink of an eye. Now, consider all eight pounds of a Havanese jumping into your lap. You may get a disapproving look from a family member or two, but in many cases, everyone lets it slide.

Mealtime is just one scenario where guardians of little dogs let them get away with what would be considered bad manners in larger dogs. Large jumping dogs can knock down children and the elderly; small dogs that jump could, at worst, scratch grandma's calves. Bites from a large dog also have the potential for more physical damage, compared to those of a small dog. Because small dogs get more free passes than their bigger counterparts, they do not learn critical life skills early on: sitting instead of jumping, walking on a loose leash instead of pulling, dropping a sock instead of guarding it. These free passes add up over time, and lead to a dog that ultimately has a complicated, sometimes confrontational, relationship with his human family.

Reason 2: Making small dogs feel unsafe

Secondly, the world really does look different to little dogs. Our home, yards, and vehicles were not designed for them, and even the simplest daily routines can be a challenge for our tiny sidekicks. Imagine the vulnerability of climbing a stair that's taller than you. And if the delivery person were to hurl boxes ten times your size in your direction, you'd probably yell at them, too! While owners don't intentionally make their dogs feel unsafe, it is hard to put yourself in the position that small dogs face on a daily basis.

See the world through their eyes

I'd like you to try this activity. Lie on the floor, stomach down, head pointed straight in front of you. Once you've recovered from the shock of how dusty your floor really is, then you'll start to notice the magnitude of your furniture, and how daunting that leap up to the couch would be. If you have a helper available, ask them to walk directly toward you while you're lying there. As this person approaches, you may feel acutely vulnerable, ready to cry out, "Please don't step on me!" This is a bit like how your small dog sees the everyday world: imposing and often overwhelming. If you'd like to take this activity a step further, then do the same thing at the top of your staircase, looking down to the bottom landing and those fourteen spine-snapping obstacles required to get there. No wonder many small dogs ask to be carried down the stairs.

Because it's so challenging for us big, bumbling humans to see the world from our small dogs' perspectives, we unknowingly put them in uncomfortable or threatening situations. You may bring your little Klee Kai puppy to a family barbecue, where a toddler twice his size chases him to the point of exhaustion. Or we may squeeze him tightly to trim his nails, not realizing how painful and frightening this experience is.

This doesn't mean we small-dog owners are intentionally scaring our dogs. In reality, most of us are simply not trained to notice a dog in distress until it's too late. Our dogs are always communicating their emotions to us, but all too often, small dogs' attempts to communicate their fear or pain go unnoticed, resulting in even more stress.

Reason 3: Missing the subtle signs of stress

Dogs have several telltale signs indicating that they are becoming frustrated, scared, angry, overstimulated, and so on. However, some dogs are easier to read than others, and size plays a role here. Imagine you're sitting on your couch. A shepherd or a large hound, roughly eye level with you and having a head at least as big as yours, has features that are easy to see. A furrowed brow, a hard stare, a relaxed smile. With time, many owners learn what emotions those expressions convey. For instance, guardians of large resource-guarding dogs can usually accurately describe their dogs' increasing warning signs: "When Roscoe has a bone, first he'll stare at me, not blinking. Then his lip will curl, with a low growl. If I don't back off, eventually he'll lunge at me." In situations like this, we are incentivized to pay attention to a large dog's body language. If we don't heed the dog's early warning to back off, we may be putting ourselves in danger as we continue to walk toward him.

Unfortunately, you are less likely to perceive these stress signs as easily with small dogs. This is partly because our little lowriders are more challenging to see, unless they are atop a piece of furniture. Their eyes, lips, feet, and body carriage can be especially challenging to read when you're hovering above. Additionally, because a stressed-out Scottie does less damage than a St. Bernard, we are less inclined to take their early signs of stress seriously. But when you really watch your small dog, you'll notice he does give you plenty of body language cues about his emotional state if you know what to look for, well before it gets to the "SOS" level.

For instance, before Max the Min Pin begins barking wildly at a passing dog outside the window, there are numerous subtler signs that his humans might fail to see. First, the ears perk up as little Max wakes from a seemingly deep sleep. He stops breathing momentarily and his body stiffens. Both his body and his whiskers lean slightly forward. As his eyes harden, he lets out a low growl. Finally, the explosion – Max leaps toward the window, barking frantically, keeping it up even after the "threat" has passed. This is a common scenario and the whole sequence may only take a second or two to escalate. Therefore, Max's family may only notice the last, noisiest part of the sequence, failing to realize that Max was telling them, "Hey, I'm a little concerned." Then, "Uh oh, I'm getting super stressed over here." And finally, "SOS, SOS, I'm gonna blow my lid!" Had someone intervened at the first level of "I'm a little concerned," the drama that ensued could have been prevented.

One of the goals of this book is to help you recognize and respond when your small dog tells you, "I'm a little concerned." Think about Max the Min Pin when he's taken to a friend's outdoor party. Children are kicking soccer balls bigger than Max, tipsy adults are reaching down to pet him, a 50-pound Lab puppy is repeatedly tackling him, and if all that weren't bad enough, there is no safe place to hide in this unfamiliar environment.

Max may well be giving warnings again and again. These signals might include:

- Yawning
- Tongue flicks
- Looking away
- Sniffing the ground

These behaviors are known as **calming signals**. Your dog does these seemingly odd behaviors to indicate that he is not comfortable with the current situation. Other dogs will often, but not always, respond to calming signals by backing off. People, however, don't always understand what the dog is trying to communicate. If these polite warnings aren't heeded by the people and pets there, what choice does Max have but to use his teeth to communicate "stay away!"? Most dogs don't want to injure a person or another dog, but in too many cases, they feel they are left with no choice. It's just as if you were being followed by a stranger, and your warnings of "give me space" and then "I'll call the police" aren't heeded. What options do you have when backed into a corner but to physically defend yourself?

All too often, I see small dogs in situations that overwhelm them and their humans are not stepping up to protect them. Just like any panicked person, a dog that feels vulnerable may resort to biting. It's up to the guardian to be that dog's ally, to ensure he feels safe. As you will read in the next chapter, trust is essential to having a good relationship with your pup. But how can your dog trust you if you put him in scary situations and fail to keep him safe?

In the photo, you'll see one individual having a nice moment, and another who clearly is not. Beans is turning her head and averting her eye (since she only has one), expressing that she is clearly uncomfortable with this interaction. I recommend looking through your own photos. Do you have any photos of someone holding, hugging, or kissing your dog? And if so, what body language is your dog demonstrating?

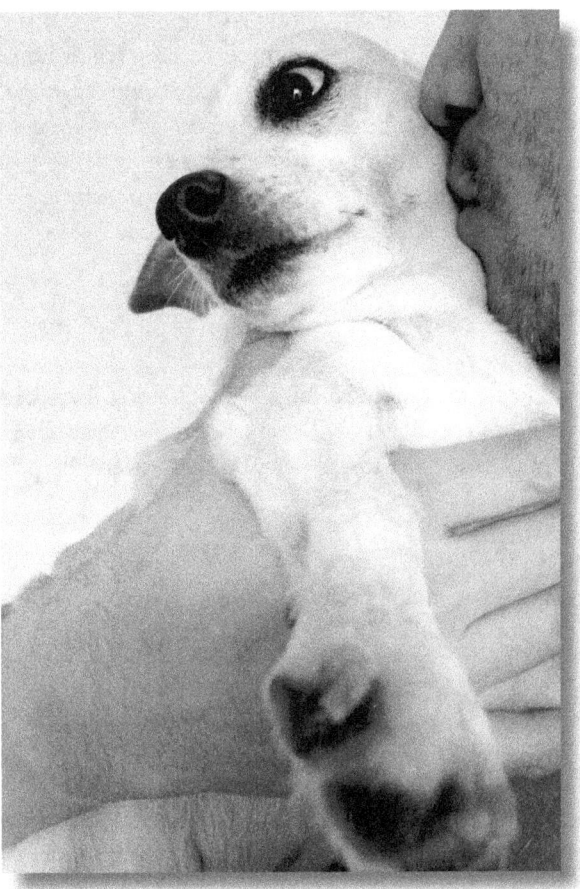

*By averting her gaze and turning her head, Beans is clearly
saying that she is uncomfortable with this interaction.*

For more examples of calming signals, read "The benefits of grrrowling" section (page 23). For an even deeper dive into calming signals, check out a book by Turid Rugaas called *On Talking Terms with Dogs: Calming Signals*.

Reason 4: Waiting too long to address problems

There is a final reason why little dogs seem to act badly, and like the previous one, it comes from misunderstanding rather than malice. It is, in a word, procrastination. We often don't address a small dog's behavioral issues with a professional until it's gotten extremely bad. I get *a lot* of lesson requests right after a holiday. Why? Nester the Mini Goldendoodle went to a Thanksgiving family gathering where a young niece kept pinning him down and hugging him. She was bitten, strong words were exchanged among family members, and holiday travel plans for December are now on hold. In truth, Nester's discomfort around children had been on the owner's radar for quite some time. The dog's emotional challenges were not new, and in fact, may have been brewing for years. So why wait until an accident happens to address this behavior issue? With small dogs, there is a misconception that it's not a problem unless he is lunging or biting. But once a dog is lunging and biting, he is at the end of his rope. If Nester's concerns had been addressed months ago, when he was showing more subtle stress signs like licking his lips, averting his eyes, and yawning around the niece, this bite incident could have been prevented. Were Nester a large dog, it's much more likely the owners would have reached out for professional help earlier. The guardian of an aggressive Mastiff will probably seek help the first time they hear a warning growl. A Chihuahua may not get the "doggie therapy" he needs until there is a police report filed or family left divided.

This is important because early intervention improves a dog's prognosis. A young dog that has just started growling at people or other dogs generally has a good chance of improvement with behavior modification. When it's a dog that already has a long bite history, things get more complicated. While I believe you can always make progress, the extent of that progress depends, in part, on how severe the problem has become over time.

So that's the bad news. The good news is, the solutions to all of these are within the control of you, the dog's guardian. By following the guidelines in the following chapters, you will ensure that you're bringing out the absolute best in your canine companion.

How to seek professional help

If you're feeling overwhelmed, don't wait to contact a professional for help. Even if it's day one with your new dog—that's OK! Early interventions are often the most successful ones. If you need personalized help, contact the right kind of trainer to help you make a tailored plan for your pup. But how to find one?

Don't be lured in by promises of fixing a behavior issue in a matter of days or weeks. I am very suspicious of any trainer who promises these results. What methods are they using to get there? Are they using aversive tools such as e-collars (shock collars) or prong collars, or utilizing techniques meant to scare or hurt dogs? As Kristina Spaulding, PhD, CAAB, describes in her excellent book, *The Stress Factor in Dogs*:

Most of the research suggests that aversive methods are associated with increased distress and, therefore, decreased welfare in dogs. For example, Schilder and van der Borg (2004) found that German Shepherd Dogs undergoing guard dog training showed signs of immediate distress when experiencing shocks, including lowered body posture, redirected aggression and yelps, barks and squeals. The dogs trained on electronic collars (also called e-collars or shock collars), also showed more signs of stress both during the training session and outside of the training context (2022, p. 107).

Our dogs deserve better than this from us. Safe, humane training takes time and a lot of work on everyone's part. If your dog is struggling with aggression or extreme fears, there are no humane quick fixes for these serious behavior issues.

Unfortunately, there are no required credentials for a dog training professional (at least, not in the United States). Literally anyone in the US can do it, no experience or education necessary. Would you hire a child therapist with no credentials? Or a doctor who learned to perform surgery from watching videos online? Or almost any other professional where a creature's welfare is at stake?

The good news is that even though there is no federal or state requirement, we do have certifying bodies that educate and assess dog trainers. I recommend that you seek out a professional who has gone the extra mile to attain a certification and then maintains it by earning continuing education credits annually. Or, at least look for a trainer who has learned from certified professionals. You can usually find this information on the trainer's website. Look up any names the trainer mentions as mentors or influences and see what training methods they use or which credentials, if any, they hold.

If you're looking for help with your dog's manners, the following organizations are among those known to have reliable trainers, and you can search for a trainer on their websites.

- CCPDT (The certification is CPDT-KA or CPDT-KSA)
- IAABC (The certification is IAABC-ADT)
- Karen Pryor Academy
- The Academy for Dog Trainers
- Peaceable Paws Academy
- Victoria Stilwell Academy
- CATCH Canine Trainers Academy

A puppy or dog having a behavior concern such as aggression, fear, or anxiety, will require a professional with a different skill set. The previously mentioned trainers might also be qualified to help, but you will have to ask each individual. There is a specific kind of professional called a behavior consultant, who specializes in behavior issues. There are only a few organizations in the US that offer certifications for behavior consultants, such as:

- IAABC (The certification is CDBC or CABC)
- CCPDT (The certification is CBCC-KA)
- Family Dog Mediation

For serious behavior concerns, the most highly educated professionals are called behaviorists. But beware! There are also some uncredentialed professionals out there who call themselves behaviorists. True behaviorists are almost always DVMs or PhDs who have passed rigorous testing in dog behavior. So if you see a dog professional using this title, you should also see some very impressive credentials to back it up. Look for:

- CAAB
- DACVB (DVM board certified in behavior)
- DVM plus additional credentials in training or behavior

Chapter 3

Build Trust with Your Small Dog

Think of a person you don't trust. Would you take advice from an acquaintance who has lied to you repeatedly in the past? Or would you be comfortable alone with a person who has acted inappropriately toward you before? Probably not. The same holds true for your small dog. If you don't have your dog's trust, you can't communicate clearly, train effectively, or expect to improve your dog's behavior issues.

While dogs of any size can lack trust in their guardians, little dogs are particularly susceptible. All too often, we pick up little dogs against their will or put our much larger faces into theirs, or allow family members to play too roughly with them. Over time, these unpleasant experiences shape a small dog's perception of the world, and it's no wonder they learn that the best defense is a good offense. This chapter is designed to ensure that you have earned your dog's trust in a variety of interactions.

Trust goes both ways and your emotional health is important, too. If you have been living with a dog that acts aggressively, as much as you love her, you have good reason not to trust her. I found myself in this situation in 2019, after adopting Margaret, the most affectionate dog we've ever had. She also turned out to be the scariest little creature to set foot in our home. Margaret, a four-or-so-year-old Chihuahua mix, has what you might call a memorable face: underbite and fully exposed snaggletooth, shifty little eyes, whiskers shooting in all directions, one ear up and one ear undecided. She also had some personality quirks. My husband and I quickly learned the extent of her distrust when we attempted to put on her harness the first day. As my hand reached toward her, a switch flipped in her brain. She instantly went into attack mode, lunging and snapping at my hand twice, then scampered into a corner and braced herself, probably expecting a hit in retaliation. Clearly, it was a pattern she had practiced many times. It was equally shocking and heartbreaking. At that moment I felt crushed under the gravity of what must have happened to her in the past, plus the seemingly overwhelming task of teaching her to trust me, my husband, our vet, and essentially anyone else with hands. Not to mention, teaching myself to trust her.

Your dog need not be aggressive, as mine was. In fact, many dogs will never bare a tooth or muster a growl, but they may be showing fear and distrust all the same. You may have a dog that backs away when you approach her, runs under the couch as you grab the leash, or hovers over her bone when you come close. Situations like these often involve a lack of trust, even if you were not the one who caused it. The only way you'll be able to trim your dog's nails or remove a dirty napkin from her mouth is to teach her that she can trust you. To do that, you may have to look at your dog in a whole new light.

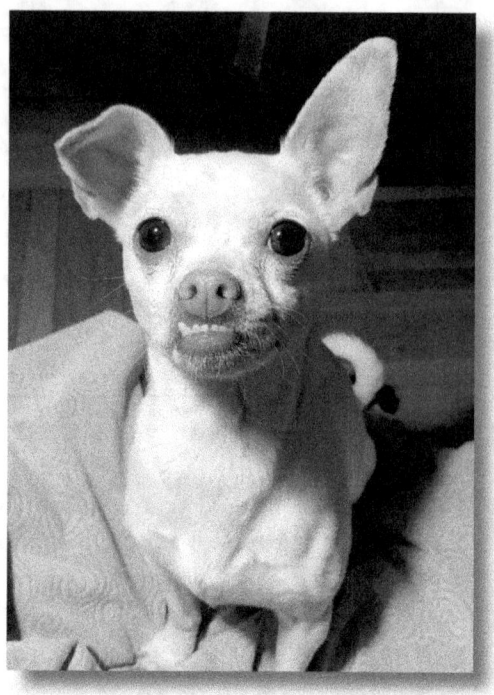

At first, teaching Margaret to trust people was a challenge.

Trust and security are intertwined

Before we proceed, a note on the word "trust," and how I'm using it in this book. What is trust, and what does it look like in the context of little-dog concerns? A trusting dog expects a positive and safe outcome from an interaction with you, another dog, or a situation. For instance, when you pick your dog up, you give her access to your lap—which is her favorite thing in the world. Therefore, she trusts you every time you pick her up, smiling and wagging as you lift her onto your lap. This is because she feels secure, which Allie Bender and Emily Strong in their book *Canine Enrichment* describe as "the feeling of being protected from harm" (2019, p. 58). In your dog's mind, your hands and your lap are directly associated with security, which allows her to trust you when you handle her.

A distrustful dog, on the other hand, has learned that an interaction with a certain person, dog, or situation has an unpleasant and potentially unsafe outcome. Therefore, she will aim to avoid that interaction because she does not feel secure. If you only pick your dog up for nail trims, she will likely begin to distrust you when you reach your arms toward her. Can you blame her? Your reach implies that she will be held against her will and possibly feel significant pain. Naturally, during this interaction she doesn't feel secure or "protected from harm." As time goes on, she may start to run away, cower, or even show aggression as you approach her.

When a dog is being handled in a way that makes her feel insecure (as in, not feeling safe), she will likely give you one or more body language cues. If your dog shows any of these signs, it means she is feeling fearful, anxious, or stressed:

- Averts her eyes
- Yawns, especially with tight lips
- Turns her head or body away
- Licks her lips
- Lifts a paw
- Shows whale eye, when the dog turns her head but keeps her gaze on you, meaning you will see some whites of the eyes
- Has dilated pupils
- Lowers or tucks her tail
- Pull her ears back
- Trembles
- Urinates
- Flight: leans away or tries to escape, often in addition to other signs above
- Freeze: becomes immobile, often in addition to other signs above
- Fight—defensive aggression: piloerection (raised hackles), direct eye contact, commissures pulled back as if forming a "V," baring teeth, body low and retreating
- Fight—offensive aggression: piloerection (raised hackles), lunges toward you, ears and tail raised, commissures pulled forward as if making a "C," teeth bared

Be your little dog's advocate

From the day your puppy or dog comes home, it's critical to show your dog that she can trust you, your family, and the environment. Research has shown that dogs frequently look to us to decide what's safe and what's potentially dangerous. In one study, Dr. Claudia Fugazza and her associates put puppies to a trust test of sorts (Fugazza, 2018), to evaluate this concept of **social referencing** in dogs. 48 eight-week-old puppies were presented, one at a time, with an unfamiliar object, such as a table fan with pieces of ribbon attached, blowing in the fan's breeze. In some of the sessions, a human was also in the room with the puppy and novel object. The human provided either positive or neutral emotional signals, meaning that, in some cases, the human interacted happily with this new, strange object; in other cases, the human remained neutral to the object. What the researchers found was that the puppies were using **referential looking** to determine if this funny new contraption was safe to approach, based on the human's interactions with it. That is, in Fugazza's words:

> Puppies alternated their gaze between the stimulus and the social partner
> with all the partners. Puppies tested in the presence of a human expressing
> positive emotional signals toward the stimulus were more likely to approach

it than puppies tested with a human expressing neutral emotional signals (behavioural regulation).

What we see here is that domesticated dogs, even at eight weeks old, will naturally look to our social cues for information about the world. "Hey human, is this weird new thing safe?" It's up to us to show our dogs that, yes, it is safe.

I sometimes joke with guardians of anxious or fearful dogs, telling them, "You are your dog's emotional support animal." This is especially true for small dogs, for whom the world really is bigger and scarier. Jokes aside, research demonstrates that an unsure dog will look to her guardian for security. You can only provide emotional support to your dog if she trusts you, so let's show your dog that interactions with you are safe. If your dog trusts that you will keep her safe, then she won't feel the need to defend herself every time you pick up the nail clippers or when an unfamiliar guest comes by for a visit.

Myths that erode trust
There are a few doggie myths that can hinder your dog's ability to trust you. Let's put these myths to sleep for good.

Myth 1: Don't pick up your small dog if she's afraid
If your dog is afraid or in danger, it is your responsibility to make her feel secure. And if the only way to make your dog feel secure is to pick her up, please do so immediately. This is a matter of protecting your dog and showing her that she can count on you. As Dr. Kristina Spaulding states, "You may have heard that you should not comfort a frightened dog because it can reinforce their fear. The truth is, for social species, the presence of another animal can often improve one's ability to cope with stress. This is referred to as social support" (Spaulding, 2022, p. 87).

Those who believe this myth say that the dog needs to learn how to face her fears, and that picking her up will "reward" her fearful state of mind. However, you cannot reward fear by comforting an individual. Fear, and the fight-flight-freeze response it creates in the brain, is a natural reaction of the body—it is a survival skill. Fear happens because the animal believes she is in danger, not because someone has given her the "reward" of being picked up.

> **Still not convinced?**
> Imagine you're hiking in the woods, and you end up face-to-face with a bear. Terrifying! Your fear response is instantly triggered, and instinctively, you are about to run away. (Not the best idea when faced with a bear, mind you.) And imagine, at that moment, a park ranger intervenes, confidently gliding between you and the bear. The bear runs off and your life is spared. Has the park ranger rewarded your fear? Will you be encouraged to be more afraid the next time you see a bear, due to the ranger's intervention? Nonsense! If anything, you will be less traumatized by the bear

incident, thanks to the ranger who protected you. And you will think fondly of that individual for the rest of your life. So be like a good park ranger to your dog when she is faced with her own "bears" out in the world.

That said, there is a time to teach your dog to gain confidence around things that can cause her to be afraid, but we have a safe method for doing it, which we will cover in Chapter 8. In the meantime, if your dog is afraid of something in the environment, or if you think she might be in danger, remove her from the situation as soon as possible. And you have my permission to pick her up if it will ensure her safety and comfort.

Myth 2: If your dog gets uncomfortable in public—at the dog park, a barbecue, the vet, or the outdoor café—you need to take her there more often

Like most bad advice, there is an ounce of truth to this one. When the dog's fear response is low enough, and the dog has sufficient resilience to bounce back from a stressful encounter, then she will likely **habituate** to certain experiences with repeated exposure. For instance, a puppy might be afraid the first time she sees her guardian put on a bicycle helmet, but after being exposed to this helmet-wearing again and again, she realizes it is nothing to worry about. However, if the dog is deeply afraid of an object or situation, repeated exposure on its own will not help, and it may actually increase the dog's fearful response. Do you really think that taking your dog frequently to the vet, which may include restraint, muzzling, needles, and thermometers, will make her like the vet more over time? Unlikely. If anything, the more unpleasant experiences your dog has at the vet, the more anxious she may feel when pulling into the parking lot, and the stronger her fear can become when she is poked or prodded.

It's the same for people, too. For example, I see spiders on a daily basis, and I panic just as intensely no matter how many spiders I've seen over the years. Exposure has not put me at ease, and depending on the size and overall creepiness of the spider, I often experience setbacks and increased fear, even spider-themed nightmares. I still remember one night, at least five years ago, when I stepped outside to find about a dozen Brown Recluse spiders on my front stoop. I was too terrified to go out that door for days and have been haunted by the image ever since. Have you ever had this kind of reaction to a scary thing or place? What about your dog?

Intense exposure to a fear-inducing stimulus can make an animal even more fearful in the long-term, and due to its risks, should never be used in a training context. You may have heard of the technique called **flooding**, which is a face-your-fears style of behavioral therapy for humans. You may also have heard of it for dogs. But here is the difference—a human can communicate to their therapist if they need to stop the therapy session; a dog cannot. A human has agreed to undergo this kind of intense therapy; a dog has not. If the dog does not have a voice in a process designed to overwhelm her (even if the goal is to help), it is not ethical to attempt it. Period.

Getting a dog comfortable with a certain place or situation requires a methodical approach to exposure. As with Myth 1, we need to expose the dog to the scary or overwhelming stimulus in small, manageable, not-really-scary-at-all doses. That might mean that you go to the vet's office just to say hello to the receptionist and give your dog some treats, and then you leave. After many repetitions of that exercise, your dog may be able to tolerate an exam once in a while, since you've introduced the location in brief, enjoyable doses over a long period of time. If nine out of every ten vet visits are simply a treat party, then that one unpleasant visit, where the thermometer goes you-know-where, doesn't affect your dog's overall impression of the vet as much. The cooperative care exercises in Chapter 4 will also give you a detailed plan to overcome certain vet-related fears.

Myth 3: The dogs will work it out themselves

This common dog-park myth shows how poorly humans understand dog body language. Just like a kids' playground, a dog park can have bullies, scaredy-cats, overly excited individuals, and other types that do not mesh well. If your toddler were getting bullied on the jungle gym by a kid five times his size, wouldn't you intervene? You should give your little dog the same support.

If all the dogs at the park were social, stable, and the same size, then yes, the dogs generally would work it out themselves. But since a dog park is a free-for-all with no temperament test, health check, size restriction, or concern for overcrowding, you need to be extremely cautious. Small dogs are especially vulnerable and should never (ever!) be in the same area as large dogs. An overly stimulated large dog can tip into predator mode, a phenomenon called **predatory drift**, when he sees a tiny, bouncy, bunny-like dog and perceives it as prey.

When it comes to dog play, choose quality over quantity. This means that a romp with a level-headed, appropriately sized doggie friend once a week in your backyard is far better than a potentially dangerous trip to the dog park every single morning. If your dog is dog-friendly, seek out neighbors and friends with suitable dogs who can participate in a play date. A high-quality day care with a separate enclosure for small dogs is also a much safer option than a public park, as the dogs' temperaments have been evaluated and there is always a staff member supervising.

If your dog is not dog-friendly, don't feel pressured to "socialize" her. Socialization is a process that takes place in the first three to four months of a puppy's life, when she is learning valuable life skills. When you try to socialize a three-year-old dog that doesn't care for other dogs, it's like asking a 30-year-old person to learn to "play nice with the other kids." Sure, some adult dogs can learn proper play skills later in life. But if your little dog is not one of them, that's fine. There are plenty of other things you can do with your dog for daily enrichment, from scent work to agility to brain games. (See Chapter 9.)

"Bad" behavior provides good information

Your dog's unwanted behavior is actually a great source of information. When your Cavapoo snarls as you pick her up, or when your Frenchie nips at your hand for attention because she wants you to play, she is telling you how she's feeling. Although we may not appreciate the way they're sending a message, your job is to listen, not to punish.

But what does "listening" mean, when we're talking about dogs? I'm not saying you need to jump up and play with your dog if she nips for attention. Listening to your dog's demand is different from obeying it. Listening to your dog means that, when she does something we consider inappropriate, we ask ourselves, "What is my dog trying to tell me? What feelings might she be conveying?" Then, our response will take the dog's needs into account. When we start to acknowledge our dog's feelings and try to understand the motivation for her undesirable behavior, it opens the door to resolving the issue. There are two main benefits to listening to our small dogs:

First, when we try to understand what our dogs are feeling, it allows us to empathize with them. So many little dogs are perpetually on edge, hypervigilant on walks and even inside the house. Should a delivery truck dare to drive past your house, your dog has instantly sprung up from a deep sleep and run to the window, barking frantically. This kind of over-the-top reaction reminds me of times I've been hypervigilant, and how quickly I've gone on the offensive, too. I remember one night, when I lived in Brooklyn, standing on the subway platform, my eyes darting back and forth on the lookout for pickpockets and boogeymen. Suddenly I felt a tap on the shoulder from behind. Thinking it was an attack, I spun around with clenched fists, and I nearly punched an elderly woman in the face. Such was the thanks that woman got for picking up my Metrocard after it fell out of my pocket. So how can I be frustrated with a hypervigilant dog for acting out when I've behaved the same way?

Second, it's important to recognize that 'bad' doggie behavior is nothing personal. Once we see our dogs' barking, growling, or biting as useful information rather than a personal attack, we can build a plan to work through it. We, the guardians, need to take on the role of coach instead of adversary. Have you ever watched documentaries about notable sports coaches? A successful coach understands that his or her team members may have big egos, challenging personalities, and inner demons. Rather than try to suppress those qualities, a top coach can motivate even the most difficult player to excel as part of a team. An empathetic, supportive coach can give team members not only tangible wins, such as trophies, but also create a sense of partnership and belonging that goes far deeper than points on the field. Likewise, for your dog, if you have compassion toward her in training sessions and in daily life, you won't see her as your opponent, a nuisance, or a problem. Rather, you'll see her as a sentient being that needs your guidance. She may currently lack the skills to act appropriately on her own, but since you are sensitive to her emotional state and privy to the training protocols in this book, you're just the person to help her build new skills. You and your dog have to be on the same team in order to succeed. And teams only work if there is trust.

The benefits of grrrowling

As strange as it may sound, dog training professionals appreciate growling. A growl, a lip curl, or a hard stare are warnings for you to "back off or else. ..." In most cases, the dog doesn't want to finish this sentence. She is growling so that she *won't* have to bite you. If you heed her stern request to give her space, you'll be safe. However, if you ignore her growl or try to suppress it by "dominating" her in any way, you've just declared war.

In my earlier story about Margaret and our first harness experience, she didn't growl. She went straight to the lunge and bite. I didn't have the luxury of a warning. Why? It's likely her stress was so intense at that moment, and perhaps her prior experiences so traumatizing, that she didn't bother with a warning. Thus, she quickly earned the nickname "Scary Peggy," for her tendency to skip the warning and dive right into aggression. One of my first strategies with Scary Peggy was to move so slowly and carefully when handling her that she had the time to give us a warning growl to tell us, "I'm starting to get nervous, please back off." As strange as it may sound, I actually *wanted* her to growl and show other subtle signs of stress. That was great information for me, allowing me to slow my approach even more, or to change how we put on the harness if needed. After a few weeks of following the techniques described later in this chapter, she began trusting us and allowing us to handle her in more and more ways.

A growl may have different meanings depending on the context. Here are some examples, particularly true for small dogs:

- **"I'm in pain" or "I don't feel well, please leave me alone."** Before assuming your dog is simply cranky, it's essential to rule out pain or illness. Ask your vet to fully examine your pup, nose to tail, to confirm that there is no medical cause for your dog's aggressive behavior. Does your little one snap when you put your hand near her face? Or shy away when you try to pick her up? These (and more) could be signs of a dog in physical pain.

- **"I'm uncomfortable with you in my space."** Imagine a dog curled up asleep on a pillow. Her owner's boyfriend, over six feet tall with the build of a linebacker, directly approaches and bends over her furry little body to say hello. While well-meaning, consider the scenario from the dog's perspective. A much larger creature has woken her up, pushed himself into her space, and is hovering over her head. This is not a position that makes the dog trust the boyfriend and she growls to ask him to back up.

- **"You're handling me in a way that makes me feel vulnerable."** Little dogs like Scary Peggy may struggle with restraint during nail trims, blood draws, or other types of handling. After just one or two bad experiences of being overpowered, a dog can become easily panicked for all future restraint. When an animal feels they're in danger, they normally go into a state of fight, flight, or freeze. If flight isn't possible due to being restrained, they may resort to fight, starting with a warning growl (if you're lucky). We'll discuss this more in future chapters.

- **"Your movements make me nervous."** Kids running and squealing, a drunken family party, a raucous dog park. All these things can make a small dog feel that her physical safety is in jeopardy. No wonder she growls to keep people and dogs away. If she doesn't try to scare them away, she might get injured.

- **"This is mine, please don't steal it."** As already mentioned, if a dog thinks you will take her prized possessions, she will start to guard them from you. Wouldn't you do the same? Imagine you just withdrew money from the ATM, your wallet fat with cash. How would you feel if your sibling grabbed the wallet from your pocket and took a few twenties? After a few incidents like this, you'd probably start hiding your wallet or slapping away anyone's hand who came close to your pocket. Likewise, a dog that repeatedly gets her food bowl, chews, and toys removed from under her nose may start to guard them.

- **"You don't belong here, go away!"** Guests, repair workers, and delivery people can be especially stressful for small dogs. For most dogs, but particularly some small breeds, the home is their safe place. When a new person barges in, your dog may feel extremely unsafe and growl to keep them away.

- **"Do it… now!"** Dogs, especially the wee ones, may communicate by growling or acting out aggressively when they are ignored. Your dog is feeling frustrated in this case, but fortunately, frustration tolerance can be learned, as in Chapter 6.

Of course, we all wish dogs wouldn't feel threatened enough to growl in the first place. By the time your dog is growling, things have already gone too far. The best thing is to not let a dog get to the point of feeling that she has to growl. But how?

1. **Know your dog's triggers and avoid stressful events.** Do you have a delivery coming around 5pm? Have a plan to avoid a confrontation. At 4:45, you could:

   - Take your dog for a walk, avoiding the "intruder" altogether.
   - Give your dog a long-lasting chewy, like a stuffed Kong or bully stick, in the bedroom, as far from the front door as possible.
   - Have a family member take your pup in the backyard to play.

2. **Look for early signs of stress.** Respect your dog's feelings by noticing when she is starting to get nervous or agitated and remove her from the situation, so her stress doesn't escalate. Once your dog is barking, biting, or lunging, it's much too late. Revisit the list of stress signals described earlier in this chapter, "Trust and security are intertwined" (page 18), to see if your dog shows any of these signals.

   This is especially important if your dog shows these signs toward you (as opposed to the postal worker). For instance, as you walk toward your dog, does she yawn, avert her eyes, or lick her lips? Your approach may actually be mildly stressful to her. This isn't to blame you. We are humans who operate based on human principles of face-to-face politeness. It's very easy to stress out a small dog unintentionally, not only because we forget about our size difference, but we also aren't naturally in tune with their low-level signs of stress. The next time you approach your dog, or put on her harness, or reach over to pet her, watch her body language carefully. Does she tightly yawn, look away, lick her lips, or exhibit any of the other calming signals? (In the photo below, you'll see all those signals! Clearly both Batman and Beans were stressed out by being asked to stand still for a photo op at the bustling New York Public Library.) If so, follow the guidelines in the next section to make yourself as non-threatening as possible.

Notice the calming signals: Batman's tight yawn (left) and Beans' averted gaze and tongue flick (right).

3. **Avoid confrontation at all costs.** If your dog thrashes and panics when you hold her tightly and trim her nails, your approach needs to change. You can still trim her nails, brush her teeth, and give her a bath, but without restraint. The grooming techniques in Chapter 4 will give you a new way to perform necessary tasks without restraining and scaring your little one.

Follow the "dog rule book" on body language

Recognizing your dog's signs of stress is the first half of the equation. The second half is modifying your own body language to appear less confrontational to your little one. Dogs tend to follow a very clear "rule book" for conduct with one another. Following certain dog-tested rules for body language can help your dog understand that you always come in peace and that she can feel secure in your presence.

Here are some Do's and Don'ts for approaching and interacting with a small dog:

Don't hover over a little dog. Do make your body "smaller."
Dogs of any size, but especially small dogs, don't appreciate another animal hovering over them. At best, it's rude, and at worst, it conveys the intent to do harm. But we humans, being hopelessly tall and bipedal, hover over our dogs' bodies constantly, especially to pick them up or clip the leash. No wonder they run under the bed when the leash comes out! Instead of hovering to do these activities, sit next to your dog on the floor or ask her to jump up on the couch to get her leash clipped. Now you're closer to eye-level and much less threatening. For a more detailed leashing protocol, see Chapter 4.

Don't pet the top of the head. Do pet under the chin or on the chest.
If your dog shows any stress signals when you pet the top of her head, try a gentle under-the-chin or on-the-chest scratch instead. Similar to hovering over your dog, petting the top of the head is sometimes perceived as rude to a dog. In fact, with small dogs, it's wise to watch for signs of stress when you pet her *anywhere* on her body. Every dog is different and some don't like their rear end, feet, or tail touched.

Don't approach head-on. Do approach indirectly, using the "death laser" technique.
While face-to-face greetings are the norm for polite humans, dogs prefer a more curved, indirect approach. You'll see this play out at the dog park, where polite dogs will approach each other in a curved or arched pattern. A dog who races head-on toward another dog lacks social skills and is asking for trouble. Likewise, a person walking directly toward a dog can be perceived as a threat, in dog terms. Especially with small dogs, I always approach toward the dog's shoulder rather than her face, and I avoid making direct eye contact.

Try the death laser technique

For dogs that are particularly uncomfortable being approached, try my "death laser" technique. It's silly, but bear with me. Imagine that there is a dangerous death laser attached to your chest, aiming straight ahead. If you point your chest toward your couch, it will instantaneously evaporate the entire couch. Aim your chest toward the front door, poof, it's gone! Now you don't want to decimate your dog with the death laser, right? So the only way you can approach your dog is indirectly, never facing her head-on. This may involve you turning your body in directions that don't come naturally to you; but rest assured, a sensitive dog will appreciate your efforts. I've been using this technique with our

Video: https://www.bklnman-ners.com/chapter3.html

the-sky-is-falling, run-for-your-life Chihuahua-mix Beans since we adopted her. Initially, it helped her feel safe when I approached, and within a few weeks, she was no longer cowering or running away when I walked toward her. But even now, a decade later, I regularly practice the death laser technique when I approach a dog, simply because it's the polite thing to do. Watch the video to see the death laser technique in action.

Don't corner the dog. Do let the dog walk away.

If I'm doing something with my dog, for example, brushing Bean's teeth, she always has an exit. I don't hold her down, and if she wants to walk away, she can. In the beginning, this meant we had very short toothbrushing sessions, because I knew after a few seconds she would get overwhelmed and want to walk away. But as time progressed, she learned that the toothbrushing wasn't so scary, and if she walked away, it meant the end of that tasty chicken-flavored toothpaste. Slowly, she tolerated longer and longer brushings, until I could do her entire mouth in one session. Had I tried to pin her down and brush all her teeth on day one, she would have made a terrible association with toothbrushing and would probably be a dog with very stinky breath today.

The same is true for other kinds of grooming and handling needs. If your dog knows she can walk away and take a break from that stressful nail trim or ear cleaning, she is actually more likely to be able to tolerate it down the road. It's when the dog feels trapped, with no options to escape, that they resist grooming more and more.

Don't trick. Do be transparent.

If your small dog doesn't like to be picked up, sneaking up on her and grabbing her from behind will probably work … once. After that, you've lost her trust, and any approach from behind could make her anxious. This is the opposite of the relationship you should be cultivating with your pup. When you approach your dog, she should think "hooray" instead of "uh oh, what are you plotting against me?" The next chapter will teach you how to be transparent and trustworthy when interacting with your dog.

The importance of choice and control

These days, research in dog behavior and cognition is revealing so much about our favorite companions. The more we study dogs, the more we find that their brains are not so different from ours (or other mammals). One area of cognition that is relevant to small dog welfare is their need for choice and control. But what do those terms mean? Englund and Cronin (2023) refer to **choice** as "the act of choosing or selecting from more than one alternative." For instance, at a crosswalk, would your dog like to turn right or left? **Control** is defined as "the ability to predictably produce desired results," and is connected to the notion of **autonomy**. As an example, a dog with a doggie door will be able to control when she goes in and out. Englund and Cronin continue, "It follows that choice is a main mechanism by which individuals can exert control over their environment." They state that, while we generally accept that autonomy is critical for the psychological wellbeing of humans, nonhuman animals also need to have a sense of choice and control in their own lives.

As humans, we already understand how necessary autonomy is to our overall happiness. When we can freely make decisions about our lives, we are more satisfied in general. We are able to choose jobs that fulfill us and we have the option of quitting an unpleasant job. A person can decide to live in the countryside because he appreciates space, or he may choose the city because he thrives on the hustle and bustle. Without the ability to make these choices and control the course of our lives, we find ourselves unhappy or chronically stressed.

Animals in the wild also exert choice and control. They decide when and where to sleep, eat, play, and so on. But what about dogs? What **agency** do they have over their own lives? We tell them when and where to sleep ("Lights out and in the crate by 9pm, Lola."), what and when to eat, and when and where they can go outside. For most dogs, even their beloved outings are limited by a leash or fence. Imagine how much stress and frustration this lack of control can cause.

You may not be able to give your dog free roam of the neighborhood or let her choose her meals from a menu of options, but throughout the day, you can let your little one make small choices that allow her to feel a sense of control over what's happening to her.

- ☐ If she walks away when you pull out the brush, respect her choice not to get brushed. Ask again later.

- ☐ Let her choose the route on your walks, at least sometimes. When you reach an intersection, tell her, "You pick," and wait for her to choose a direction.

- ☐ Teach her to push a button to communicate her needs and preferences. (See Chapter 9.) When she communicates that she wants to play, go outside, or do training, oblige her if you can.

Not all kisses mean "I love you"

Have you ever picked up your small dog, only to receive a face-full of frantic licks? Your dog may actually be asking you to give her space. And as some guardians have learned the hard way, those licks may turn to a bite if the dog isn't given the space she's asking for.

I've met several people who have been bitten in the face while holding, hugging, or resting their heads on their little dogs. Activities that humans view as a bonding experience can bring up feelings of fear and vulnerability, particularly for small pups. When you barge into a dog's personal space by picking her up or approaching her head-on, she may react with calming signals to diffuse the tension, including a "kiss to dismiss." This behavior, introduced by Jennifer Shryock of Family Paws LLC, may occur because dogs know that licking you makes you recoil. Therefore, licking your face actually becomes an effective communication strategy for the dog to make you move away.

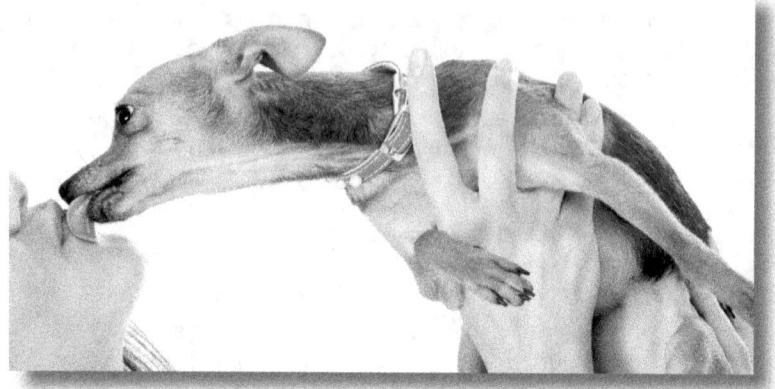

These sorts of licks do not come out of the blue. They occur when you approach, corner, or pick up a dog. As you approach, the dog is usually giving other signs that she is stressed:

- Head turns, where the dog averts her eyes or head from you, indicate a desire to create more space between you and her.

- Lip licking as you approach, as well as a tight-lipped yawn, are common signs that a dog is becoming stressed by your approach.

- Tension in the face and body also indicates a dog that is not having fun. Some dogs get wrinkled foreheads or furrowed brows. Others might close their mouths or hold their breath. Or they may simply show some tension in the eyes.

If those signs are not heeded and you put your face into the dog's, the dog may start licking your face. In some cases, this can escalate to a bite. Look for what Shryock calls the "lizard lick," with the tongue and neck extending forward. The dog is trying to create as much space as possible, and she will reach out to you before you enter her personal space any further. It's the doggie version of keeping someone at arm's length (Shryock, 2021).

If your dog's licks have ever turned to nips, there is a chance she was asking for more space by licking you, and after not being heard, she escalated to snapping or biting. Not all licks are intended to send you running, however, so look at all of the dog's body language to fully understand what your dog is trying to tell you. And if you believe your dog is "kissing to dismiss" you, avoid that kind of interaction in the future. This is another way of giving your dog a sense of control, by listening to her requests to be left alone.

The five-second petting test

Brace yourself for more surprising news. Not all dogs want to be petted, at least, not as much as we think. This is especially true for little dogs, who can easily get overwhelmed by the physical touch of us gigantic humans. But fear not, you can ask your dog if she'd like to be petted, and depending on her answer, you might get the green light again and again. This is a technique introduced by Grisha Stewart, and over the years, forms of it have been used in various contexts, including educating children about safe dog handling, use among shelter dogs, and adaptations for other species.

There are two points to keep in mind, to help you see these interactions from your dog's perspective:

Firstly, if a dog hasn't come to you on her own, then there's a good chance she doesn't want to be petted at that time. Your pup will probably tolerate petting from her family even when she's not interested but understand that you're getting a free pass because she generally loves and trusts you, even if you're bugging her at the moment. Your guests may not be treated so graciously, especially if they bend over your little dog, approach directly, or engage in other intimidating body language.

Secondly, just because your little buddy asked for pets and enjoyed them for 30 seconds, it doesn't mean she wants you to continue petting her. This may sound absurd, since she asked for the pets to begin with, but physical contact can be overstimulating at a certain point. This is true for humans, too. Do you have that friend that hugs you just a little too long and a lot too tightly? The hug starts out enjoyable, but when it's prolonged, it can make you feel awkward or even trapped. Don't be that friend to your dog.

To make sure petting is fun for both of you, do the **Five-second petting consent test**. The video below demonstrates this technique as well.

1. The dog approaches you for petting. (If she refuses to approach or shies away when you try to pet her, respect her space.)

2. Pet her gently for five seconds, in a spot you know she likes. Then stop.

3. See what she does. If she doesn't explicitly ask for more pets, then assume she does not want them. You can keep your hand casually near her (but not reaching out), to see if she tries to nudge or approach your hand to request more attention.

4. If she wants more petting, the dog may get closer to your body, paw at you, nudge you, or show other interactive body language. Her body should be relaxed or even wiggly. This is her green light signal, allowing you to pet her for another five seconds. Then stop again.

5. Continue asking for the dog's consent in this way while petting. Pause in intervals of seconds, not minutes, as a dog can change her mind and need more space at any time.

Video: https://www.bklnman-ners.com/chapter3.html

For some dogs, five seconds is actually too long. If you're not familiar with a dog, or if your dog has had handling issues in the past, shoot for only one or two seconds before stopping. As you learn to listen to your dog during these interactions, her trust in you will continue to build. She now knows that, if she gets overwhelmed when you are petting her, she can communicate her needs to you, and you will always make her feel comfortable and safe.

Now that you're able to see the world from your little dog's perspective, let's put these principles into practice, starting with handling, grooming, and other daily husbandry activities for your small dog in Chapter 4.

Chapter 4
Stress-Free Handling and Grooming

Imagine living among giants in their gigantic world. Massive feet and towering bodies, rooms with bone-crushing doors swinging to and fro, stairs the height of skyscrapers. When a giant wants to brush your hair, they hover over you and smash the brush into your tiny head. When one tries to brush your teeth, they practically knock out your incisors from the force. Feels like a pretty terrifying existence, doesn't it? This is the world that small dogs live in. And for these dogs, the most stressful parts of daily life usually involve handling, such as being picked up or leashed, hair brushing, nail trimming, and bathing. Regular grooming activities can feel threatening and even painful to our little dogs, so it's no wonder many of them become aggressive even at the sight of a brush or harness.

At the same time, we humans know that many small dogs have big maintenance needs. Since grooming, bathing, and nail trimming are all necessary to keep your pup healthy and comfortable, it pays to teach your dog to enjoy (or at least tolerate) these things. Follow the tips below to ensure your dog can handle all the spa-treatment activities that will be necessary throughout her life.

Many of the activities in this chapter include conditioning a dog to being muzzled, grooming, nail trims, or other necessary work with your dog's body. **Conditioning** refers to a systematic way to teach a dog to tolerate or even enjoy specific types of handling. We do this in two ways. First, we make sure to present the hand, brush, or muzzle only to an extent that the dog is visibly comfortable. The "Ease into body handling" (page 36) section below will show you what to look for. That means no pinning down Callie to get her sharp talons trimmed. Second, we associate the handling with a positive outcome, such as delicious food. By working at your dog's pace through the practices in this chapter, you will be reminding your dog that she can feel secure in your presence, even when you're holding a brush or nail clippers. With time and practice, your dogs can be like mine, begging, "Pleeease brush my teeth!" at the sight of their toothbrushes.

Muzzle training

Even the tiniest of teeth can puncture a hand or ankle, so if your dog is a bite risk to you, your groomer, your vet, or others, it's imperative to teach her to comfortably wear a basket muzzle for short periods of time. This is an issue of safety, liability, and consideration for those who handle your pup, regardless of your dog's size. A basket muzzle is usually made of plastic, rubber, leather, or metal wires, which form a cage full of holes around the dog's mouth. The dog should be able to pant, eat treats, and even drink water while wearing it. For most small dogs, the fit is more important than the material. This is because a small dog is unlikely to bite through a plastic or rubber muzzle; however, she might be able to paw it off her tiny face, so aim for a basket muzzle that can be properly fitted to her dimensions. For a perfect fit, consider a custom-made muzzle using your dog's dimensions, such as those from Trust Your Dog, Bumas, and Dog Muzzles Store; you can even design a muzzle for French Bulldog, Pug, and Boston Terrier faces.

If you're uncomfortable with muzzles, I understand. It feels unsettling to some dog guardians, whether for aesthetic or emotional reasons. But in reality, a muzzle is simply one more piece of equipment, like a harness or leash. And it's a piece of equipment that allows you to safely teach your dog skills while avoiding injury or a lawsuit. While our goal for training is always to keep the dog calm and comfortable, the reality is that sometimes we accidentally push too far in our training, risking a bite. Or sometimes the vet needs to handle your dog, draw blood, or perform other essential duties, even when your dog isn't in the mood for it. The fact is that your dog will probably need to wear a muzzle at some point. If she is muzzle trained, she'll be content even when wearing one at the vet, whereas a dog that isn't accustomed to a muzzle will be significantly more stressed. If you're on the fence about this tool, visit the Muzzle Up Project (muzzleupproject.com) to learn more about muzzles and how to muzzle train.

The key point with muzzle training is to teach the dog to push her face into the muzzle, not to push the muzzle into the dog's face. Imagine if someone were shoving a hockey mask toward your face; you would immediately back away. But now imagine that someone was holding a hockey mask still, with a hundred-dollar bill right on the other side of it. Wouldn't you be tempted to move toward the mask in order to snatch the money?

Follow these steps to ensure your dog thinks muzzle training is a fun game.

How to teach muzzle training

Take the muzzle out of its packaging and place it on the floor for your dog to investigate. Don't touch it yourself or do any training yet. Just leave it on the floor for a few hours to let your dog get used to it. If your dog backs away from or avoids the muzzle, repeat this a few times a day, over several days. You can sprinkle treats around (but not in) the muzzle to encourage your dog to walk around it.

1. Present the muzzle in your cupped palm, as if the muzzle is a bowl. Put a few treats inside the muzzle (which is inside your hand) and let your dog eat out of it. Do not touch the straps or attempt to put the muzzle on in any way. Repeat until your dog sees the muzzle and thinks, "Yay, food bowl!"

2. Now, steps 2-4 will happen in the same session. You'll hold the muzzle in its normal upright position, at nose-level with your little dog. Place a long, thin treat in a hole of the muzzle, as in the photo. Use the hole that lines up with the dog's mouth.

Place a long, thin treat in a hole of the muzzle and let the dog bring her face into it.

3. Hold the muzzle still, a few inches in front of your dog. Let your dog dig her face into the muzzle to eat the treat. Repeat a few times, until your dog is happily sticking her face into the muzzle for a treat.

4. Then, when your dog reaches her head into the muzzle, draw it away from her, just a few millimeters. Your dog will have to reach farther and move toward the muzzle in order to get the treat. Repeat until your dog is walking right into the muzzle. This may take several sessions.

5. Repeat the same sequence, but without the treat poking through the muzzle. You will let your dog walk into the muzzle, wait one second, then pop a treat through the hole. Do this a few times while the dog's face is still in the muzzle: pause one second, pop a treat into the muzzle, then pause one more second, and pop another treat into the muzzle. Repeat this over several sessions until your dog is comfortably holding her face in the muzzle. We want your dog to think this is just a fun training game.

6. Increase the duration of the muzzle on your dog's face, with you still holding it. Pause two seconds before giving the treat through the muzzle, then two

more seconds, and another treat. Keep working your way up to about five seconds between treats.

7. Now, let's incorporate the straps. During those five second pauses, with one hand, you'll fiddle with the straps for only a second or two. Your other hand is still holding the muzzle in place, so you won't be able to clip the straps yet. Practice until she's unfazed by your fiddling.

8. It's now time to clip the straps. Show the muzzle, let your dog put her face in, quickly clip the straps, and then have a big treat party of five or more treats, one after another, while your dog is wearing the muzzle. Remove the muzzle immediately. Practice until your dog loves this game.

9. Once your dog can get the muzzle strapped on comfortably, you will ask her to wear it for several seconds while you give some treats, and then pause, give some treats, and then pause. Remove the muzzle before she gets annoyed.

Leveling up
Add duration to your dog's muzzle experience. Continue to make it really fun!

- While your little dog is muzzled, start walking around the room together. Give a treat, walk a few steps, then give another treat.

- With your dog wearing the muzzle, ask for easy, fun cues she knows well. Sit, paw, spin, touch (nose/paw target) are all good options.

Continue practicing this on a maintenance level long-term. Depending on how often you need to use the muzzle in real life, it could be a daily practice or a weekly practice. For instance, with Margaret, I do one very short practice weekly. However, if I know we have a vet appointment coming up, I will practice two to three times a week for at least two weeks beforehand.

Ease into body handling
Handling your small dog's body is inevitable. Practice the following activity for a dog that shows signs of stress during body handling, grooming or nail trims, including at the groomer or vet.

How to ease into body handling
Start acclimating your dog to handling, touching, and grooming with some simple touch activities.

1. Set your dog up so that you are relatively level with each other, to avoid hovering over her. Choose a spot where she can walk away if she wants to. For instance, sit on the floor with her or on the couch together. She should never feel trapped, as that could increase her stress and take away her choice and control.

2. You'll say a **communication cue**—a word or phrase to tell your dog that you're about to touch her. You could say "groom" or "clippers." Mine is the somewhat embarrassing "brushy brushy." Then you'll very gently run your hand along your dog's body for a few inches, going in the direction of the hair. Choose a part of the body that your dog is comfortable with. This may be her back, her chest, or her shoulder. Feet, legs, rump, tail, and top of the head may not be good starting points, as some dogs dislike being touched there.

3. Continue this for several strokes, as long as your dog seems to be enjoying it. Remember to say your word before each stroke. Revisit the "Trust and security are intertwined" section (page 18) for the signs of fear, anxiety, and stress. Some of the common signs in a handling context include:

    • Turning her head toward your hand (as in, "Don't make me bite you.")

    • Whale eye

    • Leaning away or cowering

    • Freezing or stiffening

4. Stop the session before your dog gets tired of it or shows any signs of stress. A few strokes is plenty.

5. For the next several sessions, only touch parts of your dog's body that she is comfortable with, and continuously watch her body language for signs of stress.

6. Now, you will use a Fear-Free® technique called **touch gradient**, where you start with a comfortable part of the dog's body, and gently glide your hand to a less comfortable part, such as a leg. This is far less scary to a dog than simply grabbing her leg or tail. As you do this, continue to assess your dog for signs of stress. It may take several sessions, but over time, you want to be able to touch every part of your dog, from nose to tail and from ears to toes, using this gliding motion. Always continue to assess for signs of stress.

You can repeat these activities in short doses on a regular basis. For dogs that require a lot of grooming, give them a short daily reminder of how nice it is to be touched. For lower maintenance dogs, weekly sessions should be enough.

During husbandry activities at home, it's important to listen to what she is telling you and use the conditioning exercises in this chapter to ensure she feels secure when you are interacting with her. But what about at the vet or groomer? If your dog is showing multiple signs of fear, anxiety, or stress, consider talking to your vet about an as-needed medication for certain vet or groomer visits, as well as using a basket muzzle for safety. This will prevent your dog from escalating to detrimental SOS-levels of stress, and in turn, will make future vet or grooming appointments more tolerable for everyone. One terrible experience can make a dog fearful of grooming or nail trims for life, and I urge you to prevent that at all costs. To learn more you can visit the Fear Free website for pet guardians, www.fearfreehappy-homes.com. It has a number of resources.

Grooming

Initially, when grooming with a brush or comb, expect to only do a few brush strokes in one sitting. This means you will not be removing matted hair or fully de-shedding your pup right away. Going slowly pays off in the long run, so be patient. This is a sample progression, but make sure your dog is comfortable at each step before proceeding. You will probably need to spend several sessions at each level. Your dog will tell you when you've gone too quickly through the steps, by showing signs of stress or discomfort as mentioned in the previous section.

As with body handling, you should position your dog and yourself in a way that is comfortable for your dog. Avoid hovering over or restraining your pup. The photo of little Morti the Chihuahua and his guardian, Ryan, demonstrates this. Notice how Ryan keeps his body from leaning over Morti, and Morti isn't shying from the brush, turning away, or cowering during grooming.

Aim to position yourself like this to avoid hovering over your pup when grooming.

1. Say your communication cue word(s), and do a very gentle stroke, barely touching the dog's hair. Start at the least sensitive part of the dog's body. As you do this, look for signs of stress to ensure you're not pushing her too far out of her comfort zone.

2. After the brush stroke, you may give what I call a *thank-you treat*. This is a small, low-value treat that reinforces how nice it is to tolerate brushing, but not so delicious that it makes the dog excited or distracted.

3. If your dog did not show any signs of stress and appeared to be comfortable with the first gentle stroke, do another stroke and thank-you treat. Repeat this along the whole body, but be ready to stop at any time your dog shows any sign of stress or discomfort.

4. The next session, say your communication cue word(s), and do a slightly firmer brush stroke, with the bristles touching the hair, but not the skin. Start at the least sensitive part of the dog's body. If your dog did not show any signs of stress, do another stroke. Repeat along the whole body, but stop any time your dog indicates she needs a break, by displaying behaviors that indicate stress.

5. As the sessions continue, press a little more firmly, until you're grooming your pup with normal pressure.

Thank-you treats

Throughout this book, you'll see mentions of a thank-you treat. These are rewards I give my dog when she makes a desirable choice. In the case of grooming, I'm thanking my little pup for standing quietly and tolerating a brush stroke. She could have just as easily walked away, but she chose to accept the brushing.

You'll see the use of thank-you treats for other training exercises in the following chapters, too. For instance, if your skateboard-reactive dog chooses to calmly look up at you when she sees a passing skateboard, that behavior is worthy of a big "thank you!" In this case, she chose to give you eye contact rather than bark, lunge, or frantically twirl. As you work with your little dog, you can tailor this concept to your dog's particular needs.

As far as brushing equipment is concerned, I will admit that I'm not an expert on this topic. For brushing equipment, I recommend Agnes Murphy's *Dog Grooming: An Owner's Handbook*. But from a behavioral perspective, I'd recommend a small brush that feels comfortable on the dog's skin. Stiff bristles that poke the skin are less tolerable for some dogs, so at least in the early days of brushing, I encourage you to look for the softest brush you can find, even if it's not the most efficient from a grooming perspective. With my short-coated dogs, I usually start by acclimating them to a soft bristle brush, and in the weeks and months that follow, add in an undercoat rake, which is less enjoyable to them, but more effective at removing hair.

Nail trimming

Just the thought of doggie nail clippers sends many owners and dogs into a panicked sweat. As with brushing, don't expect to trim all your dog's nails—or any of them—on day one. This is usually a process of trust-building that spans a period of time.

In part, trust comes with choosing the right kind of trimming device, so let's decide what's best for your dog.

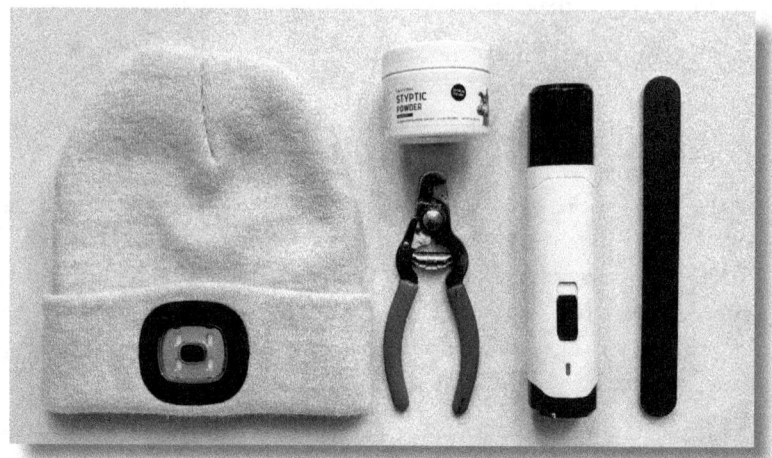

My nail trim tools may include a headlamp, styptic powder, clippers, nail grinder, and nail file.

Nail Clippers: First, the standard nail clippers offer the quickest way to cut a nail, by placing the nail in the center hole and compressing it with one little snip. Another benefit is that they do not make any noise, except the sound of the nail crunching. But before you run out and buy a pair, consider these caveats. Some dogs have intense aversions to them, probably due to the way in which their guardians clip the nails. Do not pinch off the tip of the nail all at once, as if you're chopping a tree. This can cause intense pain and bleeding if you misjudge the location of the **quick** (the area containing the blood vessel and nerves inside the nail). Even if you don't "quick" your pup, the crrrrunch of the nail is upsetting to many dogs. You can avoid this problem by shaping the nail, as if you're shaving the tip of each nail into a sharp point. You'll thinly slice bits off the tip, diagonally, until the sides have been shaved down like a newly sharpened pencil. And after doing so, I recommend taking your dog for a walk on the pavement, to dull that sharp dagger.

Dremel: If the description of the clippers gives you shivers, then perhaps a nail grinder (also called a Dremel) is a better option. This tool allows you to shape the nail more easily than clippers, making smooth, rounded edges. The chance of quicking your dog is reduced, and because the process is slower, your dog can safely pull her paw away if she feels discomfort. The down side of a nail grinder is that it makes a whirring noise and vibrates against the nail. While many dogs are able to overcome this aversion, dogs with sound sensitivity may struggle.

Nail File: Finally, you can file your dog's nails with an emery board designed for people. This is the most labor-intensive option, but also the safest. It is virtually impossible to quick your dog and cause bleeding because of how slowly the filing goes. Because you are manually filing each nail, the vibration and noise is far less than a grinder. If you choose this option, be prepared to file your dog's nails frequently, since you can't take off a huge amount of nail all at once (unless you have the most patient dog on the planet). As you'll see in the video, this is the option I chose for Beans, after having had an unpleasant experience with the clippers and being too sound-sensitive to tolerate a nail grinder. After about two weeks, she started jumping for joy at the sign of the emery board, so we've stuck with this trimming style for years.

Video: https://www. bklnmanners.com/ chapter4.html

Scratch Board: This is a great alternative to traditional nail trimming, particularly for fearful or aggressive dogs. You can teach your dog to file her own nails, especially for the front feet, by pawing at a scratch board (also called scratch pad). This tool is essentially a piece of sandpaper adhered to a board. I use a scratch pad for Margaret, who came to us with extreme aggression when her front feet were handled. She adores doing this trick for a few scratches every day and this regular scratching has made formal nail trims unnecessary on her front paws. Similar to the emery board, you shouldn't expect to file a large amount of nail in one sitting, so it requires a little bit of maintenance on a regular basis.

Teach your dog to file her own nails with a scratch board.

How to condition to nail trimming

This sample progression uses a nail grinder, since it requires an extra step of acclimating your dog to the noise. However, the steps for acclimating your dog to nail clippers or an emery board would generally be the same.

1. With the tool off, let your dog investigate it on her own. Do not push it toward your dog. Either hold it still or leave it on the floor.

2. Decide the most comfortable position to file your dog's nails and practice this position without the nail grinder. These are some options:

The dog is sitting on your lap, in a typical sit position. The nail trimming video in this chapter demonstrates this position.

The dog is being held by a helper, with the legs dangling below, as shown in the photo. For some dogs, this seems to feel the most secure and comfortable, but other dogs might feel trapped, which can increase their stress about nail trims. Watch your dog's body language to ensure you're not causing stress.

Some dogs feel the most secure during nail trims when a helper holds them with legs dangling.

She is reclining with her back pressed against your lap and chest, her legs sticking outward, baby-bjorn style.

She is standing on a cushion. You should be able to use the grinder without having to pick up the feet. (If it has a safety cap, it will not destroy the cushion.) However, for clippers or emery boards, you will need to hold each foot while trimming, meaning your dog needs to be able to balance on three legs.

3. Practice the same position, with your finger gently touching one toe on each paw for one to two seconds. Your dog can have a thank-you treat after each touch.

Watch your dog's body language to gauge how she feels. Does she pull her paw away? Move her nose or mouth toward your hand? Squirm or cower? Show aggression? If so, reduce how intensely you are handling her paws. Do not proceed past this point until you have conditioned your dog to enjoy brief touches on every foot.

Your dog should be able to walk away at any point. If your dog walks away, respect her choice and give her a minute to calm down. You can stay there quietly, and if she returns, you can start again. Avoid bribing with treats, picking her up, or begging her to come back. Respect her choice, even if it's not what you want.

4. Increase the difficulty by touching every toe on every foot. You can give a treat after each toe, or after each foot, depending on how tolerant your dog is. Continue at this level until you have conditioned your dog to enjoy toe touches.

5. Hold each toe as you would when grinding it. You are essentially miming the nail trimming with your fingers. This means you may have to hold the foot as you touch a toe, or you may need to gently grab onto the nail. Give a treat after each toe or foot. Practice until your dog enjoys this.

6. Now get the dog in the same position, and gently tap the nail grinder to each toe, with the tool still off. Treat after every toe or foot. Practice until your dog is comfortable.

7. In a separate session, show your dog that the sound of the nail grinder is really cool. Hold the grinder and have either a favorite toy or some extra tasty treats in your other hand. With at least a few feet between you and your dog, turn on the grinder to the lowest setting. Immediately toss the toy or treats onto the floor. The idea is to associate the sound with a happy outcome. Do not push the grinder into your dog's space. Practice this game until your dog hears the grinder turn on and looks happily at you, waiting for the game to start.

8. Have the grinder next to you and get your dog in her nail trim position. Turn on the grinder, but do not move it toward your dog. Give her some treats as she sits (or lies or stands) in the position. If your dog is comfortable, gently touch her toes with your hand, not the grinder. Then turn off the grinder and stop the treats. Practice until your dog is comfortable with this.

9. Now a big step! You will start grinding for a split second. Get your dog in the proper position. Turn on the grinder, on the lowest setting, if possible. Hold one toe as before, and touch the grinder to that toe for a split second. Give a thank-you treat. If your dog is still comfortable, repeat this for one toe (not every toe!) on each foot. Practice at this level until your dog is comfortable being touched with the grinder on all four feet.

10. Repeat the above sequence for every toe. Plan to start with a split-second grind on each toenail of one foot. You may need to take a break after every foot, which is fine. Short, low-stress sessions now will allow you to do longer, stress-free sessions later.

11. From here, you will very gradually extend the amount of time you are grinding each toenail. Plan to grind all the nails on one foot for one to two seconds each, rewarding after every toe. After trimming all the nails on one foot, you may need to take a break.

   Remember to shape the nails by rounding the edges and smoothing out any sharp points.

12. Continue extending how many seconds you are trimming each nail, as well as how many nails you can trim in one session. Always listen to your dog and watch her body language to see if she tells you she needs a break.

When your rewards aren't rewarding

The relationship between you, your dog, and treats can be complicated. Simply putting a treat in front of your dog's nose will not automatically fix serious behavior problems. In fact, when used improperly, treats can actually increase a dog's stress.

You might be thinking, "Wait, what? Treats can make things worse?" In some cases, yes. If your dog is highly stressed during a training session and you use treats, she can actually form a negative association with that particular food. Imagine you need to trim your dog's nails, right now, even though your pup is absolutely terrified of the clippers. So you use a spoonful of peanut butter to sweeten the deal. You crrrunch a nail and feed some peanut butter, crrrunch another nail and feed a little more. If your dog's stress is very high during this experience, you can turn her off of both the clippers and the peanut butter. This is because the peanut butter now triggers a conditioned fear response, as it predicts something overwhelming and terrifying. In essence, when the dog sees peanut butter, she thinks, "Uh oh, they're going to trick me into doing something I won't like." At that point, even the tastiest goodie won't convince her that a nail trim is OK.

But now, imagine you go through a nail trimming protocol very slowly, always making sure your dog is comfortable at one level before increasing to the next. Your dog gets a lick of peanut butter each time you touch the clipper to her toe, and over numerous short training sessions, you eventually trim a single nail. Then multiple nails, and so on. By going at your dog's pace, you are making a positive association with the clippers and the peanut butter. Wins all around!

The takeaway here is that using treats alone, no matter how tasty, will not help a dog overcome an intense fear. Rather, treats are a means to accelerate behavior modification and make it more fun for your dog, provided you do not breach the upper limits of her comfort zone.

How to file nails with a scratch pad

A scratch pad is a great method for getting shorter nails on the front paws, no clippers needed. To get started, you'll need a small square of fine-grained sandpaper and lots of small, stinky treats. Eventually, you'll need to purchase a scratch pad, or you can make your own by gluing a sheet of sandpaper to a board, a plastic cutting board or sturdy cardboard.

1. First, you'll teach your dog to paw at the small square of sandpaper. Place a stinky treat on the ground and cover it with the square of sandpaper.

2. At first, your dog may try to push the paper away with her nose to get at the treat. Just hold the sandpaper still and stay quiet. Eventually, your dog will use her paw to try pushing the sandpaper away. The moment she touches her paw to the sandpaper, mark "yes" and quickly remove the sandpaper to let her eat the treat. Repeat this for a few sessions until she is easily pawing at the sandpaper.

   If your dog won't paw the sandpaper, mark and reward for any movement of a paw toward the paper. As time goes on, she will learn that it's her paw movement you're marking and rewarding. She'll start to paw more dramatically, eventually hitting the sandpaper.

3. Now stop placing the treat behind the sandpaper. You will hold the sandpaper out or place it on the floor, the same as before, with nothing behind it. When your dog paws at the sandpaper, immediately mark and reward with a treat from your treat pouch or pocket. Practice until she can enthusiastically hit the sandpaper.

   When you give the reward, toss it behind your dog a few feet, so she has to run and find it. Once your dog has eaten the treat, she'll run back to the sandpaper with some momentum and paw at it more enthusiastically.

   If your dog is pawing hard enough to actually file her nails, don't overpractice this. You don't want her nails to get so short they become tender or bleed.

4. Present the scratch board, with the sandpaper securely fastened to it. Mark and reward, same as before, when your dog paws at it. Practice until she's happily pawing at the board.

5. Once your dog can reliably do at least one full scratch, then you can wait to mark and reward until she offers multiple scratches and eventually scratches with both paws.

   For multiple scratches, simply delay the marking and rewarding. Your dog will scratch once and look at you for reinforcement. You can cheer but don't reward yet. Once she scratches twice or more, mark and reward with a jackpot of several treats.

   To make sure she scratches with both paws, you can jackpot when she scratches with her non-dominant paw. This will make using her non-dominant paw more rewarding. You can also try angling the board closer to her non-dominant paw for a few scratches.

Video: https://www.bklnmanners.com/chapter4.html

6. At this point your dog is fully doing the scratching behavior. If you'd like a verbal cue, I say "Scratch It" right before I present the sandpaper. Usually presenting the sandpaper is enough to get the dog interested in scratching, even without a verbal cue.

Mark and reward

For many of the training behaviors in this book, you'll see the phrase **mark and reward**. This is an integral part of the training sequence. Before you start training, get comfortable with these terms. Here is an example of a training sequence when teaching a dog to use a scratch pad.

1. You verbally cue, "Roxie, Scratch It" as you hold out the visual cue of the sandpaper.

2. Roxie swipes her paw on the sandpaper.

3. At that moment, you mark the behavior. Most commonly we use the words "Yes," "Good Dog," or the click of a clicker. The marker identifies that the thing she just did—swiping her paw on the sandpaper—was what you were looking for. The timing of the marker should be precise.

4. Follow that up with a reinforcer, which can be anything the dog wants. It might be a treat, initiating play, or pets from you. The dog, not you, determines what is rewarding. So if your dog is averse to petting, then pets are not a reward. And if your dog really dislikes chicken, then a chicken treat won't motivate her to scratch the sandpaper again. Experiment with different rewards to let your dog tell you what motivates her.

Chin rest for handling, grooming and nail trim issues

This protocol is meant to give your dog a way to communicate with you, to tell you either "yes, I'm ready for some grooming," or "no, please stop." We call these **consent cues**, and they give the dog a way to consent to certain procedures. Consent cues are particularly useful for small dogs whose natural body language can be hard to read. If you aren't sure if your dog is stressed or not during grooming, then teach her how to do a **chin rest** using the instructions below. When her chin is resting on a certain object, she is giving you the green light to move forward with a few brush strokes. And if her head pops up, detaching from the object, it's a red light, indicating she needs a break.

You'll need an object for your dog to rest her chin on. A firm pillow, padded stool, or a rolled towel work well. You can even use your palm, or for taller dogs, your lap. Keep your dog's height in mind, so her chin can comfortably settle onto the object. As you'll see in the video, I may use a padded stool, my palm, or my lap, depending on the dog's height. Choose a location with non-slip flooring, and have lots of little treats handy.

How to teach a chin rest

1. Start by setting up the object (we'll use a folded towel for this example) at chin-height for your dog. You and your dog are on opposite sides of the towel.

2. If your dog puts her chin on the towel, mark "Yes" and reward calmly with a treat. If your dog doesn't naturally put her chin on the towel, use a treat to lure her head into the position, so her head is lightly resting on the towel. Then mark and reward.

   If you are luring, point your finger to the towel as you lure. This pointing gesture can become a visual cue in the next step.

3. Once your dog is comfortable with luring, take the treat out of your pointing hand. You will still point, empty handed. Reward immediately from your other hand while the dog's chin is still on the towel. Release with "OK."

4. Repeat this until your dog is offering to put her chin on the towel when you point to it. For several reps, reward her as her chin is touching the towel, then release with "OK." And then occasionally, say "Get It" as you toss a treat reward a few feet behind your dog, so she has to reset her body position from scratch.

   Your dog might be pawing at the towel, climbing on the stool, or doing other undesired behaviors. Ignore those. If your dog needs a reset, toss a treat a few feet behind her.

5. Now add the verbal cue, which for me is "Chin." Say "Chin," point if needed, and then wait for her to put her chin on the towel. After a split second of her chin touching the towel, mark, reward, and release. Repeat until she's able to respond to the "Chin" cue over several repetitions.

6. Start adding duration. This means you will teach your dog to keep her chin on the towel for longer and longer. The sequence is: cue "Chin," pause one second and reward, pause one second and reward, pause one second and reward, release with "OK." Repeat until she's comfortably holding the position for several repetitions.

7. Continue adding duration. Now it's two seconds in between treats. Over several sessions, work your way up to five seconds between treats.

   Be very methodical about increasing duration. Count in your head, and record how many seconds your dog can do the chin rest in each session. It may take several sessions to get a few seconds of duration.

   Occasionally throw in some short, easy reps, too! Just like human students, canine students gain confidence and motivation with an easy win once in a while.

8. Once your dog can hold the chin rest for about five seconds of duration, it's time to incorporate distractions. I recommend distractions that simulate a

very, very toned-down version of grooming. Start by choosing your groom-ing position, which might be different from the face-to-face position you're currently in. So you'll cue the chin rest with you sitting at your dog's left and right sides. After several seconds of each chin rest, mark, reward, and release as before. Practice over several sessions.

9. Now add the mild distraction of hand movements that simulate groom-ing. You are not holding a brush yet, nor are you even touching your dog. Your air-brushing hand will be several inches away from the dog's body. Cue "Chin," and sweep your hand, a few inches at a time, past your dog's body. Start with the least sensitive parts of her body, and as you do more and more practice sessions, sweep the air near the more sensitive parts—usually legs, rear end, tail, or top of the head.

Does your dog stay in the chin rest position as your hand sweeps? Great! Give her a treat after each hand sweep. Holding the chin rest position will become your dog's "green light" behavior to tell you to keep grooming.

Does your dog pop her head up as you move your hand? That's OK too! This will become your dog's "red light" cue to you, telling you to stop grooming for a moment. When your dog lifts his head off the towel, immediately stop moving your hand. Give her a few seconds, and then cue the chin rest again, moving your hand less dramatically next time.

Does your dog walk away or lose interest? Does she keep giving "red light" head lifts? She's telling you she needs a break.

Video: https://www. bklnmanners.com/ chapter4.html

Leveling up

As time goes on, you'll gradually increase the level of distraction by making movements closer to the dog's body and eventually adding a brush. You'll also add duration, mean-ing how long the dog is being asked to hold the chin rest position. These are some of the future levels, which would take place over several sessions, at your dog's pace.

1. Sweep your hand closer to the dog's body. (This adds distraction.)

2. Reward after every two-to-three sweeps instead of every sweep. (This adds duration.)

3. Use your fingers as a very gentle comb, touching your dog's body. Reward for every stroke. (This adds distraction.)

4. Use your fingers as a very gentle comb, touching your dog's body. Reward for every two-to-three strokes. (This adds duration.)

5. Hold the brush and sweep the air around your dog, not touching her body. Reward for every stroke. (This adds distraction.)

6. Hold the brush and sweep the air around your dog, not touching her body. Reward for two-to-three strokes. (This adds duration.)

7. Brush your dog gently for one stroke and reward. (This adds distraction.)

8. Brush your dog gently for two-to-three strokes and reward. (This adds duration.)

As you continue to practice, remember to sprinkle in short reps with no distractions, so your dog isn't overly challenged. And remember to watch her head—if she lifts her head from the chin rest, she's telling you she needs a break. And if, after a few seconds of break, she is reluctant to do another repetition of chin rest, end the session. We want the dog to know that she has control over what happens to her body.

Beyond grooming, chin rest can be applied to a number of other situations, many of which happen at the vet clinic. Nail trimming, body handling, vaccinations, ear cleanings, tick removal, or checking eyes and teeth are all made easier when the dog can hold her head still for a short period of time. In all of these cases, you should introduce new kinds of touching or restraint just as you did for the grooming, by starting with a very toned-down version of the action and slowly increasing the level of distraction and duration. You may find other useful scenarios for it, as well. I've used it as a recall game for some dogs, by cuing "Chin" from a distance. Get creative with your pup, too!

Toothbrushing

It's generally believed that small dogs are more prone to dental issues than their larger kin. This may be due to crowding of the teeth inside those tiny jaws, retention of baby teeth to create even more crowding, and bite abnormalities among brachycephalic (flat-faced) breeds. While there are plenty of supplements, water additives, and chews to help maintain healthy teeth and gums, nothing works as well as daily brushing. Yes, daily!

If your dog has never had her teeth brushed before, it's important to have the right tools and to go slowly. You'll need toothpaste specifically for dogs, as some human toothpaste is toxic; look for flavors that your dog already loves, such as poultry. If your dog thinks toothpaste is a special treat, as mine do, then she will literally jump for joy at the sight of the toothbrush and paste. You'll also need a brush that can fit inside that little mouth. A finger brush may be too bulky for some tiny dogs' mouths, so consider a toothbrush made specifically for small dogs or even for (human) babies. I use a C.E.T. pet toothbrush for Beans, which is small enough to fit under those tight Chihuahua jowls. For Margaret, I decided on a circular 360-degree baby's toothbrush, as she has more dental issues, and this brush seems to cover a bit more surface area.

To acclimate your dog to toothbrushing, choose a position where your dog is securely next to you, but can walk away if she gets overwhelmed. As you'll see in the video, I like to sit next to my dog on the couch. Plan your brushing sessions for times when your dog is already relaxed. These are typical stages of acclimating a dog to toothbrushing.

How to condition to toothbrushing

1. Show your dog the toothbrush, but don't pick it up yet. Leave the toothbrush next to your dog as you practice steps 2 and 3.

2. Start by letting the dog lick the toothpaste off your finger. As she licks, occasionally move your finger around the outside of her gums and teeth, even just a centimeter or two. This simulates the feeling of a toothbrush in her mouth, but only for a few seconds at a time. You're alternating a few seconds of gently sweeping your finger around the mouth, and another few seconds of regular licking.

   If your dog turns up her nose at the toothpaste after several tries, look for another flavor or brand.

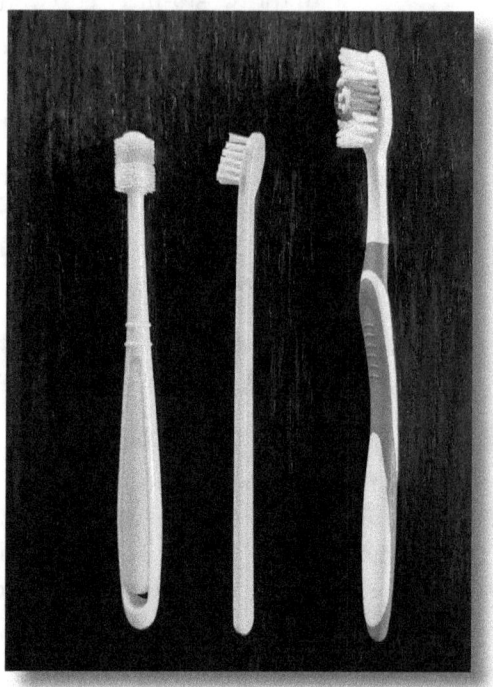

From left to right: a circular 360-degree baby's toothbrush, a small pet toothbrush, and a human adult toothbrush for comparison.

3. Repeat Step 2, but as your finger "brushes" her teeth for a few seconds, you'll take your other hand to gently cradle her snout, as you see in the video, to stabilize her head. You may or may not need to also lift up her lips to brush her teeth.

   Make sure your dog isn't showing signs of fear (cowering, turning away, trying to escape) or aggression (stiffness, hard stare, growling, snapping). If she is, do not push it. Do the brushing less invasively, or stop altogether if you have concerns.

4. Once she's enjoying Step 3, then you'll incorporate the toothbrush. Let your dog lick the toothpaste off the toothbrush. As she licks, hold the toothbrush on both sides of her mouth, behind the canines, as well as right in front of her mouth.

5. If your dog is showing no signs of stress with Step 4, occasionally do a quick sweep along a few teeth with the brush, as you gently stabilize your dog's snout with the other hand, if needed. Start with the teeth that are most

accessible, such as the upper canines (fangs). Aim for about 90% licking and 10% brushing.

6. As time goes on, gradually add in more brush strokes and less licking. For instance, 80% licking and 20% brushing, then 70% licking and 30% brushing, and so on.

7. When your dog is comfortable with the more accessible teeth being brushed, then you can start pushing the brush gently toward the back teeth.

Take lots of short breaks while brushing, so you're brushing for a few seconds, and then taking a break (or giving several licks) to cool off. If your dog walks away, let her have as much time as she needs before trying again.

Video: https://www.
bklnmanners.com/
chapter4.html

Bathing

Although you won't bathe your dog as often as you brush her hair or teeth, it's still wise to have a plan for occasional baths. Baths are one situation where your dog doesn't have a lot of options. Once the water starts flowing and the soap is foaming, you have to see the process through to the end. For this reason, it's important to ensure your dog has choice and control in other areas of her life, as introduced in Chapter 3. When a dog is generally able to make choices and have her personal space respected, it's less stressful during those infrequent moments when she has to tolerate something unpleasant.

However, even for baths, you can make the experience more enjoyable for your pup. Get a lick mat with suction cups, which can be stuck on the bathtub or sink wall. Load the mat with peanut butter or your dog's favorite wet food. Adhere the lick mat to your bathtub at doggie eye-level, and she can happily lick, lick, lick while you lather, rinse, and towel dry. While bathing, make sure you use lukewarm water—neither hot nor cool—and products specifically designed for dogs. And then, once your shivering little one has been towel dried, give her a warm spot to dry off. In our home, when

On spa day, Niles enjoys baths thanks to his lick mat adhered to the bathtub.

there are no suitable sunbeams post-bath, I pull out a space heater and let the trembling Chihuahuas huddle in front of it until they're dry.

Calorie considerations

You'll notice that many of the training and behavior modification protocols in this book utilize treats. This is partly because food is motivating to almost every dog. Treats make training rewarding and meaningful, especially in the early stages when we're asking them to contort their bodies into strange positions and do activities they would never choose to do on their own. Treats also add precision to your training. For instance, when teaching your dog to go to her place on the couch, the placement of the treat will help your dog understand exactly where to go.

The issue for small dogs is calorie consumption. It's worth knowing how many calories your dog takes in on a daily basis, which you can calculate using the labels on your dog's food and treat containers. On days when you do more training than usual, be prepared to reduce your dog's next meal accordingly. The rule of thumb is that treats should comprise no more than 10% of your dog's caloric intake.

Look for treats that can easily be divided into tiny pieces. I prefer the "soft and stinky" variety, meaning the treats can be broken into very small portions without crumbling, and they're smelly enough to be motivating. With your fingernail, you can slice one little round training treat into six pieces or more. This will allow you to be generous with your rewards, without the guilt of overstuffing a tiny tummy.

For low-level tasks, use a portion of your dog's regular meals as treats. Simply measure your dog's meals in the morning, and then put aside a certain amount for training sessions throughout the day.

Get Carried Away: Teach your dog to love being picked up

Small dogs sometimes need to be picked up. This isn't coddling or spoiling them—it's a matter of safety. If I'm walking my two dogs past their greatest fear, the dreaded garbage truck, I scoop one pup in each arm and jog past. The garbage truck is so unpredictable and noisy, with bins flying and trash crunching, I fear my dogs would try to escape their harnesses in a panic. Perhaps you don't experience this particular terror, but there are likely other situations in your daily life that require a quick pickup.

Imagine if my dogs were afraid of being picked up, and they darted away when they saw my approaching hands. Or worse, if they tried to bite me as I scooped them up. On garbage day, it would be a serious safety concern. By picking your dog up in a way that makes her feel safe, you'll be building another layer of trust. Follow these steps to show your dog that she has nothing to fear when you come near.

How to condition your small dog to being picked up

1. You approach your dog indirectly, as described in "Follow the 'dog rule book' on body language" on page 26, with a treat in your hand or pocket. Think hot dog, not kibble. You do not need to show the treat.

2. When you reach your dog, avoid hovering over her. If she is on the couch, sit next to her. If she is on the floor, kneel next to her. See the photo on page 38 of little Morti, whose guardian, Ryan, is taking care not to lean over his itty-bitty Chihuahua.

3. Have a treat in the hand that is farther from your dog. The hand closer to your dog is empty; this will be the picking-up hand. The photo demonstrates this.

4. As you sit or kneel down, facing parallel to your dog's side, you give her a treat. This makes a positive association with you getting into her space.

5. Practice at this level until your dog is comfortable. Is she turning her head toward your pick-up hand? Stopping eating? Moving her body away from you? Lowering her body or tucking her tail? Growling, showing whale eye, or snapping? These are signs that she is uncomfortable. Stop for this session, and next time, reach your hand only half as far. The goal is for your dog to happily eat the treat, unfazed by your picking-up hand.

6. Next, let your dog gnaw on the treat as you bring your picking-up hand around the top of her back. Your pick-up hand will aim toward your dog's shoulder, but stop the motion before you get to the shoulder. Do not touch your dog yet; you are simply going through the motions of moving your hand and arm part-way around your dog, as in the photo on page 54.

7. Practice at this level over a few sessions, until your dog shows no signs of stress. Keep sessions short, under one minute, and if your dog decides to walk away at any point, respect her decision and take a break.

8. Now, repeat the same motion, but delay the treat by half a second. So you will gently reach around your dog (still not touching her), and half a second later, give her a thank-you treat for tolerating your movement around her body. The timing here allows you to gauge your dog's response to the reaching. If she is simultaneously eating the treat as you reach, she won't be able to tell you if she is uncomfortable until it's too late. You want to be able to read your dog's reaction and then give her a quick thank-you treat for being so lovely and tolerant.

9. Moving forward, you will be following this pattern of reaching your pickup hand slightly more around your dog, and within one second, giving a treat with the other hand.

10. Take your time and keep sessions short. Inch by inch, your pickup hand will wrap around your dog's torso, touch her belly, lift her up with the tiniest bit of pressure, and eventually, pick her up for less than one second. After each rep, she gets a treat right away.

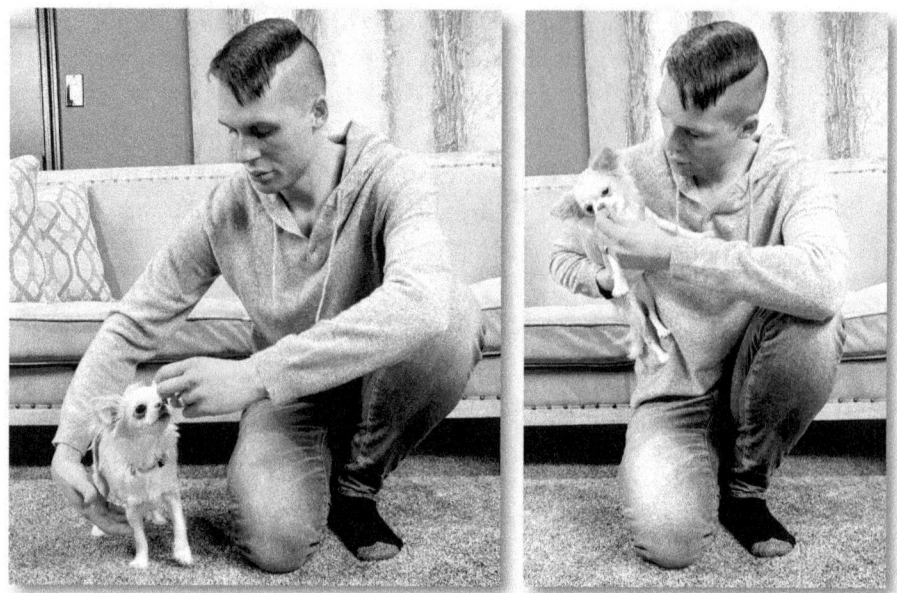

Avoid hovering over your small dog during pickups.

Leveling up

Once your dog is enjoying being picked up in this manner, it's time to name the inter-action. You can verbally give her a heads-up the moment before you reach down. I say "Up Up" right before I pick up any dog. These dogs hear "Up Up" and actually start to hop up into my arms, in anticipation of being picked up. Make sure to only add the "Up Up" when your dog is comfortable being picked up. If you add this (or any) verbal cue to an activity your dog finds unpleasant, it will actually cue her to stiffen, run away, or cower.

Repeat this every time you need to pick up your dog, until your approach is something that elicits wagging rather than recoiling. For some dogs, you will move through the steps quickly. For others, it will take longer. Remember our dog Margaret's nickname, Scary Peggy? Because a lot of her scariness was related to handling, we were in no rush to wean her off the treats. The first several weeks, she earned numerous treats per pickup. As the months passed, fewer and fewer pickups were paired with treats. Now, years later, she is agreeable to almost any pickup, no treats needed. However, even today, if she's comfy in her bed, I will gladly give her a thank-you treat for being picked up at a time when she would really prefer not to be touched.

Considerations for multi-dog households

When you have multiple dogs, you may need a few extra precautions to ensure your little one feels safe during pickups.

If your dogs are getting excited or cranky at one another, be cautious when picking one dog up in the presence of the others. This is especially true if your other dogs are bigger or stronger. While you are lifting up and holding the small dog, there is a risk that the other dogs will jump and snap at this moving target. Rather than picking up your small dog in a chaotic moment, it is usually safer to ask all the dogs to "Come" and "Sit" for you. (See Chapter 6 for "Sit" and Chapter 7 for "Come.") This will diffuse the tension and get the dogs all focused on you, not each other.

Do this any time your small dog is feeling overwhelmed by the play of bigger, younger, or more energetic canine housemates. Do not expect them to work it out, especially if your small dog is older and less energetic than the other dogs. In nature, adults are bigger and stronger than juveniles, which means they can protect themselves from youthful exuberance, but a middle aged MaltiPoo doesn't have the size or strength to defend herself from a forty-pound Golden Retriever puppy. The responsibility here falls on you, the guardian, to make sure that you can always call your larger dog to you, restrain him with a leash, or block his access to certain areas with gates and fences. When the dogs can't be supervised, they should be separated.

Happy harnessing

Body harnesses are often the best equipment option for small dogs, from a health perspective. (See Chapter 7 for suggestions on harnesses.) However, getting that harness on can be a scary experience for your pup. It often involves you hovering above, reaching over her head, and fidgeting your hands all around her torso.

If your dog has had a negative association with a particular harness or leash, get a new one for the following practice. Sometimes it's better to start fresh with equipment that doesn't give your pup bad vibes. For instance, you may know that your previous harness had snaps that scared your dog, so consider a new harness with Velcro™ or magnetic clips instead. Or perhaps the clip was under her belly, which caused her to snarl at you as you tried to snap it. For the new harness, make sure the clip is higher up, toward the dog's spine.

With this method, you'll be asking your dog to walk into the harness, rather than pushing the harness onto her body. You'll have some treats in your pocket or hand, ready to go. As with all handling exercises, if there is a bite risk, put on your dog's basket muzzle for this practice.

The steps here represent practice sessions over several days or weeks. Go at your dog's pace and make a note of how far along you are in the process after every session. The video demonstrates the progression from start to finish.

How to condition your dog to a harness
1. Sit in a position that allows you and your dog to be at about the same level. You could sit on the couch together, side by side, or on the floor. Or sit on the lowest stair, with your dog at floor level.

2. Let the harness hang from your forearm, so your arm goes through the neck hole. Put a treat in that hand and let your dog eat the treat. Do not attempt to bring the harness closer to the dog; just let it hang on your arm. How did your dog seem to feel? If she confidently approached your arm and took the treat, then proceed to the next step. If your dog hesitated, or if she grabbed the treat and then backed away, stay at this step until she is happily coming to your hand for the treat.

3. With each rep, you'll draw the harness an inch closer to your hand. It is still hanging on your forearm, just slightly closer to the dog's face each time. Do this in numerous increments with the harness dangling on your arm, then wrist, then hand, then fingers.

4. Now you will use your other hand to hold the harness up, with the neck hole wide open. Your treat hand will hold the treat right in the center of this hole. Your dog is now almost sticking her head into the neck hole to get the treat. This is a big change, so your dog may be hesitant at first. Continue with this step until she can confidently stick her head into the center of the hole.

5. From here, you will be asking your dog to reach her head into the harness, little by little, to get the treat.

6. Once she can poke her entire head through the hole, you will briefly rest the harness on her neck and shoulders. Remove it right away. Repeat until she's comfortable with this.

7. Now, once she's poked her head through and the harness is resting on her body, you'll start to touch the belly strap. Give another treat as you do this. At first, you may only be able to make a slight touch to the strap. That's fine—don't push your dog past her comfort level.

8. As she grows comfortable with this, you'll be able to move the belly strap closer and closer to the buckle or Velcro. At this point, you may need both hands for the strap. Each time you make this movement, treat your dog as quickly as you can.

9. When you are ready, fasten the strap calmly. Give your pup a jackpot (several treats in a row) as quickly as you can. You may also need to give a treat when you unfasten it.

10. If your dog likes going out for walks, immediately take her out in her snazzy new harness. What fun! But if your dog isn't looking thrilled about her new outfit, remove it.

Video: https://www.bklnmanners.com/chapter4.html

Sit side-by-side with your little dog when putting on the harness.

Leveling up

As your dog becomes more comfortable with the process, you can delay the treats by a second or so. This means you will put the harness onto her shoulders and then give her a thank-you treat. Snap the clasp and then give another treat. Watch your dog's comfort level in that one second between the action and the treat. She should be relaxed and happy. If you notice signs of stress, go back to the last point where your dog seemed comfortable or decrease the time between your action and feeding a treat.

Eventually, most guardians are able to get the harness clipped on, then give one thank-you treat at the end. In many cases, the dog becomes so comfortable with the process that treats are not required at all. Watch your dog's body language as you reduce the treats. If she is still enjoying the process, you're good to go. But if you see a regression in her enthusiasm for the harness, then continue with the treats for at least another few months. If your dog always needs some level of treats to be comfortable with the process, that's fine. When looking at the bigger picture, it's far better to have a trusting relationship with your dog, even if that requires paying her for tolerating an unpleasant handling activity.

Here comes the airplane: giving your dog pills

Have you ever used the "here comes the airplane" technique to convince a reluctant baby to eat? It works for your pup as well! For small dogs, pills are literally hard to swallow. With so many human medications being used for dogs, there is a real mismatch between the size of the pill and the size of the mouth ingesting it. If your tiny Toy Poodle has a negative experience taking pills, she may then become picky about accepting treats or even get aggressive when you approach her to give medication. In addition to emotional stress, a reluctance to take medication can limit the kind of lifesaving care a dog receives. Here are some tips to ensure your pup loves taking pills, even the big ones.

To start, choose a suitable treat to fully wrap around the pill. You can purchase pill pockets or pouches or try your own varieties. Consider peanut butter (it's stiffer and less sticky if refrigerated), pâté style wet food, a piece of banana, or a chunk of semi-soft cheese like mozzarella. The ideal consistency is soft, and just sticky enough to envelop the pill without falling apart in the dog's mouth.

How to encourage pill swallowing

For infrequent medications, such as monthly heartworm preventative, follow these steps. The example here uses cheese, but you can get creative with the treat.

1. Pull out the cheese and grab the container of pills. Open the container and act as if you're getting a pill out. You are not actually giving the pill, just going through the motions. This helps your dog associate the pill container with yummy cheese.

2. Give your dog a little ball of cheese with the imaginary pill inside. You can use happy talk and get your dog excited for the cheese. Hype it up! The goal is for your dog to swallow the cheese whole, not even chewing it.

3. Put the pill container and cheese back. Repeat this once or twice a week, at times when you do not need to actually give the pill.

4. Then, when you do need to give the pill, go through the same motions. Make sure the medication is well hidden in the cheese.

If your dog needs daily medication, you can use this strategy.

1. Pull out the cheese and the pill bottle. Roll about five pieces of cheese into tiny balls and prep the pill inside one of the pieces. Use happy chatter and dance around as you prep the cheese, to get her excited about her snack.

2. One after the other, feed the pieces in this order: (1) cheese without pill, (2) cheese without pill, (3) cheese with pill, (4) cheese without pill, (5) cheese without pill. If your dog is comfortable with it, it's best to hand-feed each piece, and do it quickly, one treat right after the other. (The chocolate factory episode of *I Love Lucy* comes to mind, with Lucy and Ethel stuffing their

faces as chocolates whizz down the conveyor belt.) The more quickly your dog swallows each piece, the less likely she is to taste the pill.

Troubleshooting

If your doggie detective can tell the difference between a ball of cheese with a pill and one without a pill, then try this tip, compliments of Erika Austin of Dandelion Dog Training. To get your dog used to the texture of a pill inside cheese, do your practice sessions with a small piece of kibble wrapped in cheese. This builds a positive association with the crunchy center of the cheese ball.

During pill administration, if your dog makes a "yuck" face as she eats the cheesy pill, quickly tear off a few more tiny pieces of cheese and pop them into her mouth, one piece after the other. You're essentially trying to get her to swallow the pill as fast as possible and end the session with a pleasant mouthful of cheese. As before, hype it up and act as if you're having the time of your life.

Now that your little dog is comfortable with handling, grooming, and other activities, let's turn our attention to developing polite household manners—for both the dogs and humans in your life.

Chapter 5
House Rules We Can All Agree On

Home is where the heart is. But sometimes in small dog households, home is also ground zero for unruly behavior, potty accidents, and unsafe interactions among the humans and dogs sharing the space.

This chapter will guide you through some of the most common day-to-day issues that arise in the home. If your little Dachshund serenades you with shrieking cries as you prepare his meal, we've got you covered. This chapter will also teach your Velcro pup to enjoy more alone time and help you interact with your tiny whirling dervish in a calm way. Need to ensure the humans in your daily life are being polite toward your Chinese Crested? We've got a plan for that, too. Finally, we'll take a deep dive into practical housetraining solutions.

Patience at mealtime

Little dogs know what they want, and in many cases, they want it now. Doggie meal preparation is a common time for small dogs to frantically yell and jump, as if it will make you pour their food faster. If this scenario sounds familiar, let's teach your little one that patience is a virtue when you are in the middle of a task such as feeding your dog.

How to teach patience at mealtime

1. If you announce the meal, do it calmly. At home, I ask the dogs, "Hey guys, are you hungry?" in a neutral tone. No excitement, no shouting, no sprinting to the kitchen.

2. Start preparing the meal at the counter.

3. If at any point your dog barks or jumps on you, immediately step away from the counter and hold your hands up, to show you have stopped making his meal. Don't look at your dog or say anything in this case. Just patiently wait for the barking or jumping to stop.

4. As soon as there is a one-second pause in the barking or jumping, begin preparing the food again.

5. Repeat this for every single bark or jump. Make sure you step away immediately, at the first bark or jump. If you wait until the third or fourth time, your dog may not understand that his behavior is causing you to stop preparing his food.

This sequence is essentially a game of Red Light, Green Light. Barking or jumping is the red light that makes you stop preparing a meal. One second of calm is the green light that allows you to keep going. You will find that, as the days and weeks go on, your dog's barking or jumping will reduce in intensity and frequency.

Embracing alone time

Lots of small dogs were bred to be loyal companions and lap warmers. And that's why we love them so much. But what about when you—gasp—might want to take a shower without an audience? Or run errands by yourself without traumatizing your furbaby? A vital house rule is to tolerate being alone, so it's important to teach your little dog that he can indeed survive for short periods of time without you. This protocol is designed to gently introduce your dog to the idea of being away from you, whether it's in another room or entirely alone in the house.

That said, some dogs have true anxiety when they are separated from you; if your dog struggles to handle the alone-time exercise below, contact a qualified behavior professional, especially a CSAT (Certified Separation Anxiety Trainer), to help tailor a plan to your needs. Many CSATs offer virtual online training, so even if there isn't a professional living in your area, help is available.

How will you know if your dog is struggling? These are some of the most common signs of separation anxiety (but by no means a complete list):

- Vocalizing: whining, barking, howling
- Pacing, restlessness, inability to lie down and relax
- Panting, drooling, sweaty paws
- Destruction, especially around exits like doors and windows
- Soiling (for an otherwise housetrained dog)

To get your dog comfortable with being alone, it's important not to overwhelm him. You want him to think, "Eh, you're walking away. Big deal." Not because he doesn't love you, but because he trusts that you will be back. So, start with extremely short, uneventful absences.

How to teach embracing alone time

1. Wait for your dog to be relaxed. Let's imagine you're both hanging out on the couch.

2. Say something like "be right back" in a calm tone.

3. Walk away casually to do a very short activity. The examples below are organized from least to most challenging.

    *   Do one or two dishes, just for a minute.
    *   Put some laundry in the machine.
    *   Do a chore in the bathroom, door open.
    *   Put some clothes away in your bedroom closet, door open.
    *   Do a chore in the bathroom, door closed.
    *   Put some clothes away in your bedroom closet, door closed.
    *   Go outside to get the mail (assuming your mailbox is close to your home).
    *   Go outside and get something out of your car.

4. Return to your dog. You can calmly acknowledge him, but don't make a fuss.

Leveling up

By repeating these no-big-deal departures, you're showing your dog that he has the resilience to be left alone. In the beginning, I do several of these departures a day, which really only adds up to a few minutes of alone time in total. The video shows one example of separation practice, which I performed while tidying up the kitchen. As time goes on and my dog remains unfazed by my comings and goings, I start increasing the duration of some of my departures. Sometimes I'm just doing a dish, and other times I'm running to the pharmacy down the street, or taking a phone call in the bedroom with the door shut.

Video: https://www. bklnmanners.com/ chapter5.html

Let's all chill

Relaxation is important for a dog of any size, but I regularly see small dogs who struggle to relax. Once they're overly aroused, they pant, nip, spin, whine, and race back and forth until they are completely exhausted. Some people may pass it off as exuberance or happiness. But over-the-top excitement is related to the sympathetic nervous system—the same system that triggers the fight-flight-freeze response (Spaulding, 2022, p. 59). When a dog is in a state of high arousal, even if she outwardly appears happy, it is physiologically considered stress. No wonder it's impossible to get her to sit, no matter how many treats you wave in her face. If your dog fits this description, it's wise to look at the entire dog. Ask yourself a few questions:

Is the dog getting enough exercise?

Exercise can come in many forms—walks, hikes, dog daycare, agility, dog parkour, or other sports. Make sure your dog is getting the physical activity she needs in a way that satisfies her. Many of my dogs, past and present, have preferred indoor activities as in Chapter 9 over walks outside. We spend as much time doing indoor agility, parkour, and trick training as we do taking walks.

Does the dog get sufficient enrichment?

This, too, will depend on your dog's interests. In our home, we use a variety of food toys for meals, which provide a form of environmental enrichment, but enrichment doesn't stop there. Think of all your dog's senses, not just taste but also sight, smell, hearing, and touch. As for sight, sometimes we sit on a park bench and simply watch the world go by. For hearing, we play relaxing music, such as *Through a Dog's Ear*, a few times a week for our dogs. For smell, I run a diffuser with certain essential oils a few days per week. (A caveat here: some essential oils are toxic to dogs, and even for the safe ones, you only need a drop. Do your research.) For touch, I always leave cardboard boxes on the floor after we get a delivery, as the dogs love to explore the texture and smells of the box. Furthermore, daily training can provide a form of cognitive enrichment, whether it's teaching a fun trick or playing some doggie brain games.

How relaxed are you?

Finally, consider what kind of behavior you are modeling for your dog. We have evidence that a dog's behavior and stress can be positively influenced by the presence of a caring human. One study demonstrated that shelter dogs were more relaxed after fifteen minutes of petting and calm speaking from a person (McGowan et al., 2018). And at least one study has shown that dogs look to us for information about how to act (Fugazza et al., 2018). Wouldn't it follow that an excited dog can relax more easily, simply by the presence of a calm guardian?

Think about the interactions that you and your dog have. Are you the person who walks in the front door exclaiming, "Mommy's home, wheee!" while dancing and squealing? Naturally, this will get your dog dancing and squealing as well. What about when you get your dog ready for a walk, or start to prepare her food, or when the doorbell rings? If you react to these activities with a "let's party" attitude, your pup is likely to follow suit. On the other hand, if you can maintain an even-keel tone and slow, fluid movements, you're doing your part to keep your pup's arousal levels in check. When your dog gets overly excited at the sight of her food being prepared, can you use calm behavior to mitigate the intensity of her excitement? I would argue yes. Therefore, your tone of voice and body language can likely impact how excited (or not excited) your dog gets during meal prep or other high arousal times. You don't need to be a Zen master, but if you can maintain calmness in tense situations, it can help your dog remain calm as well.

House rules for kids and small dogs

Ah, the infinite cuteness of young kids and dogs together, best buddies from day one. Or are they? In reality, the child-dog relationship can be full of misunderstandings and tension. You've probably seen plenty of videos on social media of a sweet, chubby toddler running unsteadily and gaining momentum, right to her furry best friend; as she falls into the dog's soft locks, she grabs onto his jowls for support and simultaneously plants a big kiss on his wet nose.

Is this scenario cute or cringy? The answer depends on how the dog responds. If the dog has a loose smile, soft eyes, and generally relaxed body language, then he might be enjoying the interaction. If the dog is showing any of the signs of fear, anxiety, or stress from "Trust and security are intertwined" on page 18, the family should intervene immediately. Yawning, leaning away, "lizard licks," or looking to the adults for help are just a few of the body language signals to look out for.

If the dog is not enjoying an interaction with a child in your home, you must remove the child (or the dog) right away. Do not expect a dog to simply "get over it" with repeated exposure to kids. For many small dogs, every painful, stressful, or unpleasant interaction with a child only reinforces that kids cannot be trusted when they enter the dog's personal space. This is the worst possible association a dog can make with kids. If your dog doesn't trust an approaching child, how many more hugs and kisses can he tolerate? At what point will he get tired of his calming signals not being heeded, and escalate to growling or biting? This is especially concerning with little dogs, as they remain small and vulnerable while children continue to grow bigger and stronger.

Establish a doggie "safe zone"

Particularly with young children, plan to use lots and lots of **management** to facilitate a secure, trusting relationship between child and dog. Management here refers to the ways you can spatially organize the home environment to prevent stressful or unsafe interactions, which will in turn help the dog feel more secure around children. Your pup needs an easily accessible safe place, in the event he gets overwhelmed by the little humans. This could be an open crate in a quiet spot in your home, or in another room away from the kids' hangout area. An adult's bedroom or home office with a dog bed usually works well, as they are cozy, comfy spaces. Your dog should always have access to this spot, with the door open, so he can choose to give himself a break from the family if needed. Inform kids that when the dog is using this space, it is a dog-only zone, no small humans allowed. If this can't be enforced, consider if a baby gate with a pass-through opening for little dogs or even an interior dog door would be suitable.

A safe zone will only work if you make it an enjoyable spot on a daily basis. Regularly give your pup his meals in this safe zone, with the door shut if needed, to prevent little hands from digging into the food bowl while your dog eats. Not only does this prevent food guarding, but it also helps your dog see his safe zone as a wonderful place designed just for him. Whenever your dog gets a chewy or food puzzle, also give it in this area. Sometimes you can be there with your dog, as a quiet space for the two of you to relax together; other times, you can be elsewhere in the house and leave your pup alone with his chewy. The goal is for your dog to feel that this area is a place to spend time away from the excitement and potential stress of family life.

Then, when children come to visit, or when your own kids are being active, give your dog a food toy in his safe zone. Since your pup is already used to this routine, it will be met with relief rather than reluctance. If your dog is stressed out by the noise of youngsters yelling or playing, consider continuously running white noise or a box fan in this room, to offer your dog a quiet getaway any time he might need some alone time. Just as some people can't sleep without white noise, I've found this soothing *shhhhh* in the background can take the edge off for many dogs, too.

For a thorough discussion of management techniques and examples of how to implement them, I recommend the book *Manage It! Hacks for Improving Your Dog's Behavior* by Juliana DeWillems.

Let sleeping (and eating) dogs lie

The old adage "let sleeping dogs lie" still holds true. For children old enough to follow instructions, it's critical to teach them to steer clear of any sleeping dog, big or small. No hugs, no kisses, no playing dress-up-the-dog while little Trixie the Bichon is trying to sleep. When a dog is repeatedly touched or moved while sleeping, it can easily lead to a lack of trust. Trixie thinks, "Every time I lie here, someone tries to wake me up and push me around. If they won't be polite and leave me alone, I'll have to use my teeth to keep them away." And can you blame her?

For kids too young to follow instructions, plan to manage the space extremely carefully. Teach your dog to use his safe zone for naps. Beyond that, use gates, fences, or other barriers to ensure that your little dog and little human don't end up in a dangerous situation. Generally, dogs and small children should only be integrated at times when you can actively monitor them, and when you are certain the dog's sense of security won't be threatened. This could mean that your pup spends chunks of the day gated away from your toddler when he or she is active. When your child is sleeping or not home, your dog can have the run of the house.

As with sleeping, dogs should always be left alone in their safe zone when eating. This applies to meals as well as long-lasting chews or food-dispensing toys. You can also use a baby gate, exercise pen, or other physical barrier as needed to give your dog a safe place to eat. This prevents an incident from ever occurring, and by preventing dog-child tension, you are building mutual trust and a lifelong bond.

Safety first during play

Play time is an excellent way to teach both tiny humans and tiny pups to interact in a controlled, safe way. Games that involve wrestling or high-speed chasing can be dangerous for a small dog, should a child fall on him. Additionally, the high levels of arousal during these games may encourage the dog to playfully nip a child. When it's play time with young kids, always encourage them to grab a dog toy. For tug or other close proximity play, use the longest toy you can find. The goal is to keep small human hands as far away from the dog's mouth as possible. "Roadkill toys"—what I call the unstuffed floppy dead-animal looking toys—are usually a big hit with both small dogs and children. In the photo, you'll see some of Oliver's favorite roadkill toys. Even better, I recommend a flirt pole for young kids who want to play with a dog. A flirt pole looks like a fishing rod with a soft dog toy at the end. (See the video for a demonstration.) The child can hold the pole and stand several feet away from the dog, using a baby gate or fence between them for added security, to play chase-the-toy safely together. This ensures little hands will not end up between tiny teeth.

"Roadkill toys" are a small dog favorite.

With dog-human play, plan to play in short sessions—maybe as little as one minute—and then take a short break. It's easy to get a dog so worked up that he can't think straight, which can be a safety hazard for a small dog or a young child. Even after the human is done with the game, the dog may be in shark-mode, looking to sink his teeth into anything that moves (especially children's feet). This is easily fixable by taking numerous breaks during play. Here is how:

1. Before you start playing, ask your dog to sit.

2. When your dog sits, say "Get It" and start gently twitching the flirt pole or long toy. Keep the toy as close to the ground as you can, to prevent jumping

up and snapping. Avoid frantically whipping the toy back and forth. Mimic the movements of a scurrying mouse.

3. Play for about 30 seconds. Have a treat ready in your pocket.

4. After 30 seconds, stop wiggling the toy, take the treat from your pocket, put it in front of the dog's nose, and then gently toss it several inches away from the dog. This gives the dog a chance to drop the toy, find the treat, and eat it. Phew, a nice little break.

    Want to turn this into a little manners practice? Right before you place the treat in front of his nose, say "Drop It."

5. While your dog is eating the treat, remove the toy for a moment.

6. Ask for a sit again and then present the toy to restart the game politely.

7. Repeat the above sequence every 20-60 seconds, for the duration of the playtime.

Video: https://www.
bklnmanners.com/
chapter5.html

When young children play this game, let them handle the flirt pole, standing safely away from the dog. You can help them out with the sits and the treat tossing. I suggest playing the game with the dog yourself first, in order to get both you and your dog familiar with this routine before getting kids involved. Watch the video of Cooper's first polite-play session to see the steps in action.

By implementing all of the strategies in this section, you can show your dog that children are not a threat to his safety. As time passes and the dog and kids grow up together, their relationship can build from this solid foundation. If you plan to integrate children and dogs in your household, I recommend visiting www.familypaws.com to learn as much as possible about setting all family members up for success.

House rules for your "Dogs love me!" friend

We've all got one—that friend or relative who fancies himself a dog magnet, a buddy to canines of all shapes and sizes. Let's call him Uncle Jeff. Every time Uncle Jeff bursts into your home, your trembling Italian Greyhound, Biscuit, becomes frozen in fear, bug-eyed and ready to run if this overzealous intruder takes one step closer. Perhaps Uncle Jeff grew up with romping Rottweilers who loved to wrestle, and he thinks your dog should learn the same play skills. Or maybe he's binge-watched dog reality shows and can't wait to test out his newfound skills on your unsuspecting pooch. In any case, training humans to change their behavior seems to be infinitely more challenging than training dogs to do so. If you'd like to choreograph a harmonious visit with friends or family, it will require a heap of management, a bit of training, and just a dash of controlled interactions between man and mutt.

First, the training. Before Uncle Jeff comes over, make sure you have taught your dog a super solid recall. (A detailed description of recall is in Chapter 7.) Practice "Come" at least once a day, using a high value treat reward, such as deli meat or cheese. Then, when Uncle Jeff and his boundless enthusiasm come through your door, you'll also have these treats ready. At any point, if you see Biscuit in a situation where he might get overwhelmed, call him to you happily, and give him a treat. This could include:

- Uncle Jeff is coming directly toward Biscuit.

- Uncle Jeff is gesturing wildly or speaking loudly and you notice Biscuit is showing signs of stress.

- Biscuit is approaching Uncle Jeff with hackles up, barking, or other concerning body language. (See Chapter 8 if you notice any hint of aggression.)

- You see Uncle Jeff getting into Biscuit's personal space. This is especially problematic indoors, where a dog might feel cornered with fewer options for escape.

Notice we're doing this as a preventative measure. Don't wait for Uncle Jeff to descend upon Biscuit's little body, which could make any dog feel the need to act aggressively in order to have more personal space. Rather, step in as soon as you anticipate a problem, by calling the dog to you. This teaches him that (1) Uncle Jeff isn't so bad, since you never allow him to threaten your dog, and (2) whenever the dog has a problem or feels unsafe, he can come to you for support.

Now, Uncle Jeff might be a little peeved that you keep calling Biscuit away from him. But we have a plan for that, too!

Catch a Treat

Let's teach Biscuit to catch a treat in the air, so that he and Jeff can share a fun moment together without the social pressure of being touched or approached. Here are the steps, which I recommend practicing yourself with your dog first.

How to teach Catch a Treat

1. Have a handful of round-ish treats or kibble, large enough to be seen when flying in the air.

2. Ask your dog to sit, facing you, with a few feet in between you. (No reward for the sit.)

3. Gently toss a treat, underhand, aiming for your dog's nose.

4. Your dog probably won't catch it. That's fine. Let him find it on the floor.

5. Practice another toss and then another. Watch your dog's mouth as the treat flies toward him. If his mouth opens a little as you toss the treat, this means he is starting to get the point! Still, no pressure to catch it.

6.   It may take a few sessions, but eventually your dog will catch a treat mid-air. When that happens, cheer and dance and give him another few treats from your hand. This jackpot of treats will show him that catching a treat mid-air is the best!

During your practice sessions, you might find that Biscuit is not MLB material. He may watch the treats fly past his face or bounce off his nose. That's OK, possibly even better! If Uncle Jeff tosses a treat and your dog fails to catch it, then Biscuit will start searching for it on the ground. These few moments of searching offer a little decompression, where the dog isn't looking at or thinking about Jeff. Seeking out a piece of food requires curiosity and focus. It is an innately relaxing activity that brings out the natural forager in any dog. By the time Biscuit has found the treat and looks back at Jeff, it's with a renewed sense of relief and relaxation. And the more treats he fails to catch, the more find-the-treat breaks he is given, and the more relaxed he can feel around a person who otherwise makes him uncomfortable.

Housetraining issues

Regardless of how small your dog is, one essential house rule should be: go potty in the designated place. In my experience, small dogs are associated with the vast major-ity of potty-training issues. Big dogs make big accidents, and their guardians are incen-tivized to regularly take their dogs out to relieve themselves. A small dog, however, can tiptoe into a corner and leave numerous tiny "presents" before being noticed. No matter how small or old, any dog can be trained to go potty in the appropriate place. But if your dog is no larger than a guinea pig, is it really necessary to go outside for potty breaks? What about potty pads for small dogs? And what to do about those hard-to-train dogs who leave tiny puddles around your house? Let's break it down.

Potty pads

Potty pads have some advantages and I use them in my own home. If your dog is weather-averse, potty pads will make everyone's life easier on cold, wet, or dangerously hot days. In our house, we have a potty pad accessible at all times, but still encourage our dogs to go outside when the weather is Chihuahua-friendly. This means that, on pleasant (or even just tolerable) mornings, I will wake up and immediately whisk the dogs outside to do their business. On not-so-pleasant mornings, I'll take my time getting up and let them use the pads when they're ready. I might even open the front door for the dogs to say, "you want to go out in that?" Since I already know the answer will be "nope," the conversation ends there.

Furthermore, potty pads can give you more freedom. If your dog travels with you, having pads can give him a familiar spot to do his business anywhere—an airport, a friend's house, or a hotel room. If you have an irregular schedule or tend to be out of the house for long periods of time, pads will give your dog the ability to go potty while you're out. (Please don't think it's OK to leave your dog home alone all day, every day, just because he has pads. This is no way for a dog to live.) For instance,

I'm out of the house a lot, and even though my husband is home, he's wrapped up in work calls and can't always stop to take the dogs out. Thanks to potty pads, I feel comfortable stopping for groceries after work because I know the dogs won't be anxiously waiting for me with their little legs crossed.

Pads are also a good option for puppies, elderly dogs, high-rise apartment dogs, or dogs with illnesses that involve unpredictable urination or defecation. For these dogs, it may not be physically possible to take them out as often as needed, so the pads offer peace of mind. I now teach every new dog in my home to use pads while they are still healthy, because I know that by the time they are elderly or sick, it will be more stressful to attempt pad training under that kind of pressure. And let's not forget the dog guardians, too. If you have a health condition or physical limitations that make dog walks a challenge, potty pads will take the pressure off. As someone who is frequently under the weather with some gnarly virus, I'm grateful for potty pads on stay-in-bed days.

There are a few down sides of pads to consider. Firstly, dogs that have pads may prefer the pads over going outside. Wouldn't you rather use the ensuite bathroom only steps from your bedroom, instead of going to a frigid, dark outhouse in the backyard? This pad preference can be prevented by taking your little one out regularly, especially:

- As soon as he has woken up
- Shortly after meals or big drinks
- After a few minutes of play
- After he's gotten excited, such as when someone comes home

These rules are especially true for puppies, but can be followed for adult dogs, too.

Additionally, pads have a few added hassles. They require changing regularly, and unless you are using washable pads, you will be adding some heft to your local landfill. You'll also have to find a suitable location for the pad(s) and keep them there permanently. The spot depends on your dog's preferences, but I find an out-of-the-way corner or a bathroom works well. Once you commit to pads, do not remove them, ever. Would you want someone blocking access to your bathroom? Finally, if your dog is a poop eater (the technical term is **coprophagia**), you will have to watch him like a hawk and be ready to pick up the poop within a split second. If you can't commit to this level of diligence, then it's better to take him outside to poop.

Potty outside

Despite my apparent love of potty pads, I do encourage you to train your dog to go outside for potty breaks, regardless of size. If a quick potty break is all your dog needs, then designate a spot near your house. In our home, we use the back door for super-short potty breaks on a fake patch of grass, placed on the deck literally two Chihuahua-steps from the door. Your home may have a different setup, but ideally, a quick outdoor potty spot will be near the door and protected from precipitation by an awning or tree. (Keep in mind, if you use a grass patch as I do, the astroturf and the deck under it require daily cleaning.)

Many small dogs appreciate an easily accessible potty spot on cold or wet days.

You can also incorporate potty breaks into a stroll around the neighborhood. For longer walks, we use the front door. By choosing different doors for a quick potty versus a long walk, it's always clear to the dogs what the plan is. Even if you don't have multiple doors, you can use different equipment to designate "potty break" from "walk." For instance, during a potty break, you might use a flat collar and thin leash to take your dog out briefly to the designated potty spot; then for longer walks, you use a body harness and stronger leash. Your dog will quickly learn what each piece of equipment means and what the expectation is.

Secrets to potty success

Housetraining is so much easier with a new dog. Teach him the right place to go potty before he develops patterns of using your rug or sneaking off into a closet. Once a dog has decided that the living room carpet will suffice as a toilet, it can be much more challenging to retrain him. Regardless of your dog's age or past potty history, make sure you've got all the following secrets to success checked off.

As mentioned above, the timing of your dog's potty breaks is important. Particularly for puppies, they should be whisked to their potty spot after they have woken up, a few minutes after eating or drinking, after playing for a few minutes, and after getting excited by an event like guests arriving. When it's potty time, take your dog to his designated spot. If the potty spot is outside, use a leash to keep your dog from running off and turning it into playtime. If the potty spot is an indoor pad, in the beginning I use a heap of potty pads, to make it as spacious and soft as possible, like a plush carpet. Put an exercise pen around the pads, so you can close him in until he does his business. (The rest of the day, keep the pen open, so he can choose to use the pads as needed.)

What if you take your dog to his potty spot, and nothing comes out? First, wait a few minutes, calmly and quietly. If your dog is outside with you on leash, just stand there. If you are using pads, close him into the exercise pen and hang out nearby. Still nothing? You can let him out, but keep him *extremely* close to you. This means you hold your little one, or you have him on a leash which is tied to your belt loop. Alternatively, you can put him in his crate. Do not give him freedom! After about five minutes of this, go back to the potty spot and try again. And possibly again and again. Yes, it's repetitive and frustrating, but not nearly as frustrating as cleaning pee spots off your rug for the next fifteen years.

When your dog does go potty in his designated spot, even if it's taken multiple tries, cheer and give him a super tasty goodie as soon as he has finished doing his business. Scrap the kibble for this—give something extra special to encourage him to do it again (and more quickly) next time. The rewards will facilitate the process in the early stages, so be generous. Make sure your timing is correct—you are rewarding him the second he's finished going potty, not after he comes back inside.

What if your dog already uses pads and you'd like to outside-train him? Or vice versa, pad training an outside-potty-only dog? Use the weather to your advantage. For instance, if you have a dog that is already outside-trained but you'd like to begin pad training, choose a day with bad weather. I did this with my older gal Beans, by waiting for a snowstorm to introduce the new indoor potty spot. When her options were (A) go out for a walk in several inches of snow, or (B) use the fluffy stack of pads in our warm bathroom, the choice was simple. I ensured that I gave myself some extra time in the morning, because it took a few tries to convince Beans that it was OK to go potty indoors. When she did tinkle in this new spot, she got a big reward. Conversely, if your dog is only pad trained and you want him to start going potty outside, choose a calm, warm day. Block your dog's access to the pads overnight, as some dogs will have gone potty even before you wake up, and be ready to get up quickly to take him outside (with treats). If your dog does his business on the walk, cheer and reward. If not, be ready to keep him in your arms or tethered to you and go back out again in a few minutes.

Probably the biggest factor in potty training success is related to how you manage your space. In short, an un-housetrained dog must not have freedom in the house unless you are absolutely certain that he is empty. If your small dog can simply walk into another room and leave a "present" when no one is looking, then he may never become housetrained. It's as simple as that. A dog that has already learned to pee or poop in the house, with no one there to persuade him otherwise, will continue to do it. Every accident reinforces this pattern, so by allowing these accidents to happen, you are actually teaching your dog to go potty in the house. Gross! And unless you can catch him in the act, there is nothing you can do except clean it up with a made-for-dogs enzymatic cleaner and promise not to let it happen again. It's not a case of "bad dog," but rather a case of "my bad."

While housetraining, follow this general guide for when to give—and not give—your dog freedom. Let's say your dog has just done his business in the appropriate place. Yay! If you are sure he's empty, then he can have freedom for a certain amount of time. What does "freedom" mean here? It means you are not actively watching your dog for signs that he's about to have an accident. Adult dogs may be able to have freedom in the whole main living space, while puppies may still be restricted to a certain room or penned area, due to other safety concerns like chewing on electrical cords. As for the duration of free time, for puppies, plan to give them less than one hour of freedom, depending on the puppy's age and activity level at that time. As any puppy guardian knows, they seem to have an endless amount of urine that comes out when you least expect it, so always be ready to whisk them to their potty spot. For adult dogs, you should be able to give them two or three hours of freedom, maybe even more, depending on the dog.

When the designated amount of free time is up, and there is once again a chance of an accident, then you have two options:

1. Take the dog to his potty spot. If he goes potty, yay, he gets another chunk of free time.

2. Take the dog to his potty spot. If he does not go potty, bummer, he will have to go in a smaller enclosure to prevent an accident. This enclosure could be a crate, exercise pen, or on a leash that is tethered to you. Give him another chance to go potty a few minutes later. He will not get freedom until he goes potty.

Make sure you do these additional things to prevent future accidents.

- For adult dogs, close doors to all rooms except the one you're in.

- Using fences, boxes, or any other objects at your disposal, block off areas that are out of view, such as behind a couch or around a corner. This prevents sneaking off to have an accident.

- Assume that, if your dog is out of sight, he is having an accident. Don't let that happen! Watch him like a hawk.

- If certain areas or rugs have been hot spots for accidents, restrict your dog's access to them. Roll up any rug that can be rolled, and have it professionally cleaned and safely stored until this process is finished (which can take months).

- Clean your entire floor space, especially carpeted areas, with an enzymatic cleaner to remove as much odor as possible.

- Block access to rooms with a history of accidents and put furniture on top of any spots in the main living areas where your dog has had repeated accidents.

If you do catch him in the act, immediately whisk him mid-tinkle to the correct potty spot. It might be too late, but try anyway. If your dog prefers not to be picked up, then keep him on a comfortable harness and thin leash while indoors, so you can take the leash and walk him to the potty place. If he does finish going potty in the correct place—a pad or outside—big cheers and rewards! Even if you don't feel like celebrating, it's your job to make it wonderful for him to go potty in the right spot. This will encourage him to choose this spot in the future.

For nighttime, potty training gets a bit trickier because you're not awake to address accidents as they happen. This means you will have to confine your dog to a small, but comfortable, space during the night to prevent accidents. You have two options. First is an exercise pen with just enough space for a nice, soft dog bed and a potty pad. This is the best option if you're trying to pad train your dog, if you have a puppy who can't hold it all night, or if you already use pads and plan to continue using them. The second option is a dog crate, also with a comfy bed. This is the best choice if you are trying to help your adult dog hold his bladder through the night. The crate should be big enough for your dog to comfortably get into any position—standing, stretching, turning in circles, lying on his side—but not so big that he can sneak a little pee in one corner and then curl up on the other side of the crate. Whether it's a pen or crate, your dog's sleeping spot can be right next to you. If he is stressed by this change in routine, you are welcome to put your hands through the bars, talk to him, and generally make him feel loved.

In the beginning of housetraining, take your dog to the correct potty spot as many times as you can during the day, even if that means multiple times an hour for puppies. Be ready to reward for each great potty experience. Keep this up, with super strict management and frequent potty trips, until you have had zero accidents for at least one full month. This means that, if your pup has one accident, you'll go back to day zero and start counting again. How will you know if it's been a month? Write it down! There are dog potty apps out there to keep track of potty breaks and accidents, but keeping notes on your phone or with an old-fashioned pen and paper will also work. Once you've had a month of no accidents, then you can loosen one criterion slightly. There are two areas where you will make changes: (1) the duration between potty breaks gets longer and longer, and (2) the free time area gets bigger and bigger. Some options after an accident-free month:

- You take your dog to his potty spot less frequently, asking him to hold it for a bit longer. For instance, every two and a half hours instead of every two hours, for an adult dog. Puppies will still need more frequent potty trips than adults. This means he'll be having slightly longer periods of free time in the house.

- You expand his free time area by removing one barrier. You could open a door to another room or remove a fence that had been blocking off a certain area.

After another accident-free month, you can loosen one more criterion. As the months progress, your dog will be able to stay unattended in the house for longer, with fewer potty breaks in between. But any time there is an accident, your month reverts to zero.

One last point about potty training: Keeping a routine will facilitate your dog's house-training. Regular potty breaks and regular mealtimes will keep your dog's body on a clear schedule. For this reason, I recommend you give your dog a set amount of time to eat his meals and then pick up the food after about 20 minutes. This will keep your dog's eating, post-meal drinking, and potty needs on a predictable schedule.

Mealtime schedules

Set mealtimes have a number of other benefits beyond potty regularity. The main behavioral advantage is that it makes your dog value food, because food is a limited resource. When a full bowl is left out all day, dogs tend to turn their noses up at it. "Eh, that boring old food? I'll eat it later. What's the hurry?" It sends the message that food is not an important resource. Additionally, why would your dog work for food during training sessions when he can just dig into his bowl whenever he wants? It's a bit like the stereotypical heir of an unfathomably wealthy family who doesn't learn to value money because he always has access to it and never had to work for it.

In more extreme cases, free feeding can spiral out of control. Usually it begins because little Spencer the Cavapoo is picking at his food. So, the family leaves the bowl down for longer which only reinforces that food is meant for casual picking. As Spencer continues to snub his food, the family adds tastier and tastier bits to encourage eating. What happens over time is that the dog is actually being rewarded for not eating. The longer he holds out, the tastier the bits of food he'll receive. Within weeks, Spencer has trained his frazzled family to cook him chicken breast (because "Oh no, I won't touch dark meat!" he says) twice a day, but it has to be pan fried with his favorite Italian seasoning, or else.

Before switching to set mealtimes, consult with your veterinarian to ensure there isn't a medical cause for the inappetence and that switching to set meals is safe for your dog. When you do switch to a meal schedule, be prepared for a few days of confusion and skipped meals. Your dog will need some time to adjust. The video here shows you some ways to encourage your picky eater to wolf down his meal. Whether it's using kibble as training treats or putting meals in a food dispensing toy, you can kick start your dog's enthusiasm for his food by turning mealtime into a game. Many dog guardians notice their dogs' interest in meals increases when combined with fun interactions. Enrich your dog's body and mind by playing foraging and training games to bring out the dog within your furbaby. The video here provides several ideas.

If the consistency of your dog's food doesn't allow for interactive games, Plan B is to slowly reduce how long the food is left out. Start with two hours in the morning, then two hours in the

Video: https://www. bklnmanners.com/ chapter5.html

evening. For week one, pick the food up after the two hours have passed and do not offer it again until the next scheduled feeding time. For week two, reduce the duration to 90 minutes with the food bowl on the floor. For week three, reduce it to one hour. Week four is 30 minutes. Finally, 20 minutes or less per meal from week five onward.

At this point, you and your little pup have developed a day-to-day routine, and you're honing your skills to understand what your dog is trying to tell you. But don't stop there! The next two chapters focus on activities to teach polite behaviors inside the home, out on walks, and in the park—all with a small-dog spin.

Chapter 6

Essential Indoor Training for Small Dogs

If you've completed the previous chapters, you're already well on your way to developing a trusting relationship with your dog so you can communicate clearly with each other. The next two chapters will introduce you to several training activities, all tailored to pint-sized pups. Since many little dogs spend most of their time indoors, this chapter focuses on indoor training activities:

- Sit to say please
- Having an "off" switch
- Manners on the furniture
- Using a ramp
- Stay at the door

We small dog owners know that our tiny sidekicks don't present the same dangers as some large dogs do. An excited Brussels Griffon won't knock you over when she jumps on you. When your Border Terrier pulls on the leash, you're unlikely to get dragged to the ground. And every time your Maltese leaps into your lap unexpectedly, it's met with an "awww" rather than an "ooof!"

As a result, it's easy to let your tiny dog's manners slide. But when we don't provide clear guidelines of conduct to our dogs, we're actually failing to provide them with valuable communication skills and emotional support. In some cases, we're even putting their safety at risk by failing to teach a stay at the door or allowing them to jump on and off furniture. This chapter will address all the indoor manners and safety issues that small dogs face.

Your response matters

One of the main principles of dog training is this: behavior that is reinforced (i.e., rewarded) will increase, while behavior that is ignored will decrease. Now think about the ways in which you interact with your dog, especially when he barks, jumps, or nips to demand your attention. Are you rewarding this behavior with attention or a scrap of food? This pattern of reinforcement only creates more frantic, demanding behavior in the future. What happens when you don't obey your dog's demand-barks, and he has to resort to biting your pant leg or stealing your most expensive shoes to get your attention? If this is the style of communication your dog has learned from you, then it's the only way he knows how to get what he wants.

Little dogs are especially prone to this problem, and not just because they're small and harmless. Sometimes, we simply don't notice when our diminutive dogs are being polite. When Chester the Pomeranian quietly sits on his doggie bed while you are having family dinner at the table, he is unlikely to catch your eye. That's a missed opportunity to reinforce and strengthen a behavior that you like. If you don't reward or at least acknowledge the dog when he's doing something polite, he may stop sitting quietly and try a different strategy to get your attention. Surely Chester's yipping, spinning, and bouncing will easily catch someone's eye (and ear) and he is more likely to score a piece of your chicken this way. In fact, sometimes family members find this behavior so cute or entertaining that they reward the dog with both food and lots of attention. What a win for Chester! The more this frantic demanding behavior works to get your attention, the more ingrained that behavior will become. For better or worse, dogs are learning all the time, not just during formal training sessions. And in this case, Chester has learned a valuable lesson: "When I sit quietly, I don't get rewarded, but when I bounce, cry or stand on two legs, I usually get what I want."

Sit to say please, not gimme

The above scenario with Chester the Pom is exactly the opposite of the conversations we should be fostering with our dogs. Chester can have all the goodies, toys, and attention he wants (within reason), but barking in your face is not the way to get them. Instead, let's encourage a calmer, more polite way of communicating with you. What is a calm, polite way to communicate? With his rear end, of course! Offering a sit is a simple way for your dog to ask for something.

Before we continue on this path of sitting to say please, allow me to take a short but necessary detour. Decades ago, and still today in some circles, dog training regularly utilized coercion, pain, and fear to get dogs to "obey" their owners. Masked as leadership, the techniques gave the dog no choice but to be obedient to his handler or face the consequences. On the surface, the handler had achieved his goal—the dog was no longer jumping, barking, or doing much of anything, really. If you were a dog, would you try to communicate with your guardian if making the wrong move resulted in a painful leash pop, a slap on the nose, or a shock to your neck? No thanks, better to keep a low profile. However, suppressing an animal's behavior through punishment is neither a healthy nor humane way to teach any living creature, especially ones we consider our best friends.

Thankfully, we've come a long way. On the path to becoming more compassionate to our dogs, we shifted to positive reinforcement for the behaviors we liked—sitting, coming when called, and walking on a loose leash—rather than waiting for the dog to make a mistake and then punishing him for it. One popular adage used in positive reinforcement training was the notion that "nothing in life is free." Chester could get the things he wanted simply by performing a polite behavior like a sit. If he wants dinner, he has to sit first. Want to go outside? Sure, sit first and I'll open the door for you. All good things have to be earned, from toys to food to access to certain places.

This notion is still extremely useful. You do not want your dog leaping into your lap uninvited, snatching a toy out of your hand, or scratching your legs to shreds as you prepare his dinner. However, now dog professionals are asking ourselves, "Does *everything* in life really have to be earned? Is this the dynamic we want to have with our dogs, or our kids, or anyone who might look up to us?" And many guardians (including me) feel that even the notion of "sit to say please" should not be used for every single interaction we have with our dogs. Imagine if you were treated this way as a child. Mom said, "I got you a birthday present, but you'll have to clean your room before you can have it." It feels a bit like a power play, doesn't it? Because, let's face it, some things in life should be free. When certain things are free, like receiving a birthday gift with no strings attached, it makes the recipient feel loved and connected to the giver.

So when you consider the following activity, aim for a balance with your dog. Your job is to gently provide structure for day-to-day interactions, particularly when your dog defaults to undesirable or dangerous behaviors. For example, if your dog tends to jump in your lap just as you're sipping a cup of hot coffee, by all means, ask him for a sit before inviting him on your lap. If he scratches your calves asking to be picked up, a sit is a much more polite way to get noticed. On the flip side, aim to create a dynamic in which your dog gets nice things without always having to do what you want. Structure is important to living harmoniously with our four-legged family members, but too much structure can strip dogs of their agency, leaving them unable to accomplish anything without doing your bidding first. So, for situations in which your dog is already pretty polite, you may not need to ask for that sit.

When to use the "Sit" cue
Think about the interactions for which requiring a sit would be appropriate. They usually fall into two situations:

1. When your little one would bark, jump, nip, or scratch to get your attention. Perhaps he wants to be picked up, to join you on the bed, to get leashed up, or to have a taste of what you're preparing.

2. When there is a safety concern, such as sitting at a crosswalk until the light changes or sitting in an elevator until the door opens.

This is best taught in your day-to-day life, no formal training session required. Real-life opportunities to practice this will pop up naturally, so be prepared to include a sit in certain daily interactions with your dog. Remember that our dogs are always learning, and training happens every time we interact with them.

Teaching sit to say "Please"

The following chapters assume your dog has already learned to sit. If he has not learned to sit yet, this video will teach you the basic steps.

1. Hold out a treat in your hand, roughly eye level with your dog. Maintain gentle eye contact with your dog, but avoid hovering over him or moving into his personal space. This can appear intimidating.

2. If he jumps or barks to get the treat, ignore it and hold still, as you see in the video.

3. After two seconds or so, if your dog hasn't already thought to sit himself, cue him to "Sit." Make sure to say the cue only once, then wait quietly.

4. The moment he sits softly tell him what a good boy he is.

5. Say "Get It" to release him from the sit. He can then eat the treat.

As you'll see in the following video with Beans, a down position is just as effective as a sit. Choose the position that comes most naturally to your dog.

Video: https://www.
bklnmanners.com/
chapter6.html

Repeat the above exercise with the things for which your dog would otherwise jump, bark, nip, or scratch. Some examples:

- **Getting a pick-me-up**. If your little cuddle bug wants to be held, by all means, pick him up. But not until he sits first!

- **Playing with toys**. To start a game of tug or fetch, hold out the toy and wait for your dog to sit. The moment he sits, say "Get It" and the game can start.

- **Access to the couch or your bed**. In my home, I don't mind my dogs on the couch. However, if I'm on the couch, my dogs can only join me if they sit and wait for my invitation. If a dog jumps on the couch without sitting and waiting, I gently place her back on the floor and wait for her to ask politely. (Note: If no one is on the couch, this rule doesn't apply. You can't teach good behavior if you're not there.)

- **Crossing the street**. Does your dog love walks? Before crossing any street, ask your pup for a sit before you look both ways. Once the coast is clear, release him and off you go.

> ### Release me
> In training, the release word is the signal you give when the dog can finish doing a behavior like a sit. Depending on the situation, my release word for my dogs sometimes will be "Get It," and other times be "OK." But why two different terms? They have slightly different meanings when training.

"Get It" means, "You are released, and now you can get that thing you wanted." The rewards are often life rewards: getting a toy thrown, getting his food bowl, getting to jump up on the couch with you. These rewards can only come at the very end, after you have released with "Get It."

On the other hand, "OK" means, "You are released. No reward is coming." In this case, we feed for position (meaning, mark "Yes" and reward the dog while he is still in the position of sitting), and then release the dog with "OK" to signal that he can get up.

Both styles are useful depending on the training technique and goal, so you'll see them both being used in this book. You're welcome to choose other terms, as some handlers say "Free" or "Release" instead of "OK." As long as you're consistent with your dog, any word or short phrase is fine.

"Not Now" and "That's All"

With the previous technique of "Sit to say please, not gimme," you're teaching your little one how to behave when he would like something from you. But what about times when you can't give your dog what he wants? Just because your dog has politely asked for a game of fetch at 3am doesn't mean you should jump out of bed and start throwing the ball. "Not Now" and "That's All" are two cues with the same purpose: telling your dog that you won't cater to him at that moment. It is, essentially, teaching your dog to have an off switch, by indicating, "Sorry Barkley, no point in begging, jumping, or crying. I will not be entertaining you right now."

This technique is so simple, so effective, and so calorie-free, that there's no reason not to do it. When your dog requests something from you, it's important that you give him feedback. If Barkley sits at your feet, asking, "May I come up on the couch with you?" it's only fair to answer him. If it's a yes, then you invite him up. If it's a no, then you should tell Barkley, "Sorry buddy, Not Now." If you simply ignore him without telling him "Not Now," it could be confusing and frustrating to your little companion, who's trying his best to ask politely.

Use "Not Now" as your dog's off-switch

"Not Now" is the phrase I use when I can't interact with my dog at that moment. Perhaps I'm filling up the dogs' food container and they mistakenly think it's dinner time. Rather than let them sit and watch me in anticipation of food, I aim to be proactive by immediately telling them "Not Now, guys" and then turning away. As you'll see in the video (page 83), within a few seconds Margaret stops watching me, and eventually gets bored and saunters away. Dogs may not love it when I say "Not Now," but they understand and accept it.

Does saying "No" sound mean to you? If so, hear me out. Imagine two scenarios:

    A. Margaret watches me fill the food container, and I say in my little-dog sing-song voice, "I wish I could feed you, but it's not dinner time." Not understanding English, her anticipation builds, thinking food is on the way. But the food never comes. She jumps and barks and gets herself all worked up as the seconds go on. When I finally put the food bin away and leave the kitchen, she's confused, frustrated, and overstimulated. She proceeds to murder a stuffed toy, which I can only assume is a metaphor for me.

    B. Margaret watches me fill the food container, and I immediately say "Not Now" with a slightly sad, falling intonation. She understands that the food isn't for her right now, exhales deeply, and walks away. No confusion, no excitement, no frustration, and no toy-murdering.

Wouldn't you agree that scenario B is far better for Margaret's emotional health?

At first, practice this with your dog several times as a structured activity. The goal is to start with an activity that makes it easy for your dog to give up. This will teach him the words "Not Now" without frustration.

How to teach "Not Now"
1. Start an activity that will mildly pique your dog's interest. Tidy up his food area, pick up his toys, sit on the couch, or organize the bin with his leash and harness.

2. When your dog shows interest and comes close, say "Not Now" and wave your hands horizontally back and forth like a baseball umpire gesturing "safe." Then, casually turn your back on your dog and continue with your business.

3. It's critical not to give your dog any attention once you've said "Not Now." Not even a "shhh" or "no." Even scolding is attention, and that can fuel your dog's demanding behavior.

4. Wait him out. That means no repeating yourself, no eye contact, nothing. The goal is for your dog to learn that the words "Not Now" are his off-switch.

5. If your dog really can't let it go and begins barking, jumping, or nipping, add this step. The moment his demands escalate, wordlessly walk into another room and do a chore. Wash the dishes. Clean a mirror. It doesn't matter. The key is that your dog learns that when he escalates his demand-barking, he actually *loses* your attention.

6. It may take a few minutes, but wait for him to stop asking for your attention and walk away. You'll likely hear a deep "hmph" exhale as the dog settles down for a nap. Give it at least another minute to ensure he's totally cooled off, and then you have the green light to engage with him again.

Leveling up
Once your dog gets what "Not Now" means, you can start to use it in your daily life, whenever the situation calls for it. Do this when you can't play ball, pick him up, cuddle, feed him, and so on.

Use "That's All" to stop interacting with your dog

Along the same vein, there will be plenty of times when you're interacting with your dog—playing tug, petting him, having a training session—and you need to stop. Most Chihuahuas will try to extend a cuddle session indefinitely, and a committed Cairn Terrier will demand you "throw the ball, throw the ball" until he passes out. Don't feel bound to the whims of your tiny tyrant. Rather than play along until the dog gets tired of it, have a word that means, "Sorry, I'm finished doing this with you." I say "That's All," with the same horizontal wave of the hands as "Not Now." This, too, is a more compassionate way to

Video: https://www.bklnmanners.com/chapter6.html

stop interacting with your dog, by telling him, "That's All, I'm done hanging out for now." If you simply ignore him without the verbal heads-up, he may feel frustrated, not understanding that the interaction is over.

Here, too, it's best to start this as a structured activity for the first few reps. Choose an activity that doesn't get your dog too excited, so that hearing "That's All" and ending the activity will be tolerable.

How to teach "That's All"

1. Give your dog a low value treat, like a piece of dry food. (It doesn't matter if he sits for it or not.) Pause and then give another treat. Pause, and then give another treat.

2. After a few treats, say "That's All" and wave your hands back and forth as in the video.

3. Immediately turn or walk away from the dog.

4. Wait for him to walk away, lie down and sigh, or wander off to entertain himself. As with "Not Now," it is critical you do not interact with your dog, even if he escalates to jumping, barking, or nipping. Do a household chore to demonstrate that you are not going to respond. It may take a while; that's OK.

5. Once he has finally given up, wait at least a minute to ensure he's totally cooled off and then you have the green light to engage with him again.

Video: https://www.bklnmanners.com/chapter6.html

Leveling up

Once your dog starts to understand what "That's All" means, use it in your daily life, whenever the situation calls for it. Do this when you're ready to stop playing, petting, having a training session, and so on.

Furniture manners

For us humans, the couch and the bed are places to relax. But what do these locations mean to your small dog? Does your spunky Jack Russell turn into a whirlwind, buzzing around your head as you try to watch a movie? Or perhaps your chunky Chug makes a beeline for your pillow before you can lay your head to rest every night. Little dogs make great couch (or even bed) buddies, but only if they understand that it's not a play zone, a steal-the-best-spot competition, or any other rules you want to set.

This is one area of daily life where little dogs tend to use their small stature to their advantage. When a young, large dog starts to jump on furniture, the family usually makes a training plan immediately. But her diminutive canine cousin gets to hop on the couch or bed, steal the chip from your hand and bark in your face for more. Should you try to ignore her, you can expect a front row seat to her canine acrobatics, climbing all over your shoulders and gently nibbling on your earlobes for attention.

There are a lot of opinions about pets on couches and beds. I have no problem with dogs of any size on the furniture, as long as they:

- Do not growl, snap, or bite when you approach or move
- Have learned the skills to hang out politely with you
- Do not cramp your style or steal your favorite spot

If your dog doesn't tick those three boxes, the couch and bed should be off-limits to your pup until you can make noticeable progress with the training in this section. This means that young dogs, who are prone to bursts of playful energy on a moment's notice, might not earn couch access until they get a little older. It's not cruel to restrict furniture access; actually, if it prevents conflict and frustration in your home, it's the safest and most humane option, for now at least.

There are two aspects of training so you can set furniture-related house rules. First, we teach the dog to come up on invite only. No more launching onto your lap as you hold a cup of hot coffee. Then, we teach her to settle into a certain spot on the couch, so she can be with you, but not necessarily *on* you.

How to teach furniture invitations:

1. You are sitting on the couch, and your dog strolls over, interested in joining you.

2. Before she can jump up, ask your dog to "Sit." Only say it once, and then patiently wait (and wait and wait) until she sits.

3. Be prepared for your dog to ignore your "Sit" cue and attempt jumping up. Hold your arms out to your sides to block the couch, moving horizontally to prevent your dog from finding an open spot to jump up to.

4. If your dog does manage to jump up before sitting, immediately and gently remove her back to the floor. Keep your reaction neutral and calm, not

scolding or domineering. (If your dog is uncomfortable being removed in such a way, see Chapter 8.)

5. Once she has sat for one-to-two seconds, then you can reward her by picking her up onto the couch.

Repeat this sequence every single time you or any family member is on the couch, bed, or other furniture where dogs are permitted. Consistency is key, so always make it clear to your pup what behavior works (that is, sitting) and what behavior doesn't (jumping up).

Assigned seating on the furniture

Once your dog is invited up on the couch or bed, promptly cue her to settle into her place. Don't wait for your dog to get the zoomies on the couch, with you stuck in the middle. Prevention is always better than damage control, so prevent any unwanted crawling, play-bites, or zooming by guiding your dog to her place right away. This is much more effective than letting her get amped up and then attempting to calm her down.

I like to use a soft blanket as a place, so I can put it on any surface—couch, bed, floor, car seat—and fold it to my desired size. For a small dog in cold climates, burying herself inside the blanket will make her place extra rewarding. Some dogs even prefer a self-warming mat, an electric heated pad, or a burrow bed. In the photo, you'll see that Cooper prefers a doughnut style bed. In the video, I use an orthopedic mat. Regardless of the "Place" mat you choose, you want it to be the comfiest spot on the couch, in the dog's opinion.

Cooper's assigned seating is a doughnut style bed.

How to teach the "Place" behavior

Have a hand or pocket full of treats. If your dog gets very excited by treats, choose something low value, like kibble or dry treats.

1. Sit on the couch (or bed). Have the dog's "Place" mat positioned next to you.

2. Invite your dog up by asking her to "Sit" first.

3. Once your dog is on the couch, gently say "Place" and lure her to her place with a treat.

4. Once all four paws are on the place, ask her to sit or lie down. Now mark and reward with the treat.

5. If your pup doesn't know how to lie down, that's okay. From a sitting position, you can slowly lure her with a treat from her nose straight down to her toes and she may plop down naturally.

6. When you give the treat, put it on her place, between her paws. It will add value to her place if the reward comes from the mat or blanket, not directly from your hand.

7. Pause for three seconds, then mark "Yes" to indicate she's done the correct behavior and place a reward between her paws.

8. Pause another three seconds and mark "Yes" and reward. Pause three seconds and mark and reward. Do this for about two minutes, as long as your dog is enjoying it.

9. After about two minutes of this, release her with a gentle "OK" and see if she has settled in enough to stay there. You can stay on the couch and she can stay on her place and relax if she'd like.

10. After "OK," you can give her soft, slow pets if she likes that. This will continue to help her associate the couch with relaxation, even after the treats have stopped.

11. After "OK," she's not required to stay on her place, and she's welcome to get off the couch altogether. But if she gets playful on the couch at any point, be prepared to practice another round of training.

12. Practice at three second intervals until your dog is a solid B student, meaning she is able to do at least 85% of your reps correctly. Then next time, repeat the process with four seconds in between treats. Release with "OK" after two minutes or so. The purpose here is to slowly reduce how many treats are needed to get her settled onto her place.

Video: https://www.bklnmanners.com/chapter6.html

13. You can continue to increase the duration between treats by one-to-two more seconds. Always make sure your dog is at least a B student at one level (for example, four seconds) before you increase to the next level (five seconds).

Aim for a B

When you're training your pup to perform a new behavior, apply my Goldilocks rule to ensure you're not making the task so challenging that your dog gets frustrated or so easy that your dog gets bored. You need to increase the difficulty in order to make progress, but how do you know when to move to the next step of training a behavior? My rule is, aim for a B.

If you're not familiar with the letter-grade system, a B is approximately 85% correct answers. It's a perfectly good score, sufficient to move up to the next level. Your dog does not need to be an A student (about 95% correct) in order to move up. But if she's only a C student (75% correct), then she needs more practice at the current level before increasing the difficulty of the task.

As you practice the training activities in this book, read the instructions carefully. In some cases, you'll be instructed to simply shoot for a B. This means you may only need a handful of reps in order to determine, "Yep, Gracie is a B student, let's move on." In other cases in this book, you'll be asked to practice at a certain level until you reach a B over several sessions. This is usually for more complex behaviors or for behavior modification protocols where it's critical to go slowly. For those, plan on spending days or even weeks achieving a solid B grade before you move to the next step.

Leveling up

Continue to cue "Place" and reward at the appropriate intervals as soon as your dog comes on the couch. As time goes on, you should notice your dog taking more initiative; she'll head straight to her place on her own, and she'll settle in more easily once she gets there. As she learns to relax herself, you can extend the duration between treats, so you're only giving a few treats in the beginning, with many seconds in between. At a certain point, it will become clear that your dog does not need treats anymore, as the place is rewarding in itself. (Remember, it should be the softest, comfiest spot on the couch and right near you if that's what your dog likes.) You can then reward with gentle petting or just by being together.

"Place" has lots of other applications, as you'll see in the next chapter. I bring my dog's blanket when we go to the beer garden, café, friend's house, or other outings, so my dog always has a spot to relax.

Two dogs, one couch

Does your home include two dogs, as mine does? This adds a layer of challenge when enforcing furniture manners. But fear not, a little extra management will make the training go smoothly.

My current dogs, Margaret and Beans, tolerate each other, but are far from soulmates. For the first year after adopting Margaret, we kept everyone happy on the couch by ensuring each dog had her own place. As you see in the photo, my couch back then always had two pillows, one for each dog, spaced far enough for me to fit comfortably in between them. By sitting between the two girls on the couch, I was able to treat each dog equally—neither is closer to me, neither gets all the pets, and neither can claim to be Queen of the Couch by being in my lap. If you have two dogs who compete for your attention, I recommend a similar setup.

As time went on, the dogs' relationship grew and I eventually did away with the two pillows. Now they can sit anywhere on the couch without incident. However, when I join them, I still prefer to sit in between them, to prevent one dog from crawling over the other in order to get to me. Your dogs might need more (or less) management than mine have, so contact a behavior professional if there is any tension among your furry family members.

Initially, Beans and Margaret had assigned seats on the couch to prevent any prickly interactions.

Ramp it up (and down)

Small dogs and furniture—it's complicated. As you already know, I'm open to dogs being on the furniture in many cases, but one of my greatest concerns is safety. Jumping on and off chairs, couches, and beds presents a number of health risks.

But don't take my word for it. I asked Dianna Shattuck, DVM, Chief of Staff at High Ridge Animal Hospital in Stamford, CT, and she provided a veterinarian's perspective on small-to-medium dogs jumping on and off the furniture. She explained,

> The most common concern for this sort of jumping would be for neck and back injuries. It's a very common cause of new neck/back problems, generally in the category of IVDD, intervertebral disc disease. I tell my clients that a small-to-medium dog jumping off a bed is the rough orthopedic equivalent of a person jumping off the roof of their car.

> The second concern is the risk of ligamentous injury or tear. The classic example in dogs is what we call a ruptured cranial cruciate ligament, the dog

equivalent of an ACL tear in people. This may or may not be accompanied by damage to the meniscus. In moderate to severe cases these sorts of injuries are best managed by surgery. Any sort of jumping or twisting motion can contribute to this type of injury.

The third concern would be dogs with osteoarthritis. Osteoarthritis from any cause can be worsened by any activity that causes increased impact on the affected joints.

Therefore, teaching your dog to use a ramp can be a lifesaver or at least a health-saver. Make sure you choose a ramp that is sturdy, wide, and has plenty of traction, as little paws can easily slip. When ramp training, go at your dog's pace. It can be a scary contraption and your dog's early impression of the ramp can determine how likely she will be to use it on her own in the future. So consider this another form of trust-building activity, to ensure that your dog always feels safe around the ramp. As you'll see in the video, even a timid dog can embrace this new piece of interactive furniture.

Article: http://www. bklnmanners.com/ home/prevent-injury-with-ramp-training

For more details on this topic, scan the QR code to read more of Dr. Shattuck's advice.

How to train using a ramp

1. Have a handful of tiny, tasty treats. Place the ramp flat on the floor, with plenty of space on all sides around it. Get yourself comfortable on the floor, sitting about a foot away from the ramp.

2. Toss treats in various directions around the ramp and watch how your dog moves to get them. Does your dog avoid the ramp completely, or does she willingly step over the ramp to get the treat on the other side?

3. If your dog is comfortable moving near the ramp, then start to toss or place about 25% of the treats on the ramp. The other 75% of the treats will still be tossed around the ramp in various directions. The goal here is for your dog to put at least two paws on the ramp as she meanders around looking for the treat.

4. Remember not to coerce or lure your dog onto the ramp. Be casual about it, just tossing treats onto the ramp, as you would toss them on the floor. If your dog is choosing to avoid the ramp for now, that's okay. Take a break and practice Step 2 until your dog decides it's safe enough to step on the ramp.

5. Once your dog is stepping on and off the ramp like a champ, you'll now push for four paws on the ramp. Toss the treats to either end of the ramp, back and forth. It may help to walk alongside the ramp, so your dog simply follows your movement. The goal is for your dog to walk along the ramp in

both directions, from one end to the other. It may take several sessions to achieve this.

6. Now, set the ramp up where you will ultimately use it on the couch or bed. Choose a location where the dog can safely exit and enter, both on the floor end and the elevated end. That means no pillows, coffee tables, or clutter in the way and no slippery floor below. If your dog already jumps on and off the furniture from a certain spot, set up the ramp there.

7. Play a back-and-forth game, only focusing on the bottom third of the ramp. Toss a treat away from the ramp, then place a treat on the ramp, at a height where your dog needs to stretch her neck to reach it. As soon as she eats the treat, toss another treat well off the ramp.

8. Once your dog is happily running back and forth, start placing the treat higher and higher on the ramp. Increments would include: two paws on the ramp, then four paws, then ultimately all the way up. If your dog takes initiative and runs all the way up the ramp right away, go with it.

9. The first time your dog makes it all the way up the ramp, jackpot! This means feeding several treats in a row to show her what a superstar she is.

10. To guide your dog down the ramp, slowly draw a treat from the top of the ramp to the bottom, with your hand literally dragging along the ramp. Place a treat at the bottom of the ramp.

11. Be careful—if you simply toss the treat to the floor, your dog may jump off the couch rather than use the ramp. The point of this step is to help your dog slowly and carefully descend.

Video: https://www.
bklnmanners.com/
chapter6.html

Troubleshooting

When you put the ramp against the couch, is your dog struggling with the incline of the ramp? You can add an intermediate step. Instead of the couch, put the ramp against your dog's fluffiest, biggest dog bed. Set the ramp to its lowest elevation, so it aligns with the height of the dog bed. Then you'll play the back-and-forth game as above, with the ramp leading to the dog bed. Once your dog is comfortable with this version of the game, return to the steps above and repeat with the couch.

Leveling up

Once your dog is comfortable with the ramp, start using it in your day-to-day life. Be ready to guide your dog with treats for the first few days or weeks, because many dogs will need a gentle reminder to use the ramp if they want couch access. This is especially true for dogs who have been jumping up and down for their entire lives. It may take a lot of ramp practice for them to willingly choose the ramp over a leap.

Having a few treats in your pocket will let you get into training mode quickly, to help your dog make the right choice.

"Stay" as the door opens

Teaching your dog to 'Stay" at the front door is a very important safety precaution, especially for a small dog who can easily sneak past you as you crack the door open. If your dog has aggressive reactions to delivery people or guests, see Chapter 8; but if your dog simply needs to learn a little self-control at the door, follow these steps.

First, choose a spot for your dog to stay while you open the door. The ideal spot will be clearly defined by a small rug, mat or dog bed. (In our home, we use small bathmats, as they don't slip.) Place it close to the entry area, so that you can return to your dog to frequently reinforce with treats, but not so close that your dog will be in the way of a swinging door or entering guest.

Teaching your dog to stay at the door will take numerous sessions. Imagine recording yourself performing this sequence: cuing "Stay," walking away, opening the door, saying hello, and taking a package or inviting a guest in. Every frame of the recording is one step that you will train your dog. The video will give you a sense of this step-by-step progression. Asking your dog to stay put while all these exciting things happen is a big ask for a little dog! Be ready with super tasty treats, and have your dog on leash while practicing this, to avoid an escape. If you have a helper, let them hold the leash. Otherwise, choose a sturdy piece of furniture to which you will tie the leash, giving the dog plenty of room to move and shift around. You can also use a fence or gate between your dog's spot and the door to prevent door-dashing.

Security first

A note about this activity or any activity that asks a dog to be restrained and sit still: Make sure your dog is not fearful or anxious about any aspect of the training or environment. We shouldn't ask a fearful dog to sit still in close proximity to anything that makes her feel unsafe, such as a swinging door, a package, or a guest. A fearful dog should always have the ability to get away from what scares her. Imagine if you were tied to a chair as a giant spider (or snake or clown or whatever scares you) crawled around you. No thanks!

How to teach stay as the door opens

1. Set your dog up on her special spot, and cue a "Sit" or "Down," whichever is more comfortable for her. This is an informal version of stationing, meaning you send the dog to her place.

2. Say "Stay" and show the traffic-cop hand signal. Then drop the hand signal.

3. Count to three. Mark "Yes" and reward while the dog is still in the stay position.

4. Repeat at this level until your dog is at least a B student, meaning she can comfortably stay in that position for three seconds. She does not need to be a statue, but she should be able to keep her rear end on her spot.

5. Release with "OK" for a few seconds of break. Some dogs will be able to do numerous reps in a row before you release with "OK." (The video demonstrates this.) Other dogs may need an "OK" release after every single rep. Do what works for your dog. If your dog appears uncomfortable at any point, release her for a short breather.

6. For the next rep, you'll teach the dog to stay while you turn away. Cue "Stay" on the mat. Turn your body, just quarter of a turn, and boomerang back to face your dog again. Mark and reward. Repeat until she is a B student.

7. Continue increasing how much you turn away. Cue "Stay." Turn your body 180 degrees and quickly boomerang back to face your dog again. Mark and reward. Repeat until she is a B student.

8. Now you'll start moving away. Cue "Stay." Turn your body 180 degrees, walk a half step away with your back to your dog, and boomerang back to your dog again. Mark and reward. Repeat until she is a B student.

9. Continue inching your way to the door, literally step by step. Make each step natural, as if you are actually going to answer the door.

10. Now it's time to open the door. This, too, will take several steps. Walk to the door as before, reach out and touch the doorknob without opening the door, and return. Mark and reward. Repeat until she is a B student.

11. Walk to the door, turn the doorknob back and forth, and return to your dog. Mark and reward. Repeat until she is a B student.

12. Walk to the door, open the door one inch, shut the door, and return to your dog. Mark and reward. Repeat until she is a B student.

13. Continue opening the door, inch by inch, until it is wide open. If you have a screen door, repeat the sequence with that door, as well. Always make sure your dog is a B student before proceeding.

Video: https://www.bklnmanners.com/chapter6.html

14. Now incorporate anything you might say to a delivery person who's just handed you a package, or a guest who is on the other side of the door. With your dog in the stay position, walk to the door and say, "Thank you, have a nice day!" or "Hey, come on in!" Return to your dog to mark and reward.

15. The final piece is the action of literally picking up a package or making the inviting gestures as you let your imaginary guest in. As before, make sure your dog is a B student.

Troubleshooting

Issue: Your dog is struggling past a certain point.

Solution: If your dog struggles at any step, split it. For instance, perhaps your dog can handle a "Stay" with you facing her, but she struggles with you turning away 90 degrees. Try a less dramatic turn of 45 degrees. Practice that until your dog is a B student and then proceed to a 90-degree turn.

Issue: Your dog is getting up and walking away.

Solution: Remember to take breaks. Before she gets antsy or bored, release her with "OK" to take a 30-second-or-so break. It's also fine to call it a day if your dog is losing her spark.

Issue: Your dog struggles to stay as you get closer to the door or start opening the door.

Solution: The door might be too emotionally charged for your pup. Instead, start the sequence from scratch, walking in a meaningless direction—toward a wall, the bathroom, or other direction that doesn't have relevance to your dog. (Not toward the kitchen, as that can be an exciting direction, too!) The door-opening can also be practiced with a meaningless door, like a bathroom or closet door. Go through all the steps with an interior door and once your dog is a stay superstar in that context, then start the sequence from step one at the front door.

Issue: Your dog struggles to stay when you start speaking to the imaginary guest.

Solution: You can split this by adjusting your volume. Start with a whispered "hi," and speak increasingly louder over several reps.

Leveling up

Recruit a helper to be your first guest. This person should be a calm and quiet member of your household or a regular guest.

- Go through the sequence with the helper, who will walk through the door but not pay any attention to your dog as they enter. The helper does not knock on the door or ring the doorbell … yet. Once your guest is inside and the door has been shut, release your dog with "OK," at which point she can greet your guest.

- Eventually, your helper will knock or ring the bell. This is a highly arousing sound to most dogs, so only add this final step when your dog is ready. See Chapter 8 if your little one struggles with the doorbell.

Continue this training plan with as many helpers as you can recruit.

Tech support

Remote feeders can be a wise investment for training your dog to stay at the door, go to her place, or a number of other training activities you'll see in this book. A remote feeder is a treat-filled device that can be set up on the floor, a table, or a shelf. You hold a remote, or in some cases, have an app on your phone, to dispense a treat from the device at a specific

---

time. For an activity like "Stay as the Door Opens," you could set up the remote feeder next to your dog and simply push a button to reward your dog while you answer the door. Do you really need one, though? Consider these points.

- If you have physical pain or limitations, repeatedly bending down to reward your small dog can be unpleasant or even dangerous. A remote feeder allows you to simply press a button, and the device will reward the dog for you.

- If your dog is uncomfortable with you reaching over her to give a reward, a remote feeder allows you to stay near the door while rewarding your dog on her spot. No hovering, no reaching. Consider a remote feeder if your dog shows any of these stress signs as you approach to reward her: looks away, yawns, licks her lips, shifts her weight back, or hops backward as you reach down.

- If you're struggling to make progress, especially when you bring in helper "guests," a remote feeder allows you to continuously reward your dog for staying on her spot, while you focus on your guest.

One remote feeder is the Treat and Train, which includes a remote control (but don't lose it, they're expensive to replace!) and has numerous settings to dispense either a single treat or multiple treats at certain intervals. If you prefer a sleeker model that uses an app to dispense treats, Furbo and other brands have simpler designs.

Chapter 7
Essential Outdoor Training for Small Dogs

Small dogs deserve adventures, too! Rather than leave your dog home while you go out into the world, let's teach your little sidekick to come along for the ride, whether it's on her own four legs or in a carrier. This chapter covers all aspects of outdoor manners training:

- Recall, even off leash
- Leash walking
- Being carried in a bag
- Politely hanging out at the café with you

Build a strong recall

No matter the size, your dog should have a strong recall. This means that when you call Pepper the Westie to "Come," she is able to stop what she's doing, turn to you, and happily hustle over to your side. This is a deceptively complicated task, because we are often competing with the dog's innate desire to chase a squirrel, follow the scent of something foul, or tell the mail carrier to buzz off.

Think of how much humans struggle with recall. Anyone with a partner or child has felt the frustration of repeatedly calling out their names, only to be met with silence. It's not because your family member doesn't love you or respect you. Rather, they're engrossed in a video game, news article, or other activity to the point where your voice barely registers. As you practice recall, give your dog at least as much compassion as you would give your son who is wrapped up in a game or your spouse who is glued to the news.

For small dogs, there is an added layer of challenge. We're big, they're not. So when Pepper comes to you on her tiny toothpick legs, you can accidentally punish her by leaning over to give her the treat. (Dog professionals note: this is positive punishment in the operant training sense, meaning that, by hovering over Pepper, you are creating an aversive stimulus that will make Pepper less likely to come to you in the future.) As your body hovers over Pepper and closes in on her from above, it can appear quite scary from below. That's right, our body language when rewarding a dog for recall, can actually cause them stress. How will you know this? Because your dog will duck or back away as you go to reward her, or she will come to you and pause, just out of arm's reach. So, the following two styles of recall, follow-me recall and emergency recall, address that doggie discomfort and make it rewarding for your little one to trot right up to you.

Make it a win-win

There is an inherent problem with some approaches to dog training—all too often, getting the dog to do what you want means that the dog loses what she wants. If we use training to simply trick the dog into doing something she doesn't want to do, it will never stick and can even damage the dog's trust in you. For instance, if you say "Come" solely to get your pup out of the dog park, she will see it as a trick and likely stop responding to the word. If you ask her to "Stay" and then squeeze a cold, greasy cleansing solution in her ear, she has just learned that "Stay" is a four-letter word. Next time you say "Stay," she's more inclined to run.

Every single time you interact with your dog, you want her to think, "Hooray, my human is coming over!" Yes, even when little Sadie has stolen your sock and starts running away. We already know that trust forms when you and your dog are on the same team. But how can you be on the same team when you want such different things? Sadie wants to keep the sock, but you fear she'll ingest it. Naturally, you're at odds.

The goal is to show your dog that what you want is also what she wants. We help Sadie understand that when she responds to your cue, she wins big. We do this by practicing the "Come" cue to the point where, even when Sadie has a sock, she would rather come to you than bother with the stolen sock. Of course, she will be rewarded with a super special treat for doing things your way. When you pair something potentially unpleasant (leaving the sock alone) with something amazing (deli meat), it's a win-win. By following the steps for recall in this chapter, Sadie will trust coming to you, and she'll even be willing to do it when she has a sock in her mouth.

Follow-me recall

This activity has many aspects of a traditional "Come" cue, but with a small dog twist. The accompanying video features Beans, who used to struggle with coming up close to anyone who was standing, even me. Practicing follow-me recall not only improved Beans' "Come" cue, but also made our leashed walks more enjoyable, as she became comfortable being close to my feet.

How to teach follow-me recall

1. Have two values of treats, hidden in separate pockets or pouches. Your hands are empty to start.

2. With your dog near you, toss a lower value treat (perhaps a piece of kibble) behind your dog. You are effectively sending your dog away to get temporarily engrossed in an activity.

3. While your dog is eating the piece of food, start walking away and say "Come!" Walk at a normal pace, with your body facing in the direction you are going. (That is, do not awkwardly walk backwards or sideways to face your dog.

4. As you walk forward, turn your head a bit to one side, so you can see your dog in your peripheral vision. This helps maintain a connection with your dog, even as you walk away.

5. When your dog catches up to you, gently praise and reach down to give her a higher value treat. But! ... Make sure that your feet continue to point forward; do not turn toward your dog, as this will then require you to hover over her as you give the reward. Reach down to give the treat at your side.

6. Watch your dog's body language as you do this. Is her body leaning a bit backwards, or crouched low? Do you see whale eye or a low tail carriage, which may indicate the dog is uncomfortable? Does she back away as you lean down to give the treat? Does she come up to you for the treat but then retreat? If so, she is likely uncomfortable with the proximity to you.

7. If your dog shows that she is uncomfortable taking a treat from your hand, don't push it. Next time, try dropping a treat a few inches away from your side, onto the ground, instead of hand feeding. Again, watch your dog's body language to ensure her comfort.

Video: https://www.bklnmanners.com/chapter7.html

8. Practice a few repetitions of this game, in a back-and-forth fashion.

Leveling up

This is not just a recall activity, but also an assessment tool to understand your dog's comfort level. You're not trying to convince or pressure your dog to come up to you, and there are no wrong or bad results. As time goes on, you're looking for her to increase her confidence around you and her willingness to come up closer to you for the treat. This can only happen at your dog's pace, so never use coercion or bribery with the treat to get her closer than she is comfortable with. Lots of short, fun practice sessions over a long period of time are the best way to make her feel safe coming to you.

This style of recall includes elements from dog agility and other sports because it teaches your dog to follow your movements. Your dog will learn that, when your feet and body start moving in one direction, it's a great idea to follow. You'll also notice that your dog runs up to you on the side to which you've turned your head. (Make sure to turn your head right for some reps and left for others. Keep your dog on her toes!) With this activity, the verbal cue "Come" is only a small part of the bigger picture to the dog. She learns to always watch your body language and be ready to follow when you start to play this recall game.

Advance your skills methodically

Do you have great expectations of your little pup? Even the smallest of canines can learn advanced manners, tricks, sports, and more. A commonly repeated quote among dog professionals, attributed to the renowned trainer Ken Ramirez, goes something like, "Advanced training is just the basics done really well." And it's true. If you don't believe it, do an online search for musical freestyle routines at Crufts, an international dog competition venue. On the surface, you will see dogs performing awe-inspiring dance routines set to music. But what you're really watching is a series of well-practiced recalls, down-stays, paw targets, and leash walking skills.

Advanced training for many behaviors is characterized by the three Ds:

1. **Duration**: how long your dog performs a behavior. For instance, a ten-minute "Place" is significantly more advanced than a ten-second "Place."

2. **Distance**: how far you can be from your dog when she performs the behavior. Distance can take many forms, but one example is cuing "Come" from across a field.

3. **Distraction**: what kind of sights, sounds, smells are around your dog. Asking your dog to "Come" when in the living room is a great start. But that same cue in the middle of a bustling dog park would be quite advanced.

Off-leash recalls

When it comes to off-leash activities, be very careful about where you let your small dog run free. Natural areas may have predators interested in making a meal out of your beloved family member. Dog parks can also be dangerous, particularly if large and small dogs are in the same enclosure. There is a phenomenon called **predatory drift**, during which the movements of a small dog can trigger the predatory instinct of a larger one, with potentially fatal consequences. Small dogs, regardless of how confident they are, should never (ever!) mingle with large dogs in the dog park.

In theory, a long-distance recall in the park is no different from the basic follow-me style of recall. But, as most dog guardians will agree, off-leash recall in a distracting location is a whole other beast. That's because two important factors—distance and distraction—are at very high levels. This section outlines some suggestions and considerations to get your dog's recall strong enough to respond even in a park.

To kick up your dog's recall game, determine several intermediate locations to practice recall, based on both the distance from you and the distractions present. Make sure your dog is a solid B student at one level before attempting the next level. These are some sample stages, but you should write down a list of five to ten stages that fit your specific environment.

1. Indoors when it's quiet

2. Indoors when the family is home and rowdy (for distraction)

3. In a fenced yard when it's quiet

4. In a fenced yard when others are there or when squirrels are in the distance (for distraction)

5. On a safe sidewalk or cul-de-sac, when there are no cars or other dangers, on a six-foot or longer leash (for distraction)

6. In a quiet park or on a hiking trail, using a long line (for distance)

7. In a park or on a trail, using a long line, with some activity in the distance (for distraction)

8. In a bustling park or on a hiking trail, using a long line (for distraction and distance)

Even as you work your way through these stages, continue to also practice easy, basic-level recalls. Not every "Come" has to be a challenge, and occasional easy wins will ensure your dog is still having fun and feeling positive about her interactions with you.

Another important aspect of a flawless recall is its consequences. Your dog will either learn to love the sound of the word "Come," or act as if she didn't hear you calling her at all. Let's make sure you're sending the right message, by having a positive consequence for coming to you. Make sure you can check these boxes:

- Is she getting a reward? And if so, is that reward actually rewarding to her? Your dog, not you, dictates what a reward is. Some dogs will do flips for plain old kibble, but for others, only bits of ham are truly rewarding. There are plenty of dogs who will gladly come to you if it means you'll throw a ball. And there are some dogs who love nothing more than a hug and a cheer. Let your dog tell you what she finds rewarding in each situation. You may be able to use kibble for recalls in the yard, but once you get in the park, kibble is no longer considered rewarding. That's okay. Be prepared to test out different reinforcers in each location. And when she does a particularly good recall past a squirrel, pay her generously for a job well done.

- Are you rewarding her often enough? Do not dwell on fading out the rewards yet! First, focus on making recall amazing and fun for your dog. Fading out the rewards tends to come naturally, so let the process play out over time. You may find that your dog adores coming back to you, no treats needed, within a few weeks. Or you may always need a tasty reward when going to the park. There is no universal rule here; simply do what works for your dog.

• What happens after your dog has come to you? And after you've given a treat or other reward? Do you inadvertently punish her by shortening the leash and leaving the park? If "Come" starts to mean "the fun is over," no treat can override the disappointment of leaving the park. The solution is to also practice recall when there is no unpleasant consequence. As you walk around the park with your pup on a long line, look for a cool stick or stinky shrub she might like. Then call "Come" and show her this treasure. Other times, call "Come" and give a reward, then send her back to walking and sniffing. By doing this, the majority of the time, recall has enjoyable consequences. Sure, occasionally she'll have to come to you rather than roll in a mud puddle. But since you've already built a solid foundation of nice positive-only recalls, your dog will be more willing to comply even when she'd rather roll in the mud or play with her buddy a few minutes longer.

Stubborn, or something else?

Perhaps your dog has selective hearing when you're training a new behavior. Or she's only interested in training for a few repetitions before walking away. Or maybe she's snubbing your treats during training. What many guardians label as "stubborn" behavior during training is in fact something entirely different. Before you assume your dog is simply obstinate, ask yourself if she is actually trying to tell you something. Consider these reasons.

☐ **Your cues are not clear and training sessions are confusing your dog.** When you practice a behavior, like learning to sit, are you doing it exactly the same way every time? Are you sometimes saying "Sit," other times saying "Sit Down," or using different tones of voice? Is your hand gesture different every time? If so, you are not clearly communicating to your dog, and she is probably getting frustrated while trying to learn from you. Before you begin any training session, have a plan. You should run through the motions with an imaginary dog first, to make sure you know what your cues will look like. Practicing in front of a mirror or video recording your training sessions will also help you perfect your training skills.

☐ **Your dog hasn't mastered a new behavior and you are now asking for it at an advanced level or in a highly distracting environment.** This is a frequent mistake with recall. Your pup's recall may not be off-leash ready for quite some time. Make sure your dog is a B student at one level before increasing to a slightly more advanced level. If your dog is only a B student at recall in your living room, it would be unfair to expect the cue to work in a dog park. That's like putting a first-grade student into a PhD program!

☐ **You are putting your dog in an uncomfortable position.** Behaviors like "Place" ask the dog to remain in a fixed location. What if there is something stressful in the environment, such as a vacuum cleaner or children playing, that makes your little dog feel unsafe there? Asking for "Place" in this case could be stressing your dog out and making it difficult for her to follow your cues.

□ **Your dog is bored or stressed.** Some dogs get tired of repeating the same behavior more than a few times. Other dogs can become stressed by long training sessions. For these dogs, keep sessions short or take lots of breaks. It's much more effective to do two repetitions of recall and then stop while your dog is wanting more, rather than do ten reps, with your dog wishing the training session would just end already.

□ **Your rewards are not rewarding.** Just because you paid $15 for that tiny bag of organic yogurt treats, it doesn't mean your dog finds them particularly motivating. Pay your dog for a job well done and pay her in a currency that motivates her. Can you imagine if, at your job, you were paid in hugs? How long would you continue working there? Only your dog can decide what kind of currency is rewarding, and it will be different for every individual. Try different kinds of food, ranging from kibble to deli meat. Also try toys, play time, petting, and **life rewards** such as access to the couch or getting the door opened. Your dog will tell you when you've found the real reward because she will be eager to engage with you during training.

Emergency recalls

You might be wondering, "Wait, if we just practiced recall, why do we need to also teach an emergency recall?" Glad you asked! Emergency recall actually has several applications beyond just coming when called. It's a unique word or sound that your dog thinks means "free treats," and it can be used to get your dog's attention even when she is highly distracted. For a small dog who is wandering away, you must have a sure-fire emergency recall.

With this behavior, you're going to rely on your dog's love of a certain food or treat. Go big! This is where it pays to use cheese, ham, chicken, or other real foods. Then, you'll choose a certain word or sound to become the dog's cue. For our example, many of my clients use the word "Cookie." By saying "Cookie," and then presenting the treat, you are creating a strong association between the two. With practice, your dog will get as excited to hear the word "Cookie" as she will to see the treat itself.

An important detail of this protocol is that you will always, one hundred percent of the time, give your dog the food. Do not break the association between word and food. If you do, then the word "Cookie" will eventually go back to being just a meaningless word, and your dog will no longer respond to it.

In addition to being a very effective form of recall for emergencies, this technique will be a part of certain behavior modification protocols in Chapter 8. Personally, I have used it when a dog's leash slipped out of my hand, and she darted towards a squirrel in the street (and it worked!). I've also used emergency recall to catch a dog's attention when a dog fight broke out nearby and to greet new people and dogs safely.

How to teach emergency recall

1. Choose a word or sound that you don't use in daily conversation or activities. The word "Cookie" often works, as it has crisp pronunciation and, unless you're a pastry chef, you probably don't say it often. Or choose a word in another language. Or pick a sound like a kissy noise or a whistle. You'll notice in the video that I use a kissy noise with my dogs. Make sure you choose a noise that you can make loudly and that you don't already use with your dog.

2. Say your emergency recall word or sound. Within two seconds, pop a treat in your dog's mouth. Repeat this at least five times, standing still. "Cookie" and give a treat, "Cookie" and give a treat, "Cookie" and give a treat. Your dog doesn't have to perform a sit or any other behavior for this. In fact, it's critical not to ask for a polite behavior. Remember, you're just associating the word with a treat.

3. Casually walk around the room, practicing the pattern of "Cookie" and treat, "Cookie" and treat. Do at least five more like this as you stroll around. If your dog doesn't follow you, that's okay. Walk to her and give her a treat anyway! Make sure every single "Cookie" is followed by a treat, even if your dog is distracted or ignoring you. Stay relatively close to your dog, within five feet or so. This is not a typical recall that relies on long distances. It will work best if your dog gets an easy, free treat quickly.

4. Repeat this exercise indoors daily, giving a few treats standing still and a few while wandering around. You'll know when your dog is learning the connection based on her body language. If you say "Cookie" and your dog rushes over to you happily, then she's getting it! (And even if she doesn't come to you, she can have the treat anyway.)

5. If your dog isn't responding happily to the word, consider a higher value reward, like cheese or bits of meat. Don't be stingy!

Video: https://www. bklnmanners.com/ chapter7.html

Leveling up

Once your little dog has learned the connection between "Cookie" and treats, then it's time to play the exact same game outside. Most of the time, you'll keep the game easy and fun. However, once in a while, it's good to test it out in more distracting scenarios, so you know your dog's current level of skill. But remember that if your dog doesn't respond, you will give the treat anyway and then make a note of what was happening in the environment that prevented the dog from responding to your cue. Consider a balance that looks similar to this:

- 75% of practices happen when the dog is near you and not distracted, as demonstrated in the accompanying video. This can happen indoors or outdoors.

- 20% of practices happen on leashed walks or in the yard, when the dog is casually engaged in an activity like walking (not playing, digging, sniffing, or other full-attention activities).

- 5% of practices happen when the dog is thoroughly distracted by something: a squirrel, a neighbor's dog barking nearby, or during playtime. For these challenging repetitions, give several treats to your dog, which makes a big impression, and then let her go back to what she was originally doing.

Once you know that your dog can stop what she's doing and come to you, you're ready to take this technique on the road and use it for true emergencies, as well as some of the behavior modification techniques in the next chapter.

Continue practicing this exercise long-term, on a maintenance level. For me, I practice one emergency recall a day. Sometimes it's indoors, sometimes on walks. Usually there are no distractions present, but every so often I'll test it out when the dogs are intently doing another activity.

Leash walking for small dogs

Wait, leashed walks for my four-pound teacup Yorkie? Of course! Although a tiny dog might not have the same exercise needs as a Border Collie or Golden Retriever, dogs of all sizes deserve a life full of sights, smells, and exercise according to the individual's particular needs. Just like humans, dogs benefit emotionally and physically when they have sufficient environmental enrichment and physical activity.

As Dianna Shattuck, DVM, explains,

> Environmental enrichment, exercise, and social interaction (with humans and other dogs) are the three legs of the tripod for canine mental and physical health. Daily walks are essential for the mental and physical health of all dogs, including our littlest friends. Dogs experience their world through smell as much as sight, and visiting areas with interesting smells is a huge quality of life enhancer for dogs. Common misconceptions we hear from pet owners every day are, 'We have a big yard for them to run around, so they don't need walk,' 'They can look out the windows and get lots of stimulation that way,' or, 'We have two dogs so they can play with each other, and that's all they need.' While all three of those things are a wonderful part of a dog's life, they are not sufficient to meet the needs of the average dog.

Dr. Shattuck goes on the say that

> ... exercise helps maintain physical health such as optimal weight, cardiovascular fitness and muscle tone. While the exact length of walks needed may

vary based on the dog's temperament, physical abilities, and health issues, small dogs should have at minimum 30 minutes of walking per day, which may be divided into shorter segments. When considering how long or far to walk, remember to keep your pet's age, health level and physical features in mind. For example, Bulldogs, Pugs and other brachycephalic (short-nosed, flat-faced) breeds are prone to a variety of respiratory problems. They may easily overheat if exercised too much, especially in warm conditions. Always involve your veterinarian in the discussion if you have concerns about this.

Decisions, decisions: Give your little dog a choice

The tricky part with small dogs is that some of them aren't interested in walks. And the more you attempt to drag your pint-sized Pekingese around the block, the more likely she is to run from you every time you pull out the leash. This is where choice, control, and trust come into play. Let's use my household as an example. My dogs like their walks (weather permitting), but I always let them opt in or out. This gives my dog a choice, which in turn gives her a sense of control over what happens to her. As you'll see in the video, sometimes Margaret tells me "no thanks" when I offer the leash; she slowly slinks away, head and tail low, probably thinking, "Pleeease don't follow me with that stinkin' leash." I respect her choice and let her skip that walk. This is where trust comes in, because my dogs know that I will respect their decision not to walk, so they never have to run away or get aggressive when I pull out the leash. Here's the interesting part—almost without fail, when I offer Margaret the leash later that day, she jumps for joy. And off we go around the neighborhood! (Note that having pee pads or a potty spot in the yard makes it much easier to give your dogs this choice, since on-leash bathroom breaks are not necessary. See the more in-depth discussion of this in Chapter 5.)

Video: https://www. bklnmanners.com/ chapter7.html

The idea of giving your dog a choice—to walk or not to walk—is a welfare issue more than an exercise one. As Laura M. Kurtycz writes, "In fact, researchers have found that just having choices does have a positive effect on behaviour, even when animals do not take advantage of them" (2015). Much of the research in this area has been done on zoo animals, who typically have limited choices for enrichment and a lack of control over their environment. But studies have found, again and again, that offering options to animals of various species improves their quality of life and decreases their stress levels. In extending this application to dogs, it is important to give them choices when you can—whether to take a walk or not—because, like zoo animals, they already have so little control over their daily lives.

You might be wondering, "If I give my dog the choice not to walk, she might not get enough exercise. Then what?" In this section, you'll find ways to help your dog see walks as a fun opportunity to bond with you and see the world, so that she wants to go outside more and more. And if your pup turns her nose up at the leash at times, don't panic. Flip to Chapter 9 for indoor training games and canine sports that will keep both her body and mind engaged.

Walking equipment for small dogs: Safety first

When it comes to leash walking equipment for little furry bodies, safety takes priority. But as you will see in this section, your dog's safety needs might be different from someone else's dog.

Generally speaking, body harnesses are a better choice than collars around the neck. If a small dog pulls against a collar, it can do irreparable damage to the trachea and other organs around the head, neck, and back. Having lost a small dog to a collapsed trachea, believe me, it is not a fate any dog would choose. Dianna Shattuck notes that "the two most common scenarios when we strongly recommend *not* using a collar around the neck are:

1. Collapsing trachea. This is a fairly common condition in older small-breed dogs. In addition to medical management to reduce inflammation and cough, we recommend lifestyle adjustments. These include using a harness instead of a collar, avoiding exercise in hot, humid conditions, and avoiding respiratory irritants such as cigarette smoke.

2. IVDD (intervertebral disc disease) of the neck or upper back. In these cases, a well-fitting harness is necessary to prevent traction on the neck and spine. I don't recommend a specific brand, but I do recommend the type that does not restrict any joints, especially the shoulder joint."

When it comes to restricting the shoulder joint, the main concern is with harnesses that have a horizontal strap across the chest. This strap restricts the natural movement of the dog, especially when running. A better choice is a harness with straps in a Y shape across the chest, as in the photo. This shape doesn't interfere with the dog's movement.

Your dog's anatomy is not the only consideration, however.

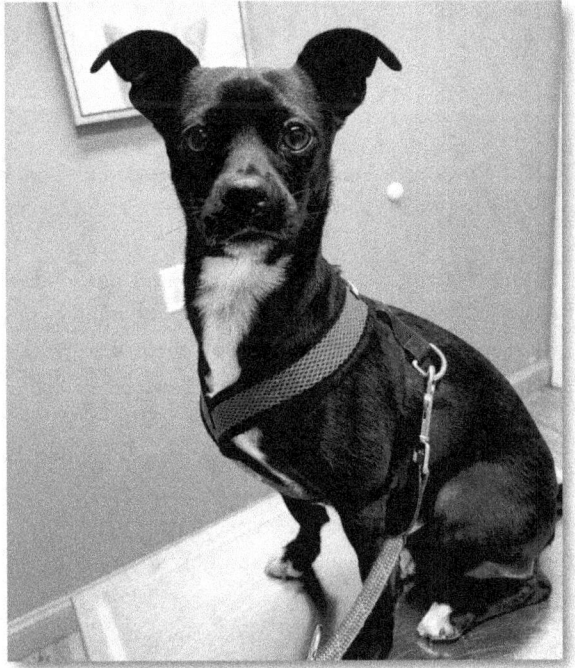

Y shape harness.

What about threats from the outside world? The equipment of choice for my rat pack is something very specific: a Coyote Vest. It's a stab-resistant vest covered in chrome spikes, offering protection from a potential dog, coyote, or bird attack. Since the vest has a loop at the back to attach a leash, the vest acts as my dog's harness. The biggest problem is that the neon-colored vests are quite a conversation piece among neighbors and passersby, so you won't get far without someone stopping to ask about it, or simply lean out their car window, snapping pictures while shouting, "Whoo yeah, punk rock!" On hot days, I will swap the vest for a spiked collar for protection, and use a regular, soft harness to attach the leash. This kind of protective equipment might not be right for everyone, but do consider safety from predators and large dogs when you choose what your little dog will wear outside.

Consider defensive gear to protect your little dog from predators.

Of the more conventional equipment choices, back clip harnesses are usually the best choice for small dogs. Because the leash attaches at the top, along the dog's spine, you don't have to worry about stumpy little legs getting tangled. These harnesses come in countless varieties: mesh ones, step-in ones, over-the-head ones, strap-only ones, and easy on/off harnesses. You may have to try out a few styles before finding one that fits your pup's body type, but it's worth the effort. Ensure that your dog can't slip out of the harness, especially when pulling backwards. And check your dog's underarms, neck, and shoulders to make sure the harness isn't rubbing uncomfortably. There is one downside of back-clip harnesses: your dog can turn into a teeny tiny sled dog, gleefully pulling you down the street. Fortunately, however, little dogs usually don't run the risk of pulling their handlers over. And the training games below will teach your dog that loose leash walking is so much more enjoyable than pulling.

If your little one has handling issues, it's important to choose a back-clip harness that requires as little fussing, clipping and hovering as possible. I recommend a secure harness with a "speed buckle" that contains a magnet, such as the one made by Brilliant K9. All you have to do is line up the belly strap to the buckle, and it practically snaps itself in place. I've used this harness with my own Margaret and several clients' dogs to reduce their stress when taking the harness on and off. There is one caveat here—all the speed-buckle harnesses I've seen are designed with one thick horizontal strap across the chest. As Dr. Shattuck had explained, this can restrict a dog's movement and negatively impact joints.

Front clip harnesses are another option, particularly for taller dogs that are less likely to get their legs tangled. These harnesses, where the leash attaches to the dog's chest, are considered a training tool to help reduce pulling without hurting the

For dogs with handling issues, a harness with a "speed buckle" is easy to get on and off.

dog. Once a pulling dog reaches the end of the leash, she'll feel some tension at her chest, and her body will naturally turn toward the handler. Therefore, the dog can't continue to pull you forward, because her own body has been turned to the side. In the early stages of training, this can be a useful tool. I prefer front clip harnesses such as the Blue-9 Balance Harness®, which are made of all straps rather than panels. This is because panels inevitably shift back and forth when the leash gets tight, making it easier for the dog to slip out or injure herself.

Collars as a backup tool

Collars do have a place, but not in the way you might think. A martingale collar is an excellent emergency backup in the event your dog sneaks out of her harness. You have a few options to create this backup system.

- Purchase a coupler with a clip at either end, which is traditionally used to walk two dogs on one leash. In this case, you would attach one clip to the harness, and the second clip to the collar as a backup. Just make sure that the strap connected to the collar is looser than the strap connected to the harness. This way, when the leash tightens, the tension happens through the harness, while the collar remains loose.

- Get (or make) a safety strap. This is a small strap, just a few inches long, with a clip at the end. You can attach the safety strap from collar to harness, or from collar to leash. The important thing is that all the equipment is attached in some way, so that if the harness pops off, you are still attached to your dog through the martingale collar. The photo here shows a harness (yes, with spikes for added safety) attached to a martingale with a short strap.

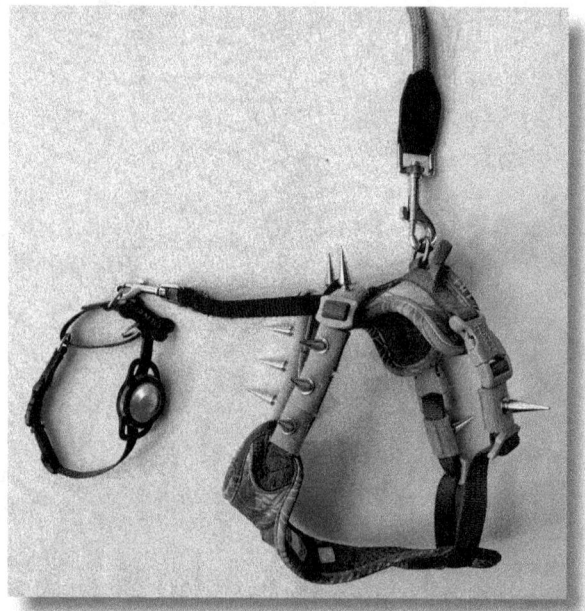

Safety first! My walking gear includes a martingale collar with a tracking device, attached to a spiked harness by a safety strap.

Regardless of the safety system you choose, make sure all your dog's equipment has a tag with your contact information on it. Even if your dog is microchipped, it would require a trip to a shelter or vet clinic to read the chip; a neighbor calling your number from an ID tag is much less stressful for everyone.

Types of leashes

As for a leash, usually a six-foot leash is best for small dogs. Four-foot leashes may be too short, given how much distance there is between your hand and your pup. Look for a clip that is sturdy enough to withstand your dog's pulling, but not so heavy it adds unnecessary weight. Retractable leashes are ineffective when teaching loose leash walking, since the leash is never actually loose. They also present too many safety risks. I had one client whose dog was startled when the retractable leash handle dropped and "chased" her, causing her to dash into the woods and be lost for two terrifying days.

For small dogs, I'm particularly fond of hands-free leashes (also called jogging leashes), which are designed to wrap around your waist. Now you have two hands free for training, and there is no risk of accidentally dropping the leash. Most styles are adjustable, so you can create the perfect fit.

Before you start leash training, practice Follow-me recall with your dog, to assess her comfort level. As much as your little dog loves you, it can be quite intimidating to stand close to a towering human's foot. So before you ask your dog to walk within inches of your moving feet, be clear about what your dog's comfort zone is.

Leash walking fundamentals

Leashed walks put both dogs and humans in a challenging position. Dogs are battered with stimuli on walks—scurrying squirrels, tasty tissues left on the sidewalk, other dogs passing by, babies crying in strollers, and cars whizzing past, to name a few. No wonder they're distracted! On top of that, dogs were never really designed to walk next to you, attached by a six-foot lead. Having been our companions for at least 10,000 years, dogs are still designed to wander freely, keeping an eye on us but not glued to our sides. It's only in the very recent past that we've stuffed them into high rise apartments with stamp-sized elevators, reduced off-leash time to cramped dog parks, and asked them to dodge strollers and joggers on narrow sidewalks. The relentless bombardment and confined spaces of modern life can be stressful to a dog.

You can't change the leash laws or live off the grid to give your dog more freedom, but you can reduce her stress by making it fun for her to engage with you on walks. By interacting with your little one outside, you build a friendly line of communication between you both, making the distractions less enthralling and the stressors less intense. With this technique, your dog will be rewarded when she interacts with you so that, over time, she will be checking in with you repeatedly on walks. And if she's thinking about you again and again, she's not getting absorbed in that squirrel hopping in front of you. She's also not grabbing leaves or trash from the grass or pulling ahead to reach the dog she sees half a block up. While you will benefit from all the techniques in this chapter, if you only teach one leash walking strategy, make it this one.

This technique uses treat reinforcers. However, you may have found that your dog is uncomfortable coming right up to you for a treat. Or you may find that bending down to reach your little dog's mouth is physically uncomfortable for you. In these cases, try a squeeze tube of treats, which extends your reach by several inches. You can buy these tubes online or at a camping store; they look like clear toothpaste tubes. Fill the tubes with:

- Pâté-style wet dog food (not the chunky "stew" stuff)

- Creamy peanut butter (avoid chunks, the natural style where the oil separates, and anything with xylitol, which is toxic to dogs)

- Another tasty paste of similar consistency. If it's too thick, you won't be able to squeeze it out of the tube, but if it's too thin, it will dribble out and make a mess.

Some other arm-extending options include:

- A mess-free pouch such as Bark Pouch, with a soft treat you can squeeze out.

- Lickable sticks that require no preparation on your part. One of my clients calls this "meat deodorant," due to the roll-on way that the meaty paste is delivered.

- A long wooden spoon, dipped in peanut butter and then hardened in the freezer. This does the trick for indoor and near-home training, where you can refuel if you run out.

Loose leash walking for the littles

Start this activity indoors first, or in an enclosed yard with no distractions. Your dog should be wearing a harness and leash. Watch the video to see the steps in action.

How to teach loose leash walking

1. Have your treats in the hand closest to the dog. Your dog and treats can be on either the left or right side, depending on safety and your dexterity.

   By safety, I mean that I always walk with the dog to the safest side of any street, sidewalk, or path. When I'm on a sidewalk or path, my dog is usually on my right side, so I can use my body to protect her little paws from an oncoming bicycle or jogger. While walking on the shoulder of the street, my dog is on my left so I can body block her from oncoming cars. (These choices are based on American norms for cars, bikes, and pedestrians.)

2. Since your treats are on the dog side, your leash will be held in the hand farther from the dog. (Even if you use a hands-free leash, you may still need to hold the leash at times.) So, if your pup is on your right side, then hold the leash in your left hand. This means you will not be controlling your dog with the leash, but rather with your treats. And that's the point!

3. Any time your dog looks at you, mark "Yes" and reward. Your dog has just chosen you over the many distractions and she deserves a treat!

4. Practice this game in short intervals as you walk around the house or yard. Choose about 20 seconds to happily talk to your dog. Then take a break for 30-60 seconds, just walking around without actively playing the attention game.

5. During that break, if your dog chooses to look up at you on her own, mark and reward! This is the best scenario of all, because your pup is thinking about you without you even asking for her engagement.

Video: https://www.bklnmanners.com/chapter7.html

Troubleshooting

Issue: Your dog swerves from side to side when you walk.

Solution: It's fine to hold the leash in both hands, to prevent swerving. If your dog is on your right side, then the bulk of the leash will still be in your left hand. But you can use your right hand as needed to stabilize your dog with the leash. This means your right hand is working double duty, holding the middle of the leash as needed, and also dishing out treats.

Issue: Your dog doesn't look at you while walking.

Solution: This is normal in the beginning. If she doesn't look at you on her own, talk happily to your dog or make some kissy or clucking noises. Ask silly questions like, "What do you want to do tonight?" and give lighthearted compliments like, "Girl, you look so good in that harness!" This technique is about engaging with your dog and being fun. It is not about saying a cue. Avoid saying the same thing over again ("Sadie, Sadie, Sadie…") and avoid cuing a behavior like "Come" or "Look At Me." Your dog should be naturally interacting with you because you're cool, not because you're explicitly telling her to look.

Issue: Your dog isn't comfortable looking all the way up at you.

Solution: That's OK! Your eyes are pretty far away from her, after all. You can also mark and reward when she is walking near you on a loose leash. Here, you're rewarding for the position next to you, not the eye contact.

Issue: Your dog is overwhelmed by passing people, dogs, or other stimuli outside. She tends to bark, lunge, growl, or snap at them, and she can't focus on you.

Solution: Flip to the "Leash reactivity" section on page 148 for strategies to help your little one feel more at ease.

Leveling up

The advanced-level training steps don't change much from the basic version. What does change, however, is the environment. You'll need to build your dog's skills in gradually higher distraction areas.

Tackle distractions methodically. Make a list of five-to-ten locations where you would like to walk your dog and rank them based on distraction level. Start with the lowest-distraction location, and using the B-student rule, work your way up. Keep in mind that one street can provide numerous levels of distraction. Perhaps your street at 6am is quiet, but by 8am it's bustling with kids waiting for the bus and adults hurrying to work. And at 6pm, oh boy, that's when everyone is out walking their dogs and mowing their lawns. These times of day would count as three separate levels.

What about fading the treats? Let's say on your quiet 6am walk, your dog is offering eye contact frequently and walking on a loose leash most of the time. That's a B, and you can now start practicing in a slightly more distracting environment. At the same time, you can start to gradually fade the treats on the quiet 6am walk. To do this, continue treating 75% of the eye contact, but the other 25% use enthusiastic praise instead. Stay at this 75/25 ratio for a few weeks, as you continue to build your dog's skills in higher distraction scenarios. If that goes well, then you can fade to 50/50 treats/praise for a few weeks. And eventually, 25/75 treats/praise. Follow this pattern to eventually fade treats from higher level distraction areas, too. However, don't be in a rush to bail on the treats entirely. Loose leash walking is hard work for your dog, and she will need a long period of reinforcement before loose leash walking feels normal to her, particularly around distractions. Expect to be using intermittent treat rewards for months or longer. You'll find that this fading happens naturally; over time, your dog will simply enjoy checking in with you and staying on a loose leash, without the expectation of a treat.

A final note about treats. Even after having my dogs for years, I still reward them with a thank-you treat about once per day for eye contact. This reward comes when there is a significant distraction—a passing dog or a delicious looking squirrel—very close to us. When my dogs look up at me instead of focusing on the dog or squirrel, I tell them, "Thank you for choosing me!" and give them a little goodie. And what about the other dozens of looks they give me on walks, sans-distraction? I continue to verbally reinforce every look, regardless of distraction level, by complimenting them when they offer me eye contact. In the long term, I want my dogs to know that when they look up at me, I will always be there to respond.

"Line Up"

In the previous loose leash walking section, I mentioned the value of body blocking your dog. Regardless of what's coming towards me, I always make sure my body is between my dogs and the oncoming person, car, bicycle, or other dog. This allows an unsure dog to feel secure because you've got everything under control. If that bicycle swerves towards her tiny paws, you'll be there to protect her. Body blocking also benefits no-nonsense little dogs. By placing your body between your pup and a jogger, it conveys that you've got it handled; she doesn't need to police every passing person or tell those kids on scooters to slow down.

"Line Up" is the training version of body blocking. Rather than hopping over your dog, or dragging her leash to the other side, why not make it a team effort? This cue asks your little one to cross in front of you when moving to your right or left side, which ensures you can see where she is at all times. Therefore, you're less likely to accidentally step on her or yank the leash as she moves so close to your feet. "Line Up" is a technique inspired by dog sports such as Rally Obedience and Freestyle, where the dog happily moves to your right or left side. If I see a bicycle approaching on my left, I can cue my dog to "Line Up" to my right side. Now she is safely body blocked. This technique will also become useful for some of the behavior modification strategies in the next chapter.

Teaching this behavior involves some bending on your part, so consider using the previously mentioned squeeze tube if either you or your dog feels uncomfortable with you bending over close to her. Or you could drop treats on the ground rather than hand-feed; in this case, avoid anything round or bouncy, as placement of the treats is important for this activity, and we don't want them rolling away. The video demonstrates treat placement, plus the steps of this exercise from beginner to advanced.

How to teach "Line Up," Part 1
Start practicing this indoors or in the yard, so your dog can be off leash.

1. Choose a side for your dog to line up on. Have a treat ready in that hand. For this example, we'll use your right side. (But in a later session, practice on your left.)

2. Stand a few feet in front of your dog. If your dog is already by your side, toss a treat a few feet behind you, to move her back.

3. Say "Line Up" and stretch your right palm down to the floor. Wiggle your fingers a little, which will catch your dog's eye. The treat in your right hand is being pinched with your thumb. If you want to be specific, you can use the cue "Right Side" instead of "Line Up." But if you're like me, always confusing right and left, then stick to "Line Up" for both sides and just make your visual cue (wiggling fingers) super clear.

4. When your dog reaches your hand, mark "Yes" and reward with that treat.

5. Release with "OK, Get It!" and toss a treat behind you. This sets her up for the next repetition.

6. Practice like this until your dog is a B student.

How to teach "Line Up," Part 2
Sometimes your dog is in front of you, or to the other side of you, when you need to cue "Line Up." Follow these steps to introduce your dog to this slightly different route. Same as before, first practice this off-leash in a quiet location. This example continues with a right-side line up, but also practice to your left side.

1. Your dog is to your left side. Toss a treat to your left, if needed, to get her there.

2. Say "Line Up" and show the visual cue, wiggling your right hand with a few treats hidden behind your thumb.

3. Slowly lure your dog in front of you and towards your right side. Once your dog reaches your right leg, hand-feed or drop one treat.

   Is your dog struggling to follow your hand? She might be confused. If so, as you lure, drop one treat right in front of your feet, and then a second one at your right side. Repeat this double-treat drop for several reps. This will clear up your dog's confusion about where you're asking her to go.

4. Now your dog has crossed to your right side, but she's facing backwards. Slowly lure her a few more steps, just behind your right leg. Then draw the treat in a U-turn back towards your leg.

5. Now your dog is on your right side and you're both facing the same direction. Good dog! Mark and reward at your right side.

6. Walk off together, as you happily talk to your dog as in the loose leash walking activity.

7. Practice on both sides, over several sessions, until your dog is a B student.

8. Once your dog is getting the hang of it, reduce the treats to only one treat at the very end of the sequence. So, if you are swinging the dog from left to right, the dog gets a treat at the completion, where next to you, facing the same direction you are, and is on your right side. Practice until she's a B student.

9. Now, cue "Line Up" and use an empty wiggling hand. Once your dog is next to you, give a treat from your pocket or treat pouch. Practice until she's a B student.

10. At first, keep your sweeping gesture the same speed as before. With more and more reps, you can speed up your cue hand slightly, but if your dog gets stuck at any point, it may be because you sped up your cue too quickly.

Video: https://www.bklnmanners.com/chapter7.html

Leveling up

Once your dog is a B student indoors, then start practicing during low-distraction moments on leashed walks. If you need to go back to luring or using multiple treats in this new environment, that's perfectly fine in the beginning.

For real life applications, use "Line Up" any time you need to pass someone or something on your walks. These things could simply be distractions, like garbage on the sidewalk, or they could be perceived threats, such as a skateboard whizzing by. Be ready to cue it well before you reach the distraction or threat. You want your dog to be safely body blocked before that thing is next to you. See the video for a real-life application of passing a distraction.

I suggest seeking out low-level distractions on your walks, such as a stinky fire hydrant or an enticing garbage can. At least ten feet before you reach the fire hydrant, cue "Line Up" to get your dog on the far side of it. Then practice loose leash walking, rewarding your pup for eye contact as you pass that distraction. Do this at least once per walk, for long-term maintenance.

Treat station game to make walks fun

Does your little dog dislike going outside for walks? Yeah, mine, too. I'm not talking about fearful behavior on walks. (If your dog is fearful, see Chapter 8.) But rather, your little sidekick would rather you two go out for a "carry" than a "walk."

If your dog isn't the outdoorsy type, it's not the end of the world. Many of us humans share this aversion, too. Think of how miserable certain people would be if they were forced to go hiking twice a day. In fact, think about how you would feel if you were forced to do any activity you deeply disliked on a daily basis. (Are you having chilling gym class flashbacks right now, as I am?) So if your dog is telling you that she's really not an outside kind of pup, this game is designed to help her see walks in a new light. She may never be a marathon runner or thrill-seeking hiker, but even a stroll around the block is a good source of enrichment and exercise.

Play the "Treat Station" game to help turn your dog's daily "carry" into an actual walk. It's fine to keep the game short, maybe just a few houses up your block to start. As your dog gets hooked on the game, you can add more distance bit by bit.

How to teach the "Treat Station" game

1. Designate three landmarks along your route. The landmarks should be no more than 50 feet (15 meters) apart, permanent, and easy for your dog to notice. For example, you can choose a fire hydrant, utility pole, or a specific tree.

2. If you usually carry your dog out the door, start by carrying her as usual. Right before you reach the first landmark, you'll exclaim, "Treat Station!" and put your dog down on the ground. She gets a treat exactly in front of that landmark.

3. Pick your dog up again and carry her to the next station. Again, say "Treat Station!" and put her down to give the treat in front of the second landmark.

4. Pick her up and do the same with the third landmark.

5. With your dog at the current end point of the game, you will stand still and let her decide what she wants to do. Would she like to continue walking? Sure, off we go! Would she prefer to go home? No problem, she can walk back on her own little legs. Let your dog decide.

Leveling up

Practice at this level for at least one week, meaning seven walks or more. At this point, your dog should be getting the pattern. Then you will:

- Put your dog down about three feet (one meter) before you reach the first station. Once she is on the ground, cheer "Treat Station" and let her walk a few steps to the first station herself. Give the treat at the station, as before. Then you pick her up and head to stations two and three. Repeat this pattern, with the dog walking about three feet to each station, for one week.

○ You're never dragging your dog to the station. Even if she walks slowly, that's fine. Keep the leash loose because pulling will only make her dig her heels in more.

○ If your dog freezes before reaching the treat station, place the treat at the base of the fire hydrant or pole. You're not luring the dog, just placing it on the ground and waiting for her to get it.

• From there, continue adding distance each week, in roughly three-foot increments. You are gradually reducing the amount of carrying and increasing the amount of walking.

• If your dog seems interested in the game, start adding more stations, one at a time.

• Once your dog can walk all the way between stations without needing to be carried, I recommend playing this game together with the loose leash walking technique. While your dog is walking between stations, talk happily to her and reward for eye contact.

Keep your small dog's preferences in mind. You'll probably have the most success if you play this game on good-weather days. You'll also be more successful if you can choose a low-distraction route, for example, a side street rather than a main road. If you need to carry your dog to a lower-distraction area simply to start the game, that's fine.

Carry on: Carrier training for small dogs

Whether you're going to a crowded farmers' market or taking a flight, it pays to acclimate your small dog to being carried in a bag. As a former city dweller who relied on public transportation for decades, I've prioritized carrier training for all my little ones. As soon as my dogs see the bag, they jump for joy and can't wait to dive inside, awaiting our next adventure together. Keep these key points in mind when training your dog to sit in a carry bag.

Make sure the bag is safe and your dog feels secure. Don't choose a bag from which your dog can tumble or a bag that makes your dog feel imbalanced. The safest bags can fully zip the dog's body inside; in fact, many forms of public transportation require a zippable bag, so a dog can't sneak out or bite someone during travel. As you see in the photo of a Sherpa bag, the sides are mesh, allowing the dog to see out and breathe normally. The trick with fully zipped bags is the fit—your dog should be comfortable inside, especially the head and neck. Other tote-style bags allow the dog's head to pop out, but partially zip to prevent an escape. You may also see a sling-style bag, with the dog's head poking out. Some styles of these bags have a short tether inside to attach to the dog's harness, to prevent an escape (though I worry about a dog partially jumping out and then dangling). There is also a baby-bjorn style of dog carriers, but I am wary of those, given the unnatural position the dog is forced to hold for an extended period of time.

Nester loves his bag because it means adventure awaits!

Take your time. For small dogs that travel or live in cities, carriers are often a *have to* rather than *want to*. So, it pays to train it correctly the first time, ensuring your dog sees the bag as a happy place. The process includes several steps: willingly hopping into the bag, staying in the bag while being carried, and tolerating the stimuli of public places or transportation. You'll see the main steps in the video. Begin your training long before you actually need to use the carrier in real life.

Plan your first real outing together. Choose a place that your dog loves—a park, a neighborhood shop that gives out treats, a pet supply store, or a beloved friend's house. The place should be a very short commute; choose a location that is either walkable or one stop away on public transportation.

How to teach "Get In"

1. Before she places even a whisker inside the carrier, get your dog curious about the outside of it. Lay the bag on the floor and sprinkle several treats around the bag. It's better not to get too involved, so you can even walk away as your dog gets familiar with the bag on her own. Repeat this daily, until your dog gladly walks near and even on the bag to find the treats.

2. With the bag resting on its side, or with a side flap opened, sprinkle some treats around and also inside the bag. The treats should still be easily accessed. Repeat this daily, until your dog willingly goes into the bag to find the treats.

3. Put the bag upright, and open the flaps as wide as possible, so your dog can hop or step in. Sprinkle some treats inside the bag, so your dog will have to partly or fully step inside the bag to get them. Repeat this daily, until your dog willingly goes into the bag to find the treats.

4. Now you'll teach your dog to step into it. Have a few treats in your hand. Toss one treat into the bag for your dog to find. Then when your dog has one or more paws inside the bag, feed her another treat or two by hand. This encourages the dog to stay in the bag for a few moments.

5. When playing this game, if your dog puts all four paws inside the bag to find the treat, jackpot! Feed several treats while your dog is still in the bag and then help her walk or hop out. Repeat this until your dog is happily putting all four paws in the bag. If your dog is too small to get in or out of the bag on her own, you will have to lift her. Make sure you're familiar with the body language in Chapter 3, to ensure your dog always feels safe. Or better yet, purchase a bag that has a side entry, so your dog doesn't have to be lifted at all.

6. Say a word or phrase, such as "Get In," and toss a treat inside the bag. Feed a few treats, one after the other, while your dog is in the bag. Then release with "OK," and encourage your dog to walk or hop out by tossing a treat on the ground outside of the bag. Repeat until your dog is enjoying this game.

7. Cue your dog to "Get In" the bag. Once she is safely inside, gently lift the bag, feeding your dog a few treats as you elevate the bag for about five seconds. Once the bag is back on the floor, continue feeding treats because you don't want your dog jumping out yet. Feed a few more treats and then release with "OK" for your dog to hop out of the bag. Practice this until your dog is happily going into the bag and can wait for the release word "OK" to exit the bag. As time goes on, you can slowly reduce the frequency of treats while your dog is being carried.

8. Add duration by walking around your home, then your yard (or if you don't have a yard, the halls of your apartment) with your dog in the bag.

9. Hit the road! Do you have a neighbor whom your dog loves, or a favorite park down the road? Take a visit there. The shorter the commute, the better. The goal is to choose a location that is very close and very enjoyable for your dog.

Video: https://www.
bklnmanners.com/
chapter7.html

Leveling up

Continue taking your dog on short adventures to fun places: the park, the pet supply store, or a friend's house … not the vet's office! If you plan to take public transportation, here are some tips:

- Bring a long-lasting food toy or chew to keep her busy, so she won't get overwhelmed by the sounds or sights.

- If your dog gets startled by a sudden noise or movement, immediately drop a few pieces of a high value treat into the carrier and use a soothing voice to reassure her she's okay. This keeps the situation positive.

- If people want to pet your dog, it's best to politely decline. This is especially true for shy dogs, but also applies to friendly dogs. You've worked so hard to keep your dog calm and safe in the bag, why set your training back by letting a stranger get your dog riled up?

"Place" at the café

Once your little one has developed a liking for her place as in the previous chapter, you can take it on the road! One of the benefits of a compact dog is your ability to take her out in public, even in cramped spaces like outdoor cafés. I recommend following these steps when you're ready to bring your dog to the café for the first time.

Prerequisites:

- Your dog should be able to relax on her place at home for up to twenty minutes. (This would be a reasonable amount of time to enjoy a coffee in public.) This doesn't mean that your dog needs to be a statue for twenty minutes straight or that she can't interact with you during this time. It just means she should be comfortable enough on her place to settle in for a while.

- Your dog should be comfortable staying on her place as people, dogs, strollers, and cars go by.

- You have researched a suitable dog-friendly café. Look for a spot with spacious outdoor seating, so you can avoid customer and server traffic. A café that lets you order and pay online will give you the freedom to leave before your pup gets overwhelmed.

The following steps are for the café, but if your dog isn't quite ready for the confines of the café yet, then follow these same steps in a park or other wide open space. This will ensure your dog isn't overwhelmed by so many movements and sounds by having the option of being further away from them.

How to teach "Place" at the café

1. Bring your dog's mat with you and set it up on the floor in the least trafficked spot available. Your body and chair should be blocking your dog from passersby, to keep her safe.

2. Your dog will remain on leash for the entire café experience. If you can't hold the leash, tie it to your belt or consider a hands-free leash around your waist. The leash should only be long enough for her to hang out on her place; do not allow her to wander to other tables or get tangled in other people's chairs.

3. Cue your dog to "Place." She can have a reward for going there.

4. The first minute or two, drop a treat onto the mat every ten seconds or so. This helps her ease into the position.

5. After that, your dog should be more settled in. Stop giving the treats every ten seconds, but you may give gentle pets or verbal reassurance as needed.

6. Any time a person, dog, or other distraction comes nearby, praise your dog for staying on her place and drop a little treat between her paws.

7. If she pops off her place at any point, don't make a fuss. She shouldn't be able to go far, since the leash is restricting her access to other tables. Gently encourage her back with your voice and gestures. If she likes attention, you can give her some slow, calming pets to help her settle in.

8. End the session after a few minutes. As you practice café manners more and more, you can extend your stay at the café, but at first, keep the trips short and enjoyable. If your dog gets restless after a certain amount of time, it means you've pushed her too far and it's time to pack up. Note how long she was able to stay comfortable, and for your next training session, leave a few minutes before you anticipate her getting restless, vocal, or seeking your attention.

Chapter 8
Aggression and Reactivity in Small Dogs

If you've followed the guidelines and practiced the exercises in previous chapters, you're well on your way to building a healthy relationship with your little one. But what if your dog is experiencing more serious behavior concerns? This chapter addresses the most common behavior issues for small dogs:

- Alarm barking

- Doorbell reactivity

- Reactivity toward house guests

- Leash reactivity

- Resource guarding of people, spaces and items

Behavior is complicated. This is true not only for humans, but for all animals. This chapter is designed to provide you with trusted, safe, and effective strategies for a number of behavior issues that plague small dog guardians. But before we get into step-by-step guidelines for behavior modification, let's address realistic outcomes. Will behavior modification transform your challenging dog into the ideal pup of your dreams? I can't guarantee that. Will this training turn your bloodthirsty mini-Cujo into everyone's perfect playmate at the dog park? Maybe not. The purpose of behavior modification is not to change your dog's fundamental personality and preferences. Behavior modification is therapy and it can have an immensely positive impact on your dog, but it is not a magic wand that will erase all your puppy problems overnight. Behavior modification will give you the tools to teach your dog new skills and healthier patterns when faced with his triggers and let him feel significantly less stressed in situations that currently cause him to overreact.

If there is one thing you take away from this chapter, let it be this: *Do not expect a greater behavior change from your dog than you would expect from a human who is undergoing therapy.*

Imagine that you have begun therapy to improve your own mental health. Would it be realistic, after a few sessions with a therapist, to be magically transformed into a completely different person? It's highly unlikely. A more realistic outcome is that you will always be susceptible to certain kinds of behavior patterns, but you have developed solid tools to help you effectively work through those difficult times. And as time goes on, you may find that the things that used to cause you stress no longer do, but the process takes time and consistency. This applies to your little dog, as well. Expect your dog to be able to use the tools you teach him to prevent him from going over his threshold, and as time goes on, his triggers will become less triggering, even if his basic personality remains intact. Sure, I have seen cases where a dog's perception of triggers dramatically improves in a matter of days and it feels like a complete 180-degree transformation. But this is not typical. I recommend you take your dog's journey one step at a time, celebrating the small victories as they add up over time, and compassionately riding through the bumps that will inevitably occur. Isn't this how you would approach your own journey of self-improvement?

Why is my dog aggressive?

Many books have been dedicated to the topic of **aggression**, most commonly defined as behavior that intends to cause harm to another individual, such as lunging, snapping, or biting. If you have a dog that acts aggressively under any circumstances, please educate yourself and consider seeking out in-person help from a professional. (Whether in print or in person, look for professionals with credentials mentioned in Chapter 2.) Aggression can be complicated and it's important not to make quick assumptions about a dog's motivations for acting aggressively.

None of us, not even professionals, have the psychic power to read a dog's mind, but we can usually make educated guesses as to why a dog is acting aggressively in certain situations. We can make observations, and even predictions, based on what's happening in the environment, as well as the dog's body language before and during the act of aggression. For instance, imagine Clarence the Toy Poodle has a new bully stick, and as you approach him, he growls at you and stiffly hovers over his treat. Were you to attempt removing the bully stick from his grasp, expect him to respond by lunging, snapping, or even biting your hand. Based on the presence of the bully stick and the body language Clarence is displaying, the best assumption is that he is showing possessive aggression (a form of resource guarding) at that moment.

This section provides a brief overview to get you thinking about your particular pup and what kind of aggression he is displaying. But keep in mind that behavior is complex. Some dogs may fit one category of aggression perfectly, others may not, and yet others may exhibit aggressive behaviors from different categories. For instance, think back to growling, hovering Clarence and his bully stick. If he is also averting his eyes and licking his lips, he could be showing signs of both possessive aggression and fear aggression at the same time. Complicated! Also be aware that the study of dog behavior is a rapidly changing field, with old ideas being challenged and current research shedding new light. So, if you plan to dive into the nitty-gritty of dog behavior, be prepared to have a curious mind and an openness to adapt your beliefs and assumptions as new information emerges.

While aggression refers to the big stuff—growling, barking, lunging, and biting—I'd like you to look for more subtle signs, too. Before your dog growls, does he hold his breath and stiffen? Do his eyes turn hard, perhaps with pupils dilated? Does his mouth close, become tense with wrinkles forming, or with a change in commissures (corners of the mouth)? Do his whiskers point ahead? Does his body lean forward tensely? Or maybe he leans back, slightly cowering? There are *so* many early signs a dog may give before he actively aggresses toward a threat. Become an expert observer of your dog, noting all the behaviors that he displays in the presence of a trigger or threat, not just the biggest, scariest behaviors.

Reactivity versus aggression

It is worth noting the difference between reactivity and aggression here, as the terminology gets a bit muddled. **Reactivity** is generally described as a reaction to a stimulus, such as the mail person, a nearby dog, or a passing truck, that is more intense than the situation objectively calls for. For example, Oreo sees an elderly dog plodding along across the street, and he starts frantically barking and standing on his hind legs. Oreo is not actually under any threat, so his behavior is considered reactive—behaving a bit "extra" in his reaction to the dog—but he is not aggressive. That is, his body language doesn't indicate that he intends to do harm. But over time, Oreo's barking at passing dogs may escalate to growling and lunging. At this point, if his leash were to slip from your hand, you fear that he might even bite another dog. Oreo's behavior has now tipped into aggression, where he is displaying behaviors that indicate a desire to harm another creature.

Common causes and types of reactivity and aggression

Pain and illness. According to a study by Daniel Mills et al., involving 100 dogs with problem behaviors, up to about 80% involved physical pain of some sort. In particular, musculoskeletal, gastro-intestinal, and dermatological issues appear to correlate to problematic behaviors. Mills et al. describe the connection between defensive aggression and pain:

> Within this category [of defensive behavior] are a range of behavior problems, but perhaps most widely recognized are forms of aggressive behavior, since agonistic behavior serves to help avoid contact with humans or other animals. … Typically, these animals are often described as having a poor and changeable temperament, with terms such as the dog having a 'Jekyll and Hyde' type of personality frequently being used. The aggressive behavior typically occurs when the dog is approached and often when the dog is lying down; further investigation of the background behavior of the dog also often reveals a more general reluctance to move." (2020)

The study describes too many other features of health-linked aggression to write here, but suffice it to say that pain and discomfort may play a significant role in a dog's behavior issues.

Dianna Shattuck, DVM, elaborates on this point, with what she sees in her patients at High Ridge Animal Hospital:

> Just recently I have seen several examples. One was a pet who was 'misbehaving' and acting 'fresh' when the owner tried to put on his leash. (It turned out he had neck pain from intervertebral disc disease.) And another was urinating in the home; the owner was sure it was because she resented the owner's new boyfriend, but it turned out she had a bladder stone.

Dr. Shattuck continues:

> There is a myth that dogs will always be vocal if/when they are in pain, when in fact they almost never are (unless there is an acute, scary pain, when they might cry immediately). In most kinds of chronic pain, the changes we see are subtle behavior changes such as being less social, hiding, being quieter than usual, interacting less with family and other pets, being slow to rise, reluctant to go for walks, these sorts of things.

If your dog is having aggression issues, talk to your vet first to rule out any medical conditions. It would be unethical to attempt a behavior modification protocol without first confirming that your dog is healthy and pain-free.

Fear aggression. Fear is a very common cause for aggressive behavior in small dogs, but not all fearful dogs will resort to aggression. We generally believe a frightened dog doesn't want to lunge or bite; he would much rather run away from the threat. However, if he can't escape, then flight turns to fight. To determine if fear (and the subsequent inability for flight) is underlying your little dog's aggression, look for body language that indicates the dog would rather escape than face the threat directly:

- Tucked tail or hunched hind end
- Hiding behind a safe person or object
- Low body carriage
- Piloerection (raised hackles)
- Backing away while barking or growling
- Chasing and possibly biting as the trigger walks or turns away

Because a fearful dog doesn't actually want to approach you, he may keep a distance as long as you are facing him, lunging forward a bit but then backing away. But when you turn away, he is more likely to lunge and bite the back of your legs. In my early days as a trainer, I had to learn this the hard way, by being bitten in the cheeks (yes, *those* cheeks) the moment I turned my back on a fearful, cornered dog.

Territorial aggression. A dog with territorial aggression tends to only growl, bark, lunge, or bite on home territory. This space could be as small as a couch, or as large as the entire neighborhood. In less familiar locations, such as a park, the dog appears to have relaxed body language and may happily interact with other people and dogs.

There is some debate whether territorial aggression is rooted in fear, anxiety, anger, or a combination; in all likelihood, it may depend on the dog. Perhaps a small dog is generally anxious and feeling threatened that strangers are intruding in his safe space, and he feels the need to scare them away to relieve his stress. Or perhaps the dog is quite confident and sees it as his job to tell intruders to buzz off. In this latter case, I wouldn't consider territorial aggression a form of reactivity, since the dog's feelings may not be over-the-top at all; he may feel it's perfectly reasonable to scare off anyone who dares enter his neighborhood. Although few small dogs have the bloodlines of guardian breeds, these behaviors could pop up in even the tiniest of dogs from time to time. To determine if your dog is displaying territorial aggression, consider these points:

- On walks, your dog only reacts inside or close to your home. Once you are away from home, he is neutral or friendly to people and dogs.

- Your dog reacts aggressively to people coming to your home. He may growl at people he sees out the window, get agitated when a delivery person is outside your door, or bark and charge at incoming guests.

- Your dog positions himself between you and the trigger. He may have an "I'll take care of this" stance, with a forward leaning body, raised head and tail, a low growl, a hard stare, and/or piloerection (hackles up).

Possessive aggression. Just like some people, some dogs haven't learned to share. And from a survival perspective, guarding your food, shelter, and loved ones means that you will have enough resources to keep yourself alive. Possessive aggression is a form of **resource guarding**, in which the dog will make threatening displays if he feels a person or animal is infringing upon his treasured items. (Note that not all resource guarding is aggressive; some dogs will take their rawhide and simply run away.) When Clarence has his bully stick, he hunkers down with it, and if you or another dog approach him, a few signs of possessive aggression might be:

- Hovering over the object
- Baring his teeth
- Showing whale eye
- Growling
- Lunging
- Biting

Possessive aggression isn't limited to food items. It can also be triggered by the presence of toys, water bowls, a preferred human, and certain furniture or dog beds. In rarer cases, dogs develop aggression around vomit, paper towels, and household objects like slippers.

On walks, a dog showing possessive aggression of the handler is similar to a territorially aggressive dog. In this case, the territory is you, not the location itself. The observable behaviors are the same as territorial aggression, except that the dog only displays it when a valued person is walking with him. This could be limited to one person in your family—and having Chihuahua mixes, I can tell you that the one-person-attachment is a real phenomenon. Or a dog might value multiple people. However, when a neutral person, such as a dog walker, walks the dog, he shows no signs of aggression at all.

Barrier frustration. Some dogs want to live life to the fullest, but a leash, fence, or window restricts them from getting to what they want. What results is an aggressive-looking display due to barrier frustration. The frustration that builds may include whining, spinning, barking, growling, and lunging at that thing he wants. In most cases, dogs that exhibit barrier frustration are friendly—maybe too friendly!

Do any of these points sound familiar? If so, your dog may have barrier frustration when restricted by a leash, fence, or window.

- He is friendly when off-leash. Many dogs are well suited to daycare, a dog park, or a backyard BBQ with humans and dogs. But when the leash clips on or he's behind a fence, he isn't able to reach the dog or person he has his eye on, and his excitement quickly turns to frustration.

- He is generally allowed to greet dogs or people on leash, but on the occasions you don't let him, he reacts by growling, barking, lunging, or other doggie acrobatics. He may even redirect his frustration toward you, by jumping on you or grabbing the leash or your pant leg with his teeth.

- His body language may look stiff and focused toward a dog or person, or it may be more playful, with an open smiling mouth, tail wagging in a circular helicopter shape, and lots of jumping and thrashing. Once he can get up close to greet the dog or person, he is wiggly and waggy. (If you've never tested out this scenario, please don't start now! It could be dangerous to let a reactive dog greet someone.)

- He never checks in with you on walks, and he's always looking for a person or dog to drag you toward.

There are other, less common kinds of aggression. Briefly:

Conflict aggression. This is a form of owner-directed aggression that may have layers, but often comes down to the dog's desire to control their surroundings. Dogs may show aggression toward all or some family members, particularly around resources, such as furniture, food, laps, etc., and when being handled or restrained. Dogs learn that aggression is an effective way to stop uncomfortable interactions (The College of Veterinary Medicine at Michigan State University, 2019). There may be elements of fear, anxiety, possessiveness, or conflict involved—meaning the dog simultaneously wants two opposite things. (Landsberg, 2018)

Protective aggression. This tends to refer to dogs that were bred to protect their owners from outsiders. While a Malinois or Doberman might come to mind, there are some small dogs that may indeed feel it's their job to "protect" their humans. Chihuahua owners, I'm looking at you!

Redirected aggression. This occurs when a dog can't reach the object of their aggression, so he redirects the behavior to a person or animal nearby. I most commonly see it with a leash-reactive dog. Due to the leash, the dog isn't able to reach the trigger, so he will bite the handler in that moment of high arousal. It may also happen in multi-dog households when the doorbell rings; in the frenzy of arousal, one dog will attack another, seemingly unprovoked.

Predatory behavior. Another category deals with predatory instinct. Technically this is not reactivity and it is not even considered aggression by many experts. That's because predation is considered **appetitive**, meaning it is actually a rewarding experience for an animal.

Stalking, chasing, catching, and killing an animal are parts of an innate predatory motor sequence, which, somewhat disturbingly to us, is a joyful experience for the dog (Huang et al., 2021). If you have a terrier, you are likely familiar with this predatory motor sequence toward small animals. As Udell et al. write, terriers "have the most wolf-like predatory sequence" when compared to herding and livestock guarding dogs in their study (2014). Like a wolf, terriers find the chase, grab, shake and kill parts of the pattern innately delightful. (Thank God they're small!) And it makes sense, as this is the job they were originally bred to do. Even though nowadays their jobs have largely been replaced by professional exterminators, terriers are still hardwired to seek, chase, and unapologetically murder small animals.

If you have a small dog who is exhibiting predatory aggression, I recommend reading Simone Muller's *Predation Substitute Training* books or seeking the help of a qualified professional.

> **Don't risk it**
> Remember, if your dog's behavior poses any threat to a human or animal, please reach out to a qualified behavior professional sooner rather than later. A professional can tailor a behavior modification plan that fits your dog's specific needs. See Chapter 2 for guidance on how to find a qualified professional.

Understanding thresholds

This chapter will frequently refer to the term **threshold**, but what is it, exactly? In dog behavior, a threshold is the tipping point at which a dog becomes emotionally aroused by a trigger, to the point where he cannot think clearly or respond to training cues. This could be due to fear, excitement, frustration, etc. The sympathetic nervous system (characterized by a fight, flight, or freeze response) activates strongly enough that the dog can no longer engage with the handler and no meaningful training can happen.

Always aim to keep your dog **under threshold** when training, meaning he is aware of the trigger but still able to focus on your cues, happily eat treats, and engage with you.

With practice, you'll likely be able to tell when your dog is right at threshold. In many cases, the dog stares just a second too long at the trigger, or he eats your treat and then quickly looks back at the trigger. Don't push it! If you're training outdoors, this is when you would give your dog more space from a trigger, such as walking away from another dog. Indoors, if your dog reacts to noises from outside, you might shut a window or move to another room to decrease the intensity of the trigger.

A dog that has gone **over threshold** might be staring, barking, lunging, growling, bolting, freezing, or rejecting your food. We aim to avoid putting our dogs into situations like this because the dog's brain is in survival mode, not learning mode.

Not all triggers are alike. You may have already noticed this when your pup barks at some dogs on the street but not others. If your dog goes over threshold, it's because the trigger was too intense for him. But what does that mean?

- The trigger is too close for your dog's comfort. A delivery person on your doorstep is much more challenging than a delivery person two houses down.
- The trigger is there for a long time. A passing jogger who stops in front of your dog to tie her shoe may be much more triggering than one who just bounces by.
- The trigger is animated. Your dog might be uninterested in a passing dog, unless that dog is enthusiastically jumping and spinning in circles. Then it's on.
- Your dog has a "type." I've worked with dogs who were much more reactive toward white vans than other colored vans. In another case, the dog was only set off by black dogs with curly hair, whereas a black dog with a short, straight coat didn't get much more than a "hmph."
- The number of triggers encountered is overwhelming. When a dog is confronted with one trigger, then another, then another, this is called **trigger stacking**. Your dog may get increasingly aroused and frazzled as the triggers stack up.

Who goes there?—Alarm barking

Yes, dogs bark. And little dogs are infamous for having a lot to say! Barking conveys many different emotions, from joy to fear, so our goal should never be to stop a dog's barking altogether. However, when a dog barks frantically at everyday sights and sounds, it's time to intervene. The mail person stopping at your mailbox. A neighbor walking her dog down the sidewalk. Cheerful kids skipping along the road. All these things are non-threatening to us humans, but to a dog, an unexpected person or animal popping into sight can cause quite a startle. To an anxious dog, surprises in his otherwise predictable environment can make him feel unsafe, pushing him into a panicked SOS mode.

We call these things **sudden environmental contrasts**, and humans are not immune to them, either. In fact, a whole genre of film—horror—plays with our innate sense of anxiety ("Oh no, the axe murderer is hiding behind you!") and the inevitable jump-scare fear response when the axe murderer leaps out at the unsuspecting protagonist. Even though you know a horror movie isn't real, it activates a fight-flight-freeze response, courtesy of your sympathetic nervous system. Your brain, whether you like it or not, has already sent out an SOS signal to the rest of your body. Your heart rate, respiratory rate, and blood pressure increase, and your body releases epinephrine and norepinephrine (also called adrenaline and noradrenaline), followed by stress hormones (glucocorticoids). When this happens, it effectively turns off the parasympathetic nervous system, the system that allows you to problem-solve and have an appetite for your theater popcorn.

It's possible your dog is put in this situation numerous times a day, living in a perpetual horror movie, to the point where he can never really relax for fear of a sudden noise or movement. Let's use Sammy the Jack Russell as an example. He's always been a little on edge around unfamiliar people, objects, and noises. While the house is quiet and Sammy is trying to nap in a sunbeam, he suddenly hears a car door nearby slam shut. First he perks up, "What's going on?" Looking out the window, Sammy's fears are confirmed—a stranger has parked his car outside your house. "Everyone, an unauthorized human is out there—panic!" He is now in full SOS mode, stress hormones pumping and higher-level critical thinking turned off. Only when the stranger walks down the road, out of sight, can Sammy calm down. But even then, is he fully calm, or simply waiting for the next threatening sight or sound? Sammy might go back to his sunbeam, but even if his body language isn't showing overt signs of arousal or stress, we can't assume that the stress hormones have stopped flowing through his little body or that he is truly relaxed. This process takes time.

The trouble with this familiar scenario is that triggers like this occur all day, every day. If Sammy startles and reacts to every sound and sight outside, he is always stressed to some extent. When the sheer number and frequency of stressors become too many for the body to overcome, he finds himself in a state of chronic stress, unable to return to a normal, healthy state. Chronic stress has been associated with a long list of both emotional and physical issues, affecting aggression, cognitive function, immune system, and more (Juster et al., 2010). Gone unchecked, chronic stress will not resolve on its own. Therefore, it's up to you, Sammy's guardian, to help him feel safer around the fear-inducing triggers.

Barking at a perceived threat

Alarm barking, as the name implies, is when a dog barks at a perceived threat. Remember the discussion of security in Chapter 3? With alarm barking, your dog may actually be safe, but he is not secure. That is, he doesn't *feel* safe. You might know that the garbage truck outside isn't a dog-eating monster, but your dog feels a genuine sense of danger. Alarm barking occurs most commonly when the dog is in your home and sees and/or an unknown person, animal, or object outside. It is often characterized by a "woo-woo" bark, so named for the woo-woo-woo sound they tend to make. This kind of bark is generally associated with fear or anxiety about something scary outside the window or door. As he barks, the dog is typically facing out the window, toward the direction of the threat, but he may turn back to face you or may run frantically from one window to another.

Every time your pup engages in this behavior, his brain and body go into full SOS mode. In the short term, this means that he won't be able to focus on your cues ("Sammy, sit!"), because his body is responding as if he were in imminent danger. He also won't be interested in your treats, because no dog wants to have a snack when he thinks, "We're all going to die!" To help Sammy overcome this stress response, it will take a whole lot of management, plus some carefully planned behavior modification.

Set the stage for success

Proper management of your space will reduce the dog's opportunities to be triggered on a daily basis. The fewer times Sammy sees a jogger go by, the fewer times he flies into SOS mode, and the fewer stress hormones are coursing through his body on a regular basis. It may not be realistic to eliminate triggers entirely, but you can always do something to reduce their intensity and frequency. This way, when Sammy is triggered, the stressor will affect him less intensely, and he won't be bombarded with trigger after trigger. Implement as many of these management strategies as you can, before you begin the behavior modification protocol.

- Play white noise or other color noises. Alternatively, a box fan or window air conditioning unit may get the same result. Place the noise in any spots where the dog is likely to hear a trigger. Perhaps you have certain windows overlooking a street, or a school to the side of your home, or construction in your backyard. Reduce the intensity of these audible triggers by running white noise continuously, day and night, any time the dog has access to those areas.

- Set up gates or exercise pens. Use these to block your dog's access to problem areas, such as front doors or rooms with low windows.

- Apply window privacy film. I use these in my home for our glass door in front, which would otherwise torture my dogs with delivery drop-offs, kids zooming by on scooters, and other constant triggers. Now the only triggers they can see are individuals who come right up to our door, which in any dog's defense, could actually be a threat and is worthy of a bark or two. Window film is easy to apply and remove—it is squeegeed on and simply peeled off.

- Draw the blinds and shades. These are perfectly suitable alternatives to window film, provided that your dog can't peek around them, and he will not destroy them in a frenzy to see out the window.

- Use food toys and activities. For prolonged auditory triggers, such as a lawn mower or construction outside, you may need extra help. Have a long-lasting food toy ready, and give it to your dog in the quietest area available to him. Add white noise and visual barriers, as well, to keep the intensity of the trigger as low as possible. The video shows an example of this.

Video: https://www.
bklnmanners.com/
chapter8.html

For alarm barkers, consider window film as a management tool.

Behavior modification for alarm barking

The goal of behavior modification is ultimately to help your little alarm barker feel secure. You can change your dog's fearful or anxious response to triggers by changing the pattern that your dog is used to. For instance, before starting behavior modification, Sammy would see a jogger outside and think, "Panic!" but using the following protocol, the sight of a jogger now predicts a much more comfortable, secure outcome and brings with it happier emotions. If you're a dog professional, you'll recognize this as **classical counter-conditioning**.

I encourage you to verbally or physically interact with your dog during this behavior modification process. If your dog notices a perceived threat out the window, I will ask you to act as if you're casually checking out the "intruder," and then reassure your dog that he's safe. In some cases, I'll even ask you to name certain things, "Ah, that's just a jogger." This uses the concept of **social referencing** to our advantage. "Social referencing is a process whereby an individual uses the emotional information provided by an informant about a novel object/stimulus to guide his/her own future behaviour toward it" (Merola et al., 2012). That is, we know that dogs look to us, as if to ask, "How should I feel about this thing? Is it safe?" Although a jogger may not exactly be "novel" as in the definition, your dog may feel uncertain about how to react, and this is an opportunity to provide meaningful information that the jogger is safe. By using a calm voice and cheerful body language to show your dog that you're not concerned, you can positively influence your dog's response to a trigger.

For the following protocol, you'll expose your little dog to the trigger in a very methodical way. Have treats ready in your pocket or stashed around the house. After you read the steps below, watch the video to see the sequence in action.

1. During each training session, you'll remove a little bit of one management barrier.

   - If it's for auditory triggers, then turn off the white noise during the training session.

   - For visual triggers, expose only a few inches of the window (pull back the curtain or peel a corner of the window film). Start with the window that typically causes the least amount of stress for your dog.

   - If you've been using gates or fences to restrict access, bring the barrier closer to a window, so your dog can partially see outside.

2. While waiting for something to pass by, you are acting casual but staying close to your dog, so you can watch his body language and act quickly.

3. Your dog perks up as he notices a trigger. Let's say it's a jogger.

4. Before your dog can bark (or as quickly as possible, even if barking has started), you'll calmly acknowledge it. Look out the window and calmly reassure your dog, "Ah, it's just a jogger, don't worry." Show him you don't care.

5. As you reassure him, put a treat in front of his nose as quickly as possible. Use the treat to lure him to a specific spot, like his place. (See Chapter 6.)

6. Once he gets to his spot, he can have the treat. If he sits, woohoo, another treat!

7. If your dog has let it go at that point, say "That's All" and go back to whatever you were doing.

8. If he is still amped up, have a relaxing food toy ready in a drawer next to his spot. For example, a LickiMat with a tube of squeezable cheese or made-for-dogs paste can be prepped in a few seconds. A minute or two of licking will help him relax himself. Make sure to keep yourself calm as well.

Video: https://www. bklnmanners.com/ chapter8.html

9. With your dog now relaxed, you'll turn the white noise back on, or put the visual barrier back up, until you have a few minutes for another repetition later in the day.

10. Practice in small, controlled doses like this. He'll need a nap or a walk or a romp in the yard before doing another repetition. We want to make sure he's fully recovered from the previous session before jumping into another one.

Troubleshooting

Issue: My dog won't follow the lure away from the trigger.

Solution: If it will be challenging to "unglue" him from the trigger, consider keeping your dog on a soft, back-clip harness and thin leash, so you can gently lead him away from the trigger without having to grab his body. Use the Loose Leash Walking technique in Chapter 7 to ensure you're not dragging your dog. Note that if you have to use the leash to move your dog away from the trigger, the trigger is probably too intense.

Issue: My dog won't follow me, even with the leash.

Solution: This means your dog is over threshold because the intensity of the trigger is too high. Avoid yanking or pulling your dog away from the trigger, as this can increase your little dog's stress. Instead, put the barriers back up and give your dog a break. Next time, reduce the intensity of the trigger by:

- Turning the white noise down, but not off

- Pushing the gate or fence back, so your dog is not so close to the window

- Starting in a new location that tends to be less challenging, like your yard, the sidewalk, or a park

> ### Hands-free hack
> Behavior modification protocols require you to be ready to train at a moment's notice. Fortunately, the alarm barking protocol can be streamlined with a little help from technology. If it's challenging for you to stop what you're doing and train, consider using a remote feeder, such as Treat and Train, right next to your dog's place. (See the "Tech Support" sidebar in Chapter 6, p. 93.) Follow these instructions.
>
> 1. When your dog notices the trigger, name it and reassure as before. "That's just a jogger."
>
> 2. Immediately hit the remote. Your dog will hear the beep of the device and run to his place, in anticipation of a treat.
>
> 3. You can dispense a few more treats if needed to keep your dog's mind off the trigger. However, I still recommend walking over to your dog to ensure he's actually lying down and relaxing on his place.

Leveling up

Once your little dog can easily play along as if it's a game, then you're on the right track. Now that he's not so stressed, let's ask your dog to do more of the work himself.

1. Your dog notices a trigger and you calmly acknowledge it, as before.

2. Reduce how overtly you lure your dog from the window to his place. See if you can encourage him with your voice and body language, rather than treat lure.

3. Once your dog is on his place, he can still have a treat, as before.

Over time, you might notice that your dog sees a trigger and takes himself to his spot before you can even tell him to go there. Amazing! This tells you he is not going into SOS mode anymore, but rather thinking clearly and able to initiate the training protocol. The video demonstrates this response. However, for more intense triggers, he may still need your guidance to go to his place.

Up to this point, you've been running white noise and maintaining visual barriers, except during training sessions. Once your dog can reliably go to his place during training sessions, let's start to remove these barriers, one at a time. Start with fading out the 24/7 white noise first. If you have visual barriers, keep them up for now. (If you haven't been using white noise, skip the following paragraph.) Currently you've only been lowering the white noise volume for occasional training sessions, but now, you'll be lowering it in general.

1. Lower the volume by one notch. Leave it at this slightly lower volume at all times when you're home and can jump into training mode. (At night or at times when you can't train, increase the volume back up, to prevent backsliding.) Any time your dog hears an alarming sound through this slightly softer white noise, immediately do the behavior modification protocol. Practice at this level until you get at least three good days in a row at this volume. What constitutes a good day?

   • Your dog notices triggers through the white noise, but doesn't get up, bark, or become restless. If he clearly doesn't care about the noise, you should calmly acknowledge it as before, but no need for the go-to-place protocol or treats because your dog is happy to let it go on his own.

   • Your dog notices triggers but takes himself to his spot for a quick treat and some gentle pets.

   • Your dog notices triggers but can easily be directed to his spot for a treat and remains calm once he's there.

2. Lower the volume by one more notch, using the same criteria as above. It may take days or weeks to reach three "good" days in a row. That's fine; go at your dog's pace.

3. Eventually, you may only need the white noise at certain times, such as when you can't be there to train. In many cases, after a while, you won't need it at all.

Once you've gotten to a point where you can turn the white noise off, then it's time to repeat the process with the visual barriers.

1. As before, you'll start by removing one visual barrier slightly, for instance, peeling a few inches of the window film off. Choose the window that typically causes the least amount of stress for your dog. You will leave a few inches exposed on this window, for as long as you are with your dog. This means that you always need to be ready to get into training mode, since triggers can appear at any time. (Put the visual barrier back any time you can't get into training mode, such as while you're showering or sleeping.)

2. When your dog notices a trigger outside the window, do the behavior modification protocol as before. Practice at this level until you get at least three good days in a row with a few inches of window exposed.

   • As with the white noise, if your dog notices the trigger but doesn't react with concern, just play it cool. You can gently assure him, "Yeah, that's a jogger" and then go back to what you were doing. No go-to-place or treats necessary.

   • If your dog becomes alert, stiff, or starts moving to his place, then follow up with the full training protocol.

3. Continue slowly peeling back the visual barriers, a few inches at a time, only after getting three good days in a row.

You will repeat this for each covered window. Depending on the size and number of your windows, this process could take a while. Be patient; you're essentially reprogramming your dog's brain and it will pay off in the long run. Fortunately, you should be able to get through windows two, three, and four faster than window one, since your dog already knows the training game quite well at that point.

You may hit a point at which your dog really struggles to do the training game. If a certain window presents too many triggers, too-noisy triggers, or too-close triggers, it is best to keep the film on it long term. We all have limits to what we can tolerate, and there is no shame in admitting your dog has reached the upper limit of his tolerance. I'm sure you can relate. Imagine something that really gives you a fight-flight-freeze response. For me, it's clowns. I've been to plenty of events with clown performers, but as long as I sat toward the back, I could enjoy myself. But I'll never forget the one time a towering clown walked down the aisle, locked his eyes with mine, and held out his gloved hand to invite me on stage. Frozen in fear, all I could do was push my unsuspecting husband out of his chair, sacrificing him to whatever clown-torture awaited. What's your version of a clown story? We all have one, as does your dog. As you go through the training, respect your dog's limits, and don't make your dog hold the clown's hand, so to speak.

The finished product of this behavior modification tends to look different for each dog. However, you can generally expect two outcomes. First, for at least some triggers, your dog will not need the training protocol long-term. He will realize that the jogger never comes to your door wielding a knife. When a car door slams from the driveway across the street, it does not result in any harm. For these triggers, your pup may perk up a bit and perhaps look to you. You should continue to reassure your dog, "That's just a car door, don't worry." If he's nearby, and finds touching to be soothing, give him a gentle pet. This tells him that you are aware of it and you're not concerned, but you do not need to engage in the go-to-place protocol. The other outcome is that your dog will continue to be concerned by certain noises and sights, such as a mail person coming right up to your door. Even for these, with practice, your dog can take himself to his place and settle in, without you cuing anything. You will still reassure him and give him a treat and gentle pets for going to his place.

A trigger by any other name ...

If you hear an unfamiliar banging noise in the middle of the night, you're likely to feel a wave of fear, thinking, "What was that? Am I in danger?" But if the person next to you says, "Oh, that's just the water heater turning on," don't you feel relieved? On the cognitive level, this is because you have an image of a water heater in your mind and you recognize it as harmless.

Your small dog may not be any different. Research has shown that dogs can learn the names of objects, and upon hearing the name of that object, a memory is activated (Boros et al., 2024). This can have significant applications to behavior modification. When your alarm barker sees a trigger—a person, dog, or object—he may growl, bark, or run to the window. But what about when he sees the same thing at the park, on a walk, or at a friend's house? Does your dog show the same signs of stress? If not, let's use this to your advantage. You can begin naming triggers in situations where they don't cause your dog to become stressed. Let's say your dog reacts to children playing on the street in front of your house, but if you are on a walk, he doesn't even give them a glance. Great, name it! By putting a name to a non-threatening thing in the environment, it adds a layer of reassurance to your reactivity training indoors.

Try this:

1. Every time you see a child in a non-threatening scenario, tell your dog happily, "That's a kid." If your dog looks up at you, make gentle eye contact back and give him a little treat. Your dog will start realizing, "Kids are pretty cool!"

2. Then, indoors, when your dog sees a child out the window, you'll label it the same way. Acknowledge what he sees, saying, "Ah, that's a kid," as you encourage your dog to move away.

Doing this adds predictability to an otherwise uncertain experience. And predictability reduces anxiety. By identifying the scary thing out the window as a "kid," it can relieve the uncertainty of what will happen next (which, in reality, is nothing). This is because your dog already knows what a "kid" is, and that children pose no threat. When the things in one's environment are predictable, they are less likely to cause stress.

Doorbell reactivity

For many small dogs, the sound of the doorbell is tied to big feelings, which leads to big reactions: frantic barking, spinning, running, and jumping up. This may also be true for the sound of knocking, the sound or sight of a car pulling into a driveway, or any other indicator that someone has arrived. You may even have a dog who reacts to any ring or knock he hears on television.

Why do doorbells trigger such intense behaviors from little (and even large) dogs? It's all about what the bell predicts. There is the excitement or stress of a guest entering, then lots of commotion as the humans do their bizarre bipedal greeting rituals. And then—what's this?—these strangers are coming into the house, walking around, and sitting on your dog's favorite spot on the furniture! Whether your dog loves guests or not, it's a lot of stimulation that your pup may not have the emotional tools to cope with. And it all starts with a single "ding-dong" of the doorbell.

The sound of the doorbell, on its own, is pretty insignificant to a dog. The ring only becomes salient when the dog makes the connection between the doorbell and arriving strangers. Because deliveries and guests create strong emotions in many dogs, the doorbell becomes a **conditioned stimulus** to "get excited" or even "panic!"

We call the dog's behavior a **conditioned emotional response**, as a formerly neutral sound now has taken on new meaning due to what it predicts, and the sound of the doorbell can trigger a frenzy before a person has even come through your door. When a dog associates the doorbell with a scary event, we call this **fear conditioning**, and it is a very strong connection. This is why your dog reacts to a doorbell on TV, even though no one is at your door. You have essentially taught your dog to respond this way, by repeatedly pairing a doorbell with a guest. So don't get mad at your dog for barking at the TV, as you (unintentionally) conditioned this response!

Anxious little dogs are particularly prone to the ill effects of fear conditioning in daily life. "Stressed animals can become sensitized to fear. Compared to unstressed animals, animals that have recently experienced stress develop conditioned fear more quickly" (Spaulding, 2022, p. 39). Like an anxious person who startles at any noise or checks the locks on windows and doors multiple times a day, anxious dogs tend to be ready to react at any moment, even waking up from a deep sleep to bark. They are also often hypervigilant, acutely aware of every small detail in their surroundings, in the event that something seems "off" or threatening. This makes them much more adept at noticing patterns, especially when a perceived threat is present. Therefore, if the doorbell repeatedly rings right before a scary guest comes in, that dog will quickly learn that doorbells are a reason to panic.

Those troublesome conditioned emotional responses got you into the doorbell drama, but it's also what can get you out. By changing the pattern of "doorbell = scary guest" to "doorbell = something nice and relaxing," we can mitigate, or resolve, doorbell reactivity.

Set the stage for success

As with any behavior concern, management is essential to success. The goal for management is to create an environment in which your dog is not surprised by the doorbell. In the beginning, the only time your dog hears the doorbell is during a controlled training session. Management techniques will depend on your environment, but may include:

- White noise (see "Alarm Barking" on p. 128), so your dog won't be aware of deliveries and mail carriers outside the door for now

- Window film, curtains, or blinds (see "Alarm Barking" on p. 128), for the same reason

- A note on your door, asking guests to call or text you rather than ring or knock. Alternatively, you may be able to get silent notifications sent to your phone if you have a high-tech doorbell.

Behavior modification for doorbell reactivity

Almost all doorbell-reactive dogs can benefit from these steps, regardless of their underlying emotions when reacting. This process allows your dog to associate the doorbell with a new, relaxing pattern. Your dog won't be rushing toward the door; rather, he will be moving away from the door and then engaging in a hobby that keeps his stress level at a much more manageable level. This technique also gives you the chance to greet your guests as a normal human would, with hugs and hellos.

Preparation includes:

1. A recording of your doorbell on your phone or other device.

2. A **don't-panic room** for your dog. Ideally this would be a room with a secure baby gate, or a sturdy exercise pen. The area should be comfortable, with your dog's bed and other treasured items in it. The location of the don't-panic room should be where your dog can see from a distance what's happening at the door, but be removed from the action itself. A pen in the far end of your living space is often a good location or consider a room off the main living space with a baby gate.

3. At least one insanely tasty, long-lasting food toy, like a stuffed Kong, Licki-Mat, chew, or bone. The more goodies, the better!

   Caution: If your dog is a resource guarder of food or spaces, this protocol will need modifications designed by a qualified behavior specialist. Don't put anyone in danger by enclosing your dog with items that will trigger his tendency to guard.

   Caution: If your dog is highly fearful of noises or guests and prefers to run away, do not force him to be in a small enclosure or room near the activity of the home. Instead, choose a room that is as far away from the action as possible, like a bedroom.

Once you've gotten that set up, follow these steps.

How to do behavior modification for doorbell reactivity

1. First, let's teach your dog that the sound of the doorbell means "go to your don't-panic room for a goodie." Do this when your dog is already relaxed, and no guests are actually coming. Stand by the front door with your phone. Then play the sound of the doorbell at the absolute lowest volume on your phone, once.

   Do your guests usually knock? Instead of a doorbell, you'll lightly tap on the door, barely loud enough to be heard at all.

2. Immediately, in a gentle voice, say, "Let's go to your room." Calmly encourage your dog to walk with you to his don't-panic room. Once in the room, you will give the food toy, shut the gate, and give your dog all the time he wants with the food toy.

   If your dog isn't used to being alone in this area, you can hang out right outside the gate. Stay nearby, but ignore him as he eats, peeking over your shoulder to ensure he's enjoying the experience.

3. Once he's done with the food toy, ask him to sit. Once he's sat for a second or two, open the gate to release him.

4. It's best to only do one repetition per day, or if you do multiple reps, space them out with a walk or nap in between. This is to ensure that your dog isn't overly stressed by the training. Even if you don't notice overt signs of stress, it's possible the doorbell sound is affecting him internally, so you don't want to push it.

5. Assess how that went before proceeding:

   If your dog showed relaxed body language when you played the recording and he went into the don't-panic room without hesitation, then proceed to the next step. His body should be loose, tail neither stiffly up nor tucked down (depending on his usual tail carriage), eyes and mouth soft. Once in the room, he should have been enjoying the food toy, not begging to be released right away.

   If your dog became agitated or excited by the doorbell sound, even a little, then don't increase the volume next time. Stay at the same volume and repeat until your dog is showing no signs of stress: no freezing, stiffening, huffing, barking, panting, restlessness, running to the door or window, etc. If your dog has an intense reaction to the recording, such as barking or running to the door, then put the phone in your pocket as you play the doorbell sound next time. This makes it even quieter. Never increase the volume until your dog is reacting calmly to the current volume.

If your dog struggles to get into the don't-panic room, you may have to do some foundation work here. Put the doorbell training on pause for a little while and simply give your dog the food toy in the don't-panic room. You can stay very close to him in the beginning, until he can happily eat the food. And then, while he is eating, start moving around your home, to get him used to being alone in the room for brief periods.

6. The next session, increase the volume by one bar or notch. Make sure you keep track of what your last volume level was. You'll repeat the same game: play the recording by the door, walk him to the don't-panic room, shut the gate, and give a tasty food toy.

   If your dog reacts by huffing, stiffening, or other signs of stress, do not increase the volume next time. Stay at the same volume until your dog can do the new pattern with relaxed body language.

   If your dog was happy and relaxed after doing that rep, you can increase the volume by one more notch next time.

7. Continue increasing the volume by one notch, as long as your dog was happy and relaxed the previous rep. It will take many sessions to reach the maximum volume. By taking your time and laying a solid foundation, you are setting your dog up for long-term success.

8. Now you're ready for the real doorbell. You'll ring it yourself at first. This probably means you will have to open your front door, so be sure your dog can't dash out. You may need a fence, gate, or other barrier to prevent door dashing. Right after you ring the bell, encourage your dog to go to his don't-panic room as before.

9. You may be at this level for a little while. That's OK. Repeat until your dog is happily following you into the don't-panic room.

Video: https://www.bklnmanners.com/chapter8.html

Leveling up

Once your dog can stay calm when hearing the doorbell at full volume, you can introduce an incoming guest.

1. Add a visitor now. If you live with family members or roommates, use one of them first. Just one guest to start. The less exciting the visitor is, the better, so choose the person in your household who interests your dog the least. The visitor stands outside, rings the bell, and you lead your dog to the don't-panic room. While your dog is eating the food, you will calmly let your visitor in. You can gently greet the person but keep your energy mellow. As you and your visitor come into the room, you'll ignore your dog and interact as you

would with any guest for a few minutes. After those few minutes, ask your dog to sit to be let out.

Your dog may want to get released from the room, jumping up at the gate or barking at you. Just continue calmly ignoring him, no "shhh," or "no," or dirty looks, until he's gone back to eating his food toy for another minute. Then release him.

Practice this until your dog is mostly disinterested in the doorbell, the guest, and the excitement at the door.

2. As you practice with your helper, you two can engage in more and more normal greetings. You can greet the helper with, "Hi, welcome back!" and engage in the chatter and movement that happens when a guest enters.

3. Finally, your dog is guest-ready. Aim to practice with a guest who can follow your instructions to stay relatively calm and not interact with your dog while he's in his don't-panic room. This will take lots of practice with several guests, but you can get there if you approach it methodically.

For real life situations, you'll need the don't-panic room and food ready to go. Deliveries will come when you don't expect it, or a neighbor might stop by at any time to chat. For packages and short conversations at the door, your dog can remain in the don't-panic room for the duration of the interaction at the door. Wait a few minutes after your unexpected guest leaves to let your dog out, to ensure he's no longer worked up.

For guests that cause your dog stress beyond just the doorbell, look to the next section. It will outline protocols for the duration of your guests' stay.

Reactivity toward house guests

You've managed to welcome your guest without encircling them in the eye of a fluffy, yapping cyclone. But that's just the first step. Now you've got to ensure that your dog, your guest, and you are all enjoying a stress-free visit. Some dogs simply get overstimulated by the doorbell, but then calm down once the guest has come in. Many other small dogs, however, don't feel secure when a stranger is in their space. They may continue to bark, growl, nip, or simply avoid the visitors throughout their stay. Regardless of how much your visitor claims to love dogs, it's up to you to ensure everyone's safety and comfort.

Dogs, and particularly small dogs, are often triggered when the visitor:

- Makes a sudden movement, such as standing up, walking into a room, or even waving their hands during demonstrative storytelling

- Makes a sudden noise, such as a burst of laughter, a gasp, or a squeal

- Bends down to pick something up from the floor

Unexpected movements and noise fall under the category of **sudden environmental contrasts**. For instance, imagine you and your guests are sitting, watching a movie.

Everyone is quiet and still on the couch. Suddenly there is a surprising plot twist, and shrieking "NO WAY," your guest shoots out of his chair, arms flailing. An unsuspecting dog will startle, his body now flooded with stress hormones to prepare for fight-flight-freeze. After all, in nature, a sudden change like this could be a predator jumping out of the bushes and an animal's body needs to be able to react instantaneously, without taking the time to weigh the pros and cons of acting. Unfortunately, the body can't differentiate between a hungry predator's attack and your guest harmlessly yelling at the TV.

You may find that different guests require different protocols. Elderly guests tend to be less triggering, given their slower movements and softer voices. Middle aged and young adults may be a mixed bag. Children are often the most challenging for small dogs to tolerate, given their sudden movements and louder volumes. But in all cases, start with your dog in his don't-panic room when guests arrive. From there, his comfort level will determine how much interaction he will have with your guests, if any. Consider which of the following strategies are appropriate for your situation. If there is a safety concern for either human or dog, contact a professional to help you work through the right protocol for your needs.

Set the stage for success

Think about these points to make sure your dog isn't pushed over threshold in the presence of your guests.

Dogs that are comfortable around guests can be given the opportunity to mingle with the group. However, if your dog is going to interact with guests, the setup is extremely important. Try to use an open space, where the dog won't feel trapped by an approaching guest or squealing youngster. This could be an open concept living area, or sometimes even better, a large yard. Avoid places that feel closed-in, or rooms full of furniture, as this often pushes a fearful dog to fight because flight isn't possible. Furthermore, any time the dog interacts with guests (if at all), there should be an easy exit for him. Avoid a setup where someone can approach your dog when he is curled under a blanket, on the couch, in a corner, in a narrow hallway, or anywhere he might feel trapped. You'll have to be constantly watching where your dog is in relation to your guests, to ensure he doesn't find himself trapped next to Uncle Jeff, who pets your ten-pound Italian Greyhound as if he were a pony-sized Newfoundland.

For any dog who reacts to guests with even a hint of aggression—lip curls, growling, lunging, biting—interactions with guests must be meticulously planned, if they occur at all. Aim to have two (yes, two!) barriers between your dog and the guests, to ensure safety. This could include:

- A gate or fence

- A secure harness and leash, held by you

- A basket muzzle (see muzzle training in Chapter 4, p. 34)

These barriers keep your guests safe from a bite, but they also ensure that a curious child, or even an adult, doesn't reach out to your pup when you're not looking. Reasonable dogs do not want to bite and will only do so when they feel they have no other option to keep a threat away. Don't put your dog in a position where he feels this threatened.

Your dog's don't-panic room is an excellent management tool, as it provides one dependable, solid barrier. Just remember that the don't-panic room should be a room for your dog only; avoid using the kitchen or your only bathroom, as your visitors will need access to those rooms. Your dog may need to be in his don't-panic room for the guests' entire visit, if:

- You have any concerns about your dog's behavior becoming aggressive
- You have concerns about your guests' behavior around your dog
- You will be too preoccupied with hosting to effectively do the necessary behavior modification protocols

Here is a real-life snapshot of what management might look like over time. In our house, Margaret is selective about which guests she tolerates and which ones she'd like to send back home. This is her stereotypical Chihuahua personality, and as much as we wish she'd roll out the welcome mat to everyone, we have accepted her us-versus-them world view. In the beginning, we used her don't-panic room for all guests, for at least 90% of their stay. The other 10%, she joined the group for structured training, as outlined in the next section. As time went on and we were able to implement the behavior modification more smoothly, we gradually gave her more and more time to interact with our guests, starting with the calmest friends and family. Over time, she built a trusting relationship with several people, preferring their laps to mine, and we no longer need to rely on structured training when these people visit. This process took weeks to months, depending on how frequently she saw the same guests. However, with every new guest, we start the process again, using her don't-panic room and highly structured interactions until both human and dog are feeling a vibe.

If your dog is as prickly with guests as Margaret is, you'll need to plan out the interactions carefully. This means deciding when to bring your dog out to interact with the guests, and where everyone will be sitting or standing during these interactions. Ahead of time, set up your hangout area so that your dog's place is in one corner or end, and your guests roughly in the other. You will be in between them, close enough to your dog to hold his leash. Even if your space is limited, make sure your seat is closest to the dog, with your guests seated on the other side of you. This spatial arrangement has a few purposes:

- It ensures that a guest won't wander close to your dog
- It shows an anxious dog that you've got his back and won't let anyone get in his space

- It shows a territorial or angry dog that he doesn't need to take control of the situation. You've got this.

The videos in this section show a typical setup.

Behavior modification for reactivity toward house guests: Phase 1

Your guests have arrived and your dog is comfortable in his don't-panic room. Keep him there until your guests have fully settled in. This means everyone has taken off their coats, gotten their beverages and snacks, and sat in the living room or other hangout area. If your guests are too active for your dog to be comfortable, or if your dog is barking or restless behind the gate, then it's not time for him to come out of the don't-panic room yet. Better to wait for just the right moment to let him interact with your guests. And if that time doesn't come, then your pup can continue to have long-lasting goodies in his room. When in doubt, keep him in his room rather than risk an unpleasant interaction with a guest.

Follow these steps if your dog is wiggly and bouncy and generally excited to see the guests, or if your dog is the take-charge kind who approaches a guest with a confident "Who the bleep are you?" strut. If your dog is fearful of guests, follow these steps but also read the sidebar entitled "Adjustment for Fearful Dogs" on page 145.

There are a few prerequisites for this behavior modification protocol.

- "Catch a Treat," Chapter 5, page 68
- "Place," Chapter 6, page 86
- "Emergency Recall," Chapter 7, page 101

How to do behavior modification for reactivity toward house guests: Phase 1

1. Prepare the space. Have your dog's place set up facing your guest, but positioned at least ten feet away if possible. If you have any safety concerns, there should be two barriers between guest and dog; in this case, a leash held by you and a gate separating the room (or enclosing your guest) would be suitable, as in the video. Give your guest a handful of treats and instruct her to remain calm and neutral—not stiff like a statue, but relaxed, as if watching a movie.

2. Put your dog in a secure harness and leash in his don't-panic room. When you are ready to bring him out, ask him for a sit, then take the leash and walk out with him. If he is amped up, use Loose Leash Walking techniques from Chapter 7 (page 103) to help him focus.

3. Walk with your dog to his place. If needed, you can use a treat to lure him there.

4. Once your dog is on his place, your guest can gently play "Catch a Treat" with five to ten treats. (See "House rules for your 'Dogs love me!' friend" in Chapter 5, page 67.)

5. If your dog can't catch the treat mid-air, that's fine. He might pop off the mat in order to chase the treat, so just lure or cue him back to his place for the next toss. This is not a manners test or a catch-the-treat test. Instead, the purpose is for your dog to have an enjoyable, controlled, and safe interaction with a guest.

6. Watch your dog's body language as this game is happening:

    Has his body gone relaxed and wiggly, tail wagging in wide, loose circles, and eyes squinty and soft toward your guest? Then proceed to the next phase, which is the short greeting.

    Does he appear excited but restless? This would look like "ants in his pants" on the mat, and he may lunge toward the guest, bark, or whimper. However, there is no hard stare, no stiffness, no growling. Your dog may be overly aroused. Bring your dog back into his don't-panic room for a cool down and try another catch-the-treat session later.

    Does he stiffen, stare, growl, bark, or lunge at the guest between treats? Are his hackles raised? This is not what we want, so bring your dog back to the don't-panic room to cool down for a little longer. Contact a behavior professional for additional help.

7. You may repeat the game a few times during your guests' stay, but always wait to do this treat-tossing game when your guest is calmly sitting and your dog is relaxed. When in doubt, return your dog to his don't-panic room after the treat tosses, and give him a long-lasting food toy to keep him happy there.

Video: https://www.bklnmanners.com/chapter8.html

Adjustment for fearful dogs
If your dog wants to move away from the guest at any point in the process, that is absolutely fine. Moving away from a stressor is a good choice that we should respect. Therefore, for a fearful dog, it is better not to ask him to stay on his place, because this could make him feel trapped, which will only increase his stress. When your guest plays "Catch a Treat," your dog can move freely (but still on leash, and with your guest behind a gate). Ensure your guests' safety by not allowing your dog to get within a few feet of them and ensure your dog's comfort by letting him move back as far as he'd like.

Behavior modification for reactivity toward house guests: Phase 2

Once your dog is enjoying the Catch a Treat game and showing soft, loose body language toward your guest, it's time to test out a greeting. Here are some safety considerations:

- Your guest may not touch the dog yet. Just because a dog comes up to a new person in a curious way, it doesn't give that person permission to hover over the dog or touch any part of his body.

- Many dogs like gentle eye contact and baby talk, but some do not. When in doubt, ask your guest to simply ignore your dog rather than engage with him.

- If there is any safety concern, continue to have two layers of barriers. The most common barriers are (1) a leash, with you holding it loosely, and (2) either a muzzle on the dog or a fence between the dog and guest. (Think of it as crating your guest, so the gate or fence is quite close to the guest, but the dog cannot make physical contact with them.)

How to do behavior modification for reactivity toward house guests: Phase 2

1. Have treats in your pocket or treat pouch. Your guest should not have treats anymore. We want to avoid a "strangers with candy" setup, in which the dog is uncomfortable approaching the guest, but is simultaneously lured in by the tasty treat.

2. Holding the leash without tension, let your pup approach the guest. Give him one-to-two seconds of a sniff.

3. Cue your Emergency Recall word, which will bring your dog back to you for a treat. This gives your dog a moment of decompression. Keep the leash loose as you do this. Pulling the dog by his leash can create tension (physically and emotionally).

4. Let your dog return to the guest for another one-to-two second sniff. Then cue the recall again, treat, and repeat.

5. Plan to play this back-and-forth greeting game until your dog is either calm and happy around your guest or he has lost interest.

   If your dog is stiff, staring, growly, barky, or unable to respond to your recall cue, then it's time for him to cool off in his don't-panic room. Contact a behavior professional for help on how to proceed before future visits with guests.

Video: https://www.bklnmanners.com/chapter8.html

Leveling up

Once your dog and your guest are having either neutral or positive reactions to each other, it may be time to integrate your dog into the hangout. Continue to be methodical, following these guidelines.

- Keep whichever barriers are necessary at this point. Dogs with any inkling of a bite risk should remain muzzled and on leash with you. Your dog may get startled without sufficient warning and you may have to intervene.

- Just because your dog is comfortable with your quiet, sitting guest, it doesn't mean he'll be OK when that same person makes a sudden movement or sound. Be prepared! If your guest is about to get up, use your Emergency Recall to bring your dog to you. If your dog shows any signs of getting over-stimulated or stressed, it's time for another break in the don't-panic room. It's possible your dog will be able to spend chunks of time with the guests as they watch a movie or casually chat on the couch. When it's time for the visitors to get up, move around, or start making noise, that becomes the perfect time to give your dog a break.

With guest reactivity, success comes in bits and pieces. It requires a series of judgment calls on your part, to ensure that your dog is exposed to the guests only when he has the ability to cope with what's happening at that moment. As time goes on, these controlled interactions will allow your dog to realize that guests are not threatening. Then you'll find that your dog can settle in faster, tolerate more noise and movement, and hang out with the gang for longer and longer. Will your pup ever graduate from the don't-panic room completely? Only time will tell, but taking a cautious approach will give him the best chance of success overall.

Overexcitement toward house guests: too much of a good thing?

What if your dog loves guests? That's great! And being little, he's less likely to hurt anyone with his jumping, which is super! But does that mean it's okay for your dog to jump, spin, yap, or nip when guests arrive? Nope. Little dogs can still scratch your grandma's legs, put holes in your friend's sweater, or injure themselves by getting underfoot. So let's give your little one the same structure that a larger dog would have, in order to keep everyone safe and healthy.

On the point of health—stress, whether good or bad, affects the body in similar ways. When a dog gets excited, it can be considered "good" stress (called *eustress*). If a dog gets overly excited again and again, this over-abundance of eustress may hormonally affect the dog in undesirable ways; it is stress, after all. "The dog exhibiting behaviours associated with eustress, driving behaviours that enhance access to a resource (such as jumping up at or pulling/lunging toward people, other dogs or items that the dog desires), however, is also exhibiting a degree of emotional arousal (Mills et al., 2013) and subsequent stress response, that interferes with the dog's capacity to pay attention to guidance from owners" (Hargrave, 2017).

I would argue that a dog who is regularly frantic with excitement is not necessarily a happy dog. Actually, an overly excited dog is stressed and in need of our help. For everyone's benefit, aim to keep your dog from getting into situations where he will default to these over-the-top reactions.

Luckily, the strategies for reactive dogs are also applicable to overly excited dogs. Consider adding these behaviors to your routine when guests visit:

- **Don't-panic room.** It's wise to have your little jumper in a safe place away from the door, so your guests can enter without drama, as described earlier in this chapter.

- **Stay as the door opens.** This strategy from Chapter 6, page 91 gives your pup a polite way to be a part of the greetings without posing a danger or nuisance. This is best for dogs that exhibit low-level excitement.

- **Catch a Treat.** This trick from Chapter 5, page 68 can be applied the same way as in Reactivity Toward House Guests, as described earlier in this chapter. Your dog can interact with the guests at a distance, by catching treats in the air. I like to play this game right after Stay as the door opens, so the dog's first interaction with the guests is a fun catch-the-treat game rather than a jump-and-bark frenzy.

- **Emergency Recall.** This is also the same as in Reactivity Toward House Guests. Any time you sense that your dog is getting a little too excited when interacting with your guest, use your emergency recall cue to bring him back for a quick break. (See Chapter 7, page 101 to learn a basic Emergency Recall.)

- **"Place" on the couch.** Perhaps your guests would like a furry little companion on the couch but not necessarily sharing all that hair on their laps. This is the perfect real-life situation to implement the "Place" cue from Chapter 6, page 86. Your dog gets attention, your guests get to pet a soft little sweetie and no one will have to lint-roll their pants afterward.

Leash reactivity

On a regular basis, I'm asked by a small dog guardian, "When I look at all the other dogs walking so nicely on leash, I get so frustrated. Why is my dog the only difficult one?" Have you felt this way, too? Having a leash reactive dog can feel isolating and embarrassing. But trust me, you're not alone. Leash reactivity—where a dog will growl, bark, lunge, or snap at a passing trigger on walks—is extremely common. Don't be fooled by all the picture-perfect dogs you seem to see on walks. There are lots of other leash reactive dogs out there, you're just not likely to see them because their guardians are reluctant to go out for walks, too!

In Chapter 7, we dove into several leash walking activities. But general manners training alone will not resolve fear, anxiety, hyperarousal, or frustration on walks. Imagine you're walking your Shih Tzu and a truck speeds by. Your dog freezes, momentarily terrified, but shakes it off a few seconds later. Then, a dog in his own yard, restrained by an invisible fence, charges at you. Magically, he stops in his tracks before he reaches the sidewalk, but at that point it's too late. Your dog is trying to run for his life and flips backward when he reaches the end of his six-foot leash. A minute later, it's a group of toddlers in strollers, giggling and waving their hands; this time, your dog responds by lunging and barking, yelling at them to "leave me alone!" Since your little dog is bound by the leash, he can't get a comfortable distance from so many of these scary or threatening things and that inability to flee only increases his stress. A walk like this is a very emotional experience for any dog, but especially small ones who are more vulnerable to threats in the environment. Manners training alone can't address these issues. Your dog isn't being naughty; he's overwhelmed and needs your support.

Set the stage for success

Management is critical when working through leash reactivity, as it will keep your little dog at a safe distance from the trigger. As you may have already noticed, a trigger that directly approaches your dog usually comes across as much more threatening than a trigger far off to the side. This is why, on your walk through the neighborhood, your dog may not be bothered by another dog sniffing in his yard. However, if that same dog were walking directly toward you on the sidewalk, your pup might stare, pull, lunge, and bark. As that dog gets closer and closer to you, your little one's stress will only increase. If that other dog makes eye contact with yours, or God forbid, dares to bark at him, then it's *on*.

When a dog is dramatically over threshold, it tends to look like barking, lunging, or trying to run away. Don't wait for your dog to reach that level of stress. Once your dog is over threshold, it is too late to do any meaningful behavior modification. Your dog may reach his threshold much earlier than you realize, perhaps when he stares at the trigger for just a second too long or when his body starts to lean forward a tad, or when his mouth goes from loosely smiling to tense and closed. Therefore, you need to be ready to jump into training mode at the earliest sign of your dog noticing a trigger. The sweet spot to implement training is the moment your dog alerts to the trigger. He takes a second or two to process, "Wait, is that a…?" and before your dog can finish that thought, you should start one of the following strategies. Don't wait for your dog to decide, "Yep, that's another dog. Panic!"

The second your dog notices a trigger approaching, you have a few options, depending on what the environment permits. Your choice will allow you to set the stage for successful behavior modification.

- Body block as you continue to walk forward. Body blocking means that, if the trigger is on your right side, you will quickly, but gently, move your dog to your left side. As you will see in the video, your body acts as a wall protecting him from the trigger. This is a good option if the trigger is off to the side, such as a dog barking in its yard.
  - Note: Has your leash-reactive dog ever redirected his aggression onto you? This can happen when a dog shows aggression toward a trigger, but cannot reach it due to the leash. Instead, in his frenzy,

he will snap at or bite the handler. If this describes your dog, it will be essential to muzzle train him first. Unless he is safely muzzled, do not put your body between your dog and the trigger, as it can result in you getting a redirected bite.

- Cross the street if possible. The more space you can give your dog, the more secure he will feel. Even when crossing the street, you should body block your dog to make it clear that you've got his back.

- Walk in a wide semi-circle around the trigger. If you are in a park or other open space, swing as wide as you can around the trigger. Continue to body block as you swing around it. The goal here is to ensure your dog doesn't have to face the trigger as it gets closer and closer, because directly approaching the trigger will send your dog over threshold much faster and more intensely.

- Make a U-turn and walk the other way. There is nothing wrong with encouraging your dog to turn away from the trigger until you can find a safer spot. I will often use a U-turn at intersections where the best option is to back up, let the trigger pass, and then turn around again to continue on my original path when the coast is clear.

- Pull over. If you can sneak into someone's driveway or a similar off-the-path spot, this will allow the trigger to pass without directly facing your dog. Unlike the other options, this one involves stopping your motion and simply waiting for the trigger to leave.

- Pick up your dog. There, I said it! There is no harm in picking up your dog when the trigger is approaching too closely or when your dog is overwhelmed. You are not coddling him or reinforcing his fear. (This is discussed in Chapter 3.) Once you pick your dog up, use your body as a wall. Just as with the other styles of body blocking, it's best to keep your dog on the far side of you, with your body between him and the trigger, to make it clear you've got everything under control.

Video: https://www.bklnmanners.com/chapter8.html

Keeping plentiful space from triggers may not resolve reactivity on its own; it works best simultaneously with behavior modification. It's the ability to manage the space that allows your dog to stay under threshold, and behavior modification gives you the opportunity to change your dog's emotional response to that trigger.

Behavior modification for leash reactivity: Anxious and fearful dogs

For small dogs, there is a lot to be intimidated by. Remember the activity in Chapter 2, where you put your body on ground level to see the world from your dog's perspective? You really are vulnerable when you're so low to the ground. No wonder short dogs act tough!

In many cases, the best defense is a good offense. Reactions that look aggressive are often (but not always) rooted in fear and anxiety. **Fear** creates an immediate fight-flight-freeze response. For example, a delivery truck beeps its horn within a few feet of you, and your dog bolts (flight) in fear. **Anxiety** is the anticipation of a scary event; for instance, after this horn incident, your dog may make the association that delivery trucks are dangerous, and any time he sees one, he will react by stiffening, barking, lunging, or snapping at it. I see this all the time—dogs who act aggressively toward men in work boots, or delivery vans, or dogs of a certain color and build. These otherwise-normal things indicate danger to your dog and his little body is flooded with stress hormones just at the sight or sound of them. Before you know it, he's at the end of the leash, hackles up and barks filling the air, trying to scare away the threat. However, not all dogs respond to a stressor with aggressive displays, some may cower, freeze, or try to escape when confronted with a trigger.

When deciding if fear or anxiety is contributing to your dog's reactivity, consider a few points. First, if your dog doesn't care to interact with dogs or people in general, you may have a fearful dog. Even in off-leash situations, your dog would rather move away from a dog or person than approach them. On leash, when moving himself away isn't possible, the dog may resort to aggression to make the trigger back off. This aggressive behavior is usually characterized by fearful body language: low head, body, or tail carriage; lunging forward and then retreating; whale eye or averting his eyes; a raised paw, especially with body tilted backward; stiff body and raised hackles; and perhaps other signs that your dog has no interest in interacting. The aggression is an act to distance himself from the trigger and although he may lunge or even bite, he would prefer that the dog or person just go away. Now, if you haven't let your dog interact with other dogs or people before, you won't have this data to work with. That's okay. Please don't encourage your reactive dog to get close to any trigger just to see what he does. That is neither safe nor ethical.

If your small dog reacts to certain noises, like a loud car engine or ambulance, there is potentially a fear or anxiety component here. Likewise, unexpected sights can trigger a fearful response. This could include your neighbor's Halloween decorations, or even a garbage bin temporarily placed on the sidewalk. The sight or sound of certain people can also trigger fear. Men in heavy boots, people carrying machinery, or children moving erratically are common triggers for fear.

While there are several strategies you could implement, arguably the most reliable one is **counter-conditioning** and **systematic desensitization**. We've already implemented this process in the doorbell reactivity process. For the on-leash application, your dog is currently conditioned to see a trigger, like another dog, and feel fear or anxiety. Counter-conditioning is the process of pairing the trigger (such as a dog) with a very enjoyable consequence (like a piece of cheese). With repetition, your dog will learn the pattern of dog-and-cheese, dog-and-cheese, dog-and-cheese. And what happens is the dog itself stops becoming such a threat. The other dog is actually the stimulus that predicts an awesome outcome—cheese! Therefore, when your dog sees his nemesis on the sidewalk, he no longer thinks, "Oh no," but rather thinks, "Oh yay!" So, on the emotional level, the pattern becomes dog-and-yay!-and-cheese, dog-and-yay!-and-cheese. The "yay!" is the conditioned emotional response, where the sight of the other dog now brings positive feelings. Because you are the holder of the cheese, you become a critical part of the pattern. When your dog looks at the trigger, he's no longer thinking much about the trigger; instead, he's thinking about you and your amazing cheese. So you get a consistent dog-and-yay!-and-look-at-my-human-for-cheese pattern. The counter-conditioning pattern becomes a game between you and your dog. Your dog finds a trigger and, hooray, he looks up at you to say, "Hey, I found one!" And you reward with a goodie.

The systematic desensitization part of this protocol is equally important. This is where the giving-space strategies come into play. Your dog needs to be in a location where he can remain under threshold. This means he is not staring, stiffening, growling, barking, or lunging. Once your dog goes into SOS mode, it is too late; no meaningful behavior modification can take place because his learning brain has turned off and his fight-flight-freeze response has taken charge. Especially in the early stages of training, maintaining a sufficient distance from the trigger is critical to being able to success-fully counter-condition.

In most cases, you can start this protocol on your regular neighborhood walk. How-ever, if your usual route is too challenging to navigate, start this practice in a park with large open spaces, where you can keep ample distance from triggers. Watch the accompanying video to see the process in action.

How to do behavior modification for leash reactivity: Anxious and fearful dogs

1. As you walk, keep a constant eye on your dog. You need to be ready the moment your dog notices a trigger. Keep in mind that a trigger is anything your dog considers a threat and reacts to. This can be a plastic bag blowing down the street, or a handbag hanging from someone's arm that kinda-sorta-maybe could be another dog, in your dog's mind.

2. The moment your pup perks up at the sight or sound of a trigger, immedi-ately reassure him "Great, you saw it!" and quickly reach for a treat. Don't wait for your dog to go into the more high-arousal stages of reactivity: a stare, freeze, growl, lunge, or bark.

    This may happen when the trigger is extremely far away. That's fine. Act at the very first sign that your dog has noticed the trigger, even if it's far in the distance.

3. Feed your dog the treat as you turn his head toward you (away from the trig-ger). This encourages your dog to disconnect from the trigger momentarily and it buys you a second or two to decide where to go from here.

    Troubleshooting: Do you have a physical limitation that makes bending down a challenge? Don't worry, you have options. See the "Leash Walking Fundamentals" section in Chapter 7 (p. 109) for tools that extend your reach.

Or simply toss a treat on the ground, angled away from the trigger, so your dog is still turning away from the trigger as he eats the treat. If tossing, use dense, flat treats, not round or super-thin ones.

4. After he eats the treat, you have some quick decisions to make.

   Is your dog happily looking up at you for another treat, with a relaxed body? Fantastic! This means he is likely under threshold. As long as the trigger isn't getting any closer, you can stay where you are.

   After finishing the treat, does your dog's head whip back to look at the trigger? If so, he might be right at his threshold, so you need to give your dog more space immediately. Choose the most appropriate management strategy to give your dog more space. You can body block, cross the street, swing wide, make a U-turn, pull over, or pick your dog up. Find a spot where you can let the trigger pass with sufficient distance between you.

   Is the trigger approaching you, closer and closer? Even if your dog isn't over threshold yet, his anxiety is likely to build as the trigger closes in on you. Use one of the "Set the Stage for Success" (page 130) strategies to find a safe place to let the trigger go by. Keep your dog under threshold by moving to a spot that is off to the side.

5. Now, once you've reached a safe spot where the trigger can pass by at a distance, you will stop moving and stay there. Cheer and treat for two things:

   Every time your dog looks at the trigger—remember to put the treat at your dog's nose and gently turn his head toward you to give the treat.

   Every time your dog looks at you.

6. Watch your dog's body language as you do this. If, at any point, you see any of these signs, you need to move farther away.

   Your dog's body is tensing up.

   Your dog is looking at the trigger more intensely, perhaps not following the treat as you bring it toward you.

   After eating the treat, he whips his head back toward the trigger.

   Your dog is getting "sharky," snatching the treat.

7. Once the trigger has passed, you can resume your walk. If your dog appears agitated or distracted, use the Leash walking for small dogs technique in Chapter 7 (page 103) to help him regain his focus.

8. Repeat this for every single trigger. Even the very low intensity ones, such as a dog far in the distance.

Video: https://www.bklnmanners.com/chapter8.html

Dogs that react inconsistently

Some dogs appear to react inconsistently, especially with reactivity toward other dogs. They can pass by one dog with no reaction at all, but then go full-on Cujo at the next dog. Look for patterns as there is usually something that can tip you off. Consider some of these points:

□ The appearance of the trigger. For dogs, the build, color, size, carriage (for example, the tall, curved tail of a Husky), sound of the collar, and other factors could be triggers. For people, vehicles, and inanimate objects, there are also defining characteristics that may indicate a threat. Your dog may well know the difference between a delivery truck and other types of vehicles, since the former predicts a scary "intruder."

□ The level of interaction. Other dogs that give direct eye contact, freeze, lie down, lunge, or bark at your dog could come across as much more threatening than a dog that simply plods on by.

□ Location. Many dogs are more reactive near their homes.

□ Time of day. If your dog reacts more on some walks than others, note the time of day.

□ Who is walking your dog. Some dogs' reactivity is heightened when a certain family member walks them.

□ Your dog's comfort and health. If your dog isn't feeling well, is wearing an uncomfortable harness, or hasn't slept enough, you may notice behavioral changes.

□ What has happened recently. Did your dog have a stressful vet visit yesterday? Did someone ring the doorbell this morning? Do you have houseguests? Stressors and disruptions to routines can frazzle a dog's nerves and make him more likely to be reactive in other contexts.

□ Number of triggers. If your dog appears relaxed the first few times he sees a trigger, but gets progressively more reactive as the walk continues, then you may be dealing with the effects of trigger stacking. At the start of a walk, your dog may be low-stress enough to keep on walking. But with every trigger he confronts, his stress level inches higher and higher, until he explodes with lunging and barking. This doesn't mean he was actually OK for the first few triggers. He simply wasn't over threshold yet, and didn't show obvious signs of stress until several reps of exposure.

When there are no discernible patterns, go through the counter-conditioning process for all potential triggers. If your dog is unpredictably dog-reactive, then do the protocol for every dog that your pup notices, even if he doesn't seem concerned. Since we don't really know what your dog is feeling inside, it's better to assume he is feeling a bit anxious and do the counter-conditioning. This will ensure your dog is making the right connection, that other dogs always mean "yay, cheese!" By counter-conditoning to all triggers, even the not-so-triggering ones, you'll enable him to follow the protocol much more smoothly with intense triggers, too.

Leveling up

There are four general levels for this protocol. Let's explore each one.

Level 1 is the trigger-and-treat pattern, in which the dog gets a treat for every little glance at the trigger. Your timing needs to be precise, to ensure you catch him glancing and not staring at the trigger. As you work through level 1, your dog's intensity will start to decline. His looks at the trigger become less focused and frantic, and he recovers more quickly after seeing the trigger pass.

Level 2 happens naturally. As your dog learns the trigger-and-treat pattern, he becomes less intense about the trigger and more interested in that treat. So, your dog will glance at the trigger, and before you can even cheer, he will be looking up at you, as if to say, "Treat please!" This is level 2, where the pattern shifts to trigger-and-eye-contact-and-treat. The trigger is now a cue for your dog to give you eye contact. With this new pattern comes an emotional shift, from fear or anxiety to happiness and focus on you. Here are the steps in detail.

1. Your dog spots the trigger. He may not even fully look at it, but just flick an ear in that direction, or briefly flash his head toward the trigger without even focusing on it. This is what you want! Your dog is no longer fixating on the trigger.

2. Before you can cheer, your dog has already made eye contact with you. You will mark "Yes" or cheer, and reward that eye contact with a treat.

   Why mark "Yes" all of a sudden? Now it's an eye contact game that uses operant conditioning. ("If you look at me, I'll mark and reward.") For dogs that already love training, we're sending the message that counter-conditioning is really just one more fun game.

3. From there, make the same decision as in level 1. Can you stay there comfortably and let the trigger pass, or should you move away to a safer spot? Let your dog's behavior guide you in making that choice.

4. For every look at the trigger or at you, you will continue to mark and reward, until the trigger has passed.

You will find that your dog goes back and forth between levels 1 and 2. When the trigger is sufficiently far away or low intensity, you may get some great level 2 responses, meaning that your dog will look up to you on his own within a second or two. But if that same trigger gets too close or intense, don't push it; go back to level 1. This is normal, and your job is to meet your dog where he's at. As the weeks and months pass, your dog should be doing more and more level 2 responses.

Level 3 is similar to level 2, except you and your dog will keep moving, rather than having to pull over for each trigger. Here is an example sequence.

1. Your dog notices a trigger approaching on the sidewalk. He glances at it and looks up at you.

2. As you mark and reward for his eye contact, you'll get him in the body blocked position but keep walking. Still swing wide around the trigger, either crossing the street or walking in a semi-circle around it.

3. As you walk, continue rewarding for every look at the trigger or at you.

4. As time goes on, you'll find that you don't have to swing as wide around the triggers.

If your dog is dog-reactive, keep in mind that most sidewalks are far too narrow for two dogs to comfortably pass each other. It's not natural for dogs to walk head-on toward one another. If you've ever seen dogs greet at the dog park, there are lots of wide circles and indirect approaches to show that they mean no harm. Friendly, polite dogs do not barrel head-on into another dog, but this is exactly what a sidewalk forces them to do. I almost always swing wide around other dogs, so that both my dog and the approaching dog understand that we're looking for neither a fight nor a party.

Ultimately, you and your dog may be able to get to Level 4, which involves fading out the treats. You can only begin this stage if your dog can comfortably pass triggers in your day-to-day walks with your dog mostly looking at you and not fixating on the trigger at all. Start level 4 in a location where you can have plenty of space between your dog and the trigger. Now, as your dog notices the trigger in the distance, he'll look up at you, and you'll give lots of praise, maybe even some pets if he likes that, and then keep walking in a different direction. So we are changing the game for these extremely low intensity and long-distance triggers. They are no longer worthy of treats, but they still give you and your dog the chance to interact with each other. As time goes on, you and your dog may continue to play this cheerful treat-free game, or your dog may stop caring about these long distance triggers altogether. As the weeks and months pass, you should be able to play this game with triggers that are gradually closer and more intense.

Every reactivity case is unique. Please don't feel pressured to reach a certain point in your training. For some dogs and handlers, reaching level 2 is perfectly acceptable for their needs. In other cases, the dogs can go all the way to level 4. Even with my own dogs, I have experienced different results. Beans, who came to us as "that" dog in the neighborhood who would bark and lunge at any dog a block away, mostly performs at a level 3, with level 4 responses for dogs that are farther away or low in energy. The process took months of diligence and practice. Margaret, who had a history of ankle-biting passersby before we adopted her, reached level 3 within a few days. She now ignores almost everyone she passes on the street, placing her firmly in level 4. She even happily greets certain neighbors to whom she's grown accustomed. Every so often she will look up at me as we pass a person, especially if the person appears unusual to her. When she checks in with me, I tell her how wonderful she is and immediately body block and swing wide around that person. Afterward, she gets a gentle scratch under the chin or a tiny treat, and sometimes she even asks for a hug (really!). I don't always know why certain passersby still elicit a mildly stressed reaction from her, but because she knows the game, she always tells me when she is a little anxious and needs reassurance. It's a conversation rooted in her trust in me, even when she feels a bit threatened.

Behavior modification for leash reactivity: Barrier frustration and more

While fear and anxiety are common causes of leash reactivity, not every reactive dog is anxious or afraid. There are a few other considerations for what's underlying your dog's reactivity, which are explained in the "Why is my dog aggressive?" section on page 122.

- Barrier frustration due to the leash

- Overexcitement

- Territorial of your home or neighborhood

- Possessive of his handler

- Predatory or chase instinct

Keep in mind that you may not always be able to pinpoint what your dog is feeling. In fact, your dog may be feeling more than one emotion at the same time. Plenty of dogs are conflicted when they see a trigger—curious about an approaching dog or person, but also fearful to get too close. As your dog's guardian, you can only interpret his feelings and motivations based on his body language, vocalizations, and history of reactivity in that environment. There is still a lot we don't know about what's happening in a dog's brain and body. Contact a qualified behavior professional if you need help understanding your dog's behavior.

If your dog's reactivity is not fear-based, I prefer to use a behavior modification protocol with an operant twist. This means that you'll ask your dog to *do* something in the presence of a trigger. I find this method works best for dogs that would otherwise feel frustrated, excited, or angry toward a trigger. By cuing your dog to do a certain behavior in the presence of a trigger, you are keeping his mind engaged and giving him a job to do. This behavior will simultaneously help you move your dog into a safe body-blocked position, which will prevent the trigger from overwhelming your pup. "Sorry, mail carrier, no time to bark at you—I've got big plans over here!"

Because you'll be using more operant conditioning here, your dog should be fluent in "Line Up" (page 112) and "Leash walking for small dogs" (page 103) from Chapter 7. Make sure you have built his skills up to the point of being able to pass a moderate distraction (but not necessarily a trigger—we'll tackle that next). When you cue "Line Up," your dog should be able to glide into heel position on either side of you. When you start to cheerfully talk to your dog, his head should pop up toward you, happily beaming at the interaction you're sharing.

This sequence is best done in a park with wide open spaces at first. This will allow you to keep sufficient distance from the triggers and then slowly close the gap between you and the trigger when your dog is ready.

How to do behavior modification for leash reactivity: Barrier frustration and more

1. Your dog notices a trigger in the distance.

2. You'll happily cue "Line Up," as in Chapter 7 (page 112). Lure or point to the far side of your body, so that you will now be body blocking your dog from the trigger. See the video for a demonstration.

3. Once your dog is safely body-blocked, you'll move together in a safe direction away from the trigger. In a park, this would probably be a wide semi-circle around the trigger. Continue roughly in your original direction, but swinging around the trigger with plenty of space in between.

4. As you walk, you'll gleefully chat with your pup, telling him how amazing he is and rewarding all eye contact on you with a little treat. Continue this Loose Leash Walking game until the trigger has passed.

Video: https://www.bklnmanners.com/chapter8.html

Leveling up

Practice this with triggers at a far distance, until your dog understands the sequence and can initiate some of the game himself. Rather than lock onto the trigger, he should be able to respond to your "Line Up" cue and then trot along with you as you swing wide around the trigger. Once he is at least a B student over several sessions, you can start to very slowly close the gap. If walking in a park, this means you'll swing a little less wide around the trigger. I don't recommend ever facing the trigger directly, as this is uncomfortable for many dogs. Instead, little by little, create less space between you as you pass. Close the gap in increments of about one foot (about 0.3 meters) and practice at each distance until your dog is consistently a B student.

Remember, though, that you're not just doing manners training. The purpose is to help your dog emotionally. So if your dog is approaching a particularly intense trigger, such as a leaping, barking dog or a flock of ten cyclists, give a wide berth. But when the trigger is mild, like an elderly dog or one person slowly gliding by on a bicycle, you can close in on the trigger a little more. Be flexible and watch your dog's body language to determine if you're pushing your luck.

Resource guarding

Resource guarding is a broad category that can encompass a variety of behaviors. In all cases, the dog has possession of something he perceives as valuable and he makes it clear that he does not want others to take it. Resource guarding is not always aggressive, and it can take many forms, such as:

- Stealing a sock and running away from you
- Hovering over the food bowl and growling if a person or animal approaches
- Sitting on your lap and lunging at a person or dog that tries to approach you
- Growling when someone pets the dog while in his bed
- Eating meals rapidly when other dogs or people are present

When resource guarding is non-aggressive, you'll often see the dog run away or hide under the bed when he has a special item in his mouth. But sometimes it *is* aggressive. The form of resource guarding that involves growling, lunging, snapping and biting is called **possessive aggression**. Unfortunately, small dogs are the poster children for this kind of aggression, as they are overrepresented for resource guarding, aggression, and biting toward familiar people (Guy et al., 2001). This section addresses the most common varieties of resource guarding among small dogs.

The conversation around resource guarding, as with many behavior concerns, is always evolving as new research emerges. It's important to ask ourselves, what is a dog feeling when resource guarding? In some cases, it may be a fear of losing the item. You might see signs of fear, such as lip licking, averting the eyes, turning the head away, yawning, or low head and tail carriage. In other cases, the emotions may be more complicated, perhaps even a mixture of fear and anger. For instance, when you see piloerection (raised hackles) during resource guarding, this indicates an adrenaline surge into a high arousal state, which may imply the dog is feeling unsure of himself in this social scenario (Martin et al., n.d.). Suffice it to say, it's complicated. As with leash reactivity, we can observe certain behaviors to make our best guess about the dog's underlying emotions, but remember that these are still guesses.

Before embarking on a resource guarding protocol, make sure you are following the guidelines from the previous chapters. Resource guarding is strongly correlated to the dog's relationship to the people, dogs, and environment in his daily life. Therefore, the way you communicate with your dog on a daily basis can either relieve or exacerbate a dog's tendency to guard. If your family and your dog have an overall healthy relationship, addressing this specific behavior issue will be smoother. However, if your dog doesn't trust you or other family members, it's only natural that his stress will be heightened when he has a valued item, whether it's a chew or a soft bed or his favorite person's lap. Revisit Chapter 3 to ensure you have earned your dog's trust in general. Then, make sure you've tackled the activities in Chapter 6, so your dog is well versed in asking "please may I" instead of "gimme now." This is because attention-seeking behavior is a comorbid diagnosis in some dogs that exhibit resource guarding (Martin et al., n.d.). In other words, there may be a connection between dogs that demand attention and dogs that guard; although we can't assume demanding behavior causes resource guarding or vice versa, it's wise to ensure your dog's attention-seeking behavior is also being addressed.

Resource guarding a valued person

Little dogs love in a big way. And it's possible that nothing makes you happier than cradling your small dog in your arms (with his permission of course), as he looks up at you with hearts in his little eyes. However, with big love can come possessive aggression. Management of the space is extremely important here, and the responsibility mostly falls on the person to whom the dog is the most attached. Follow these management and behavior modification protocols to ensure your dog understands that his love for you doesn't require him to scare the rest of the household away.

Set the stage for success

Some little ones love to rest on the couch with you. Then as another family member approaches, they'll pop up, growl, bark, lunge, or even bite the approaching person. It's essential to ensure your dog is not in a position to guard you like this on the couch. You'll notice that the protocols for owner-guarding focus on spatial orientation. Let's assume from this point on that you are the individual your dog is guarding. The relative position of you, your dog, and the "threatening" person or dog is important. If your dog is between you and the threat, then he is in the perfect spot to yell, "Hey, stay away from my person!" However, if you are in the middle, between the dog and the threat, your position is telling your dog, "No need to get involved, Fido. I got this." (A note about this. If your dog has ever shown any aggression toward you when you're between him and any trigger, do not put yourself in any danger. Contact a qualified behavior professional.)

If your dog exhibits possessive aggression—growling, barking, lunging, snapping, and biting—he should not be on the furniture at all. Furniture access is a privilege, not a right. If being on the couch brings out the dark side of your pup, it's neither safe nor emotionally healthy, for him to be there. Preventing your dog from accessing the couch or bed can be challenging at first, but here are some tips to make it easier.

- Block entry points onto the furniture. You can even put an exercise pen around your couch or bed, essentially crating the furniture, until your dog gets used to not having access.

- If your dog is about to jump on the couch, be ready to block with your arms and upper body. Make it clear that your body is a wall that your dog cannot pass. This will need to be repeated again and again at first, but trust me, your dog can learn this.

- If your dog does jump on the couch by accident, be ready to remove him. You can do this a few ways, depending on the dog.

  ○ Gently pick him up and place him on his dog bed on the floor. Only do this if he is comfortable being picked up and moved.

  ○ Get up yourself and leave the room. Now the couch has lost its value, because you've left the area, and your dog will follow.

    ○ Say "Off" and toss a treat onto the floor. This is my last choice, used only if the first two options aren't suitable. I prefer not to use treats for this activity, as it can get dogs excited and even more interested in you.

- Make an irresistible small-dog-friendly bed in another part of the room. This spot should be out of the way, so your dog will not be situated between you and an incoming person or animal. Look for a corner away from thresholds. If your dog also resource guards his bed, choose a location where he will not be disturbed. You may even need to use the don't-panic room mentioned earlier in this chapter. Here are some options for an irresistible bed:

    ○ Doughnut or bean bag style, where the dog is cradled by super-soft fluff

    ○ Burrow bed with a den-like appeal

    ○ Electric blanket (if safe), especially in winter. Otherwise, a pile of soft, fluffy blankets

Many small dogs find bean bag beds even more inviting than your human furniture.

Furthermore, if your dog guards you from other people in your household, aim to get these family members or roommates involved with your dog's care. Usually, the dog is attached to the person who provides the most attention to him. What aspects of dog care can others safely take over? Here are some ideas for family and close friends.

- They can feed your dog, especially if feeding time can be turned into a game. See the video for some ideas.

- They can walk your dog, if your dog is interested in walks.

- They can play any game that your dog enjoys, as long as it doesn't involve roughhousing or over-excitement. Options include fetch, find-the-treat, chase with a flirt pole, or a gentle version of tug as described in "Safety First During Play" in Chapter 5 (page 65).

- They can teach your dog a fun, simple trick. This isn't about obedience, but rather just having fun together with no expectations. Nose target, give paw, and sit pretty are a few options. My and Sarah Westcott's book *Play Your Way to Good Manners* has tons of ideas.

Video: https://www.
bklnmanners.com/
chapter8.html

Behavior modification for resource guarding a valued person: While sitting
Couches, beds, and other shared furniture don't always bring out the best in your pup. What should be a relaxing time together is actually stressful, causing your dog's possessive tendencies to kick in. If a person or other dog enters the room while your dog is on your lap or next to you on the couch, it's critical to have a plan. Similar to the management techniques, behavior modification for resource guarding will involve asking your dog to move away from the resource, which is you. This protocol requires some preparation. Have your dog's place mat in a safe spot, on the floor at the far end of the couch. In other words, if you are sitting on the couch, your dog's mat will be on one side of you, and the incoming person or dog will be on the other side. You will essentially be body blocking your dog from the incoming person or dog. If you are using a ramp on the couch (and I hope you are!), make sure the ramp is placed in a convenient spot to smoothly get your dog off the couch.

As already mentioned, if your pup tends to move toward the trigger (lunging, barking, biting), he should not be on the furniture to start with. He will be on the floor. Have him on a comfortable harness and leash and use a basket muzzle whenever there is a bite risk.

Have some small food rewards in your pocket, ready to go. If the trigger is a person, then you will be giving the person instructions as you go through the steps. If the trigger is another dog, have that dog on leash with a helper holding it, to prevent the dog from getting too close.

How to do behavior modification for resource guarding a valued person: While sitting
1. The dog's trigger—a person or other dog—comes into view. Your dog perks up to notice.

2. Ask the trigger to stop moving forward.

3. At this moment when your dog notices the trigger, cue him to move away from you. You'll say "Place" and lure or toss a treat onto the mat on the floor. Your tone matters here. Remain neutral and calm.

4. Once he is on the floor on his mat, cue a "Sit" (or a "Down"). Reward for the sit, using multiple treats if your dog tends to get up quickly. You want him to stay there.

5. If your dog is calmly sitting with happy body language, the trigger can approach one more step. Your dog continues to get treats for sitting.

6. As long as your dog isn't showing signs of stress, continue having the trigger approach step by step. Your dog continues to get treats for sitting.

7. If your dog pops up, just gently ask for the sit again. If you find it's hard for him to stay sitting, end the session. Sprinkle a few treats on the ground in front of your dog, while the trigger walks away.

8. If your dog starts to show any signs of stress or aggression, it means he has gone over threshold and you should end the session. Your dog may have to go into his don't-panic room with a food toy if he needs a break.

9. As your dog continues to be rewarded for comfortably sitting on his mat, the trigger may be able to approach the couch and even sit down next to you. (Do not expect this to happen on day one.) You'll see this finished behavior in the video.

Video: https://www.bklnmanners.com/chapter8.html

Leveling up

In many cases, once you remove the dog from your lap, couch or bed, there is nothing more to guard, and he is back to being wiggly and happy as the trigger approaches. For this kind of dog, you will continue asking him to get off the couch every time a trigger approaches. Then, once the person or dog has joined you on the couch, your pup can return as long as you stick to the management guidelines.

There are other dogs, however, who are not comfortable or safe to have on the couch when the resource (you) is present. If that's the case for your dog, he will not be invited up on the couch while you share it with others. However, he can certainly have a nice chew or toy on the floor, provided he doesn't guard that.

Behavior modification for resource guarding a valued person: While standing or walking

This scenario is less common, but thanks to the Chihuahua-instructors in my home, I know firsthand that it can happen. In this case, the dog and guardian might be hanging out at a picnic or taking a leashed walk. When a friend or neighbor comes over, the dog will march right up to the person and "yell" at them. So, for everyone's safety and sanity, let's use this fun technique to teach your little one that it's not his job to tell others to stay away.

How to do behavior modification for resource guarding a valued person: While standing or walking

Make sure you've taught your dog "Line Up" from Chapter 7 (page 112) before beginning this protocol. Here, you'll be using "Line Up" in the presence of a trigger. Here are the steps.

1. You are standing or walking with your dog, treats in your pocket.

2. Keep your dog on leash and muzzled if you have even an inkling of a safety concern.

3. Have a helper, who is at least ten feet away, takes a step toward you.

4. The moment your dog notices the trigger, happily cue "Line Up" and point to the far side of you, away from the trigger. Give your dog a treat when he ends up in the heel position at your side and be ready to feed a few more.

5. Ask for a sit. You may give a treat for the sit.

6. As long as your dog is comfortable and focused on you, he can continue chomping on little treats, with you still body blocking, as the helper approaches and chats with you.

7. If at any point you notice your dog becoming stressed—whale eye, becoming "sharky" toward the treats, having difficulty sitting still, or other signs—happily walk away from the helper with the Loose Leash Walking technique, to give your dog more space.

8. Once the helper has gone away, release with "OK" and go back to your regular walk or hangout.

Leveling up

In the beginning, a person or other dog may not be able to get very close before your dog starts showing signs of stress. That's okay. Stay at your dog's comfort level and with practice you'll be able to close the gap.

Once your pup can go through the full sequence smoothly, you can start asking for more of a prolonged sit-stay between treats. The progression will look like this:

- "Line Up" and sit, then treat. Pause one second and treat. Pause one second and treat …

- "Line Up" and sit, then treat. Pause two seconds and treat. Pause two seconds and treat …

- And so on, increasing the seconds between treats.

You may find that some people trigger a stronger reaction than others, so be ready to adjust your rate of reinforcement depending on the level of difficulty.

Resource guarding of spaces

We all have a favorite spot—maybe it's a recliner, the corner of the sectional couch, or a bean bag chair. If someone approached you as you sat there, would you act aggressively toward them? I hope not. So why do so many small dogs get cranky when you approach them on the couch, pet them in their dog beds, or shift your weight as they sleep next to you on the bed? In many cases, this behavior is totally understandable. They're a fraction the size of everyone else in the home, and when a large, hovering human approaches them head-on, it can appear quite confrontational and make them feel insecure. Furthermore, little dogs tend to share our couches, laps, and beds far more than their bigger canine counterparts, creating frequent opportunities for them to get stuck in unhealthy patterns: the human approaches, the dog feels threatened, he acts aggressively, and the human moves away.

With space guarding, the dog may be possessive of a cherished location, such as a bed, chair, or a certain space. Or perhaps he is actually exhibiting more of a social fear, triggered by the approach of a person while the dog happens to be settled into a cozy spot. In this case, a person's approach triggers a fight-flight response, but since flight isn't possible, he'll go right to fight as a defense. This is especially true of crate guarding, but it may apply to any space where the dog feels cornered (Martin et al., n.d.). Regardless of the reason for guarding spaces, use the following protocols to ensure everyone is interacting in a safe and stress-free way. As with the other forms of resource guarding, make sure you're following the guidelines in Chapters 3, 4, and 6, so that you have a foundation of trust and communication with your dog.

Set the stage for success

Without careful management, it's unlikely you'll be able to implement any behavior modification effectively. Of the suggestions below, incorporate any that are suitable to your situation.

If your dog's guarding is very mild, a simple rule of "do not touch the dog when he's resting" may be sufficient. What constitutes mild? Look for a fleeting moment of staring, freezing, whale eye, or other signs that the dog is uncomfortable; however, you don't notice any growling, showing teeth, lunging, snapping, or worse. Unless your pup is actively asking for pets, then assume he does not want to be touched, and leave him be. See Chapter 3 for more information about this.

If your dog shows signs of possessive aggression (growling, lunging, snapping, etc.) on the bed, couch, or other human furniture, the safest route is to revoke his access to those areas. It's best to keep options black-and-white for your dog, meaning a "no furniture, none of the time" policy is clearer and easier for your dog to follow than a "you can sit on the couch sometimes, but not always" policy. To deter your dog from jumping on the furniture, you can use fences and other barriers to block his access. For couch cushions, place flat, hard objects on top—flattened cardboard boxes, thin plywood, large coffee table books, or similar objects that aren't soft to sleep on.

But it's not all bad! If your dog's furniture access is revoked, you can give your pup an alternative that's even better. Create a no-humans-allowed hangout spot for your pup, near the family but secluded enough to be left alone. Every dog has a preference, but doughnut or bean bag beds, burrow beds, and beds with an electric blanket can be even more appealing to most small dogs than a couch. You can partially wrap an exercise pen around the bed, draped with a blanket as a visual barrier. This protects passersby from bothering the dog by accident.

A note about nighttime: This is when management is most critical, and when a resource guarder should not be in the bed with you. You can't control your movements while you're asleep. If your dog does tip into aggression, you won't know it until it's too late. Beyond that, I always worry about suffocation, falling, or other injuries that a small dog could sustain when sleeping in a bed with a much larger bedmate. For sleeping arrangements, consider an extra-comfy dog bed as described above. The bed can be inside a crate, with the door closed, so he can't jump on the bed while you're asleep. If he's not crate trained, you could "crate" yourself by separating your bed and the dog's bed with a fence.

With diligent management, you may not need to go through a behavior modification protocol. In many cases, the dog is now at ease knowing that he is not permitted to sleep in certain problematic spots. And when he's on his special doggie bed(s), his need for personal space will always be respected.

Behavior modification for resource guarding of spaces
If your dog acts aggressively, such as growling or lunging, as you approach the couch or bed, he should initially not be allowed on the furniture. However, if you'd like to invite him up someday, follow the steps below. These would be formal training sessions where your dog is given temporary couch access, just while training. Be ready with:

- Treats in your pocket
- A place mat on the couch, telling him where to go
- Another place mat off to the far side of the couch
- A muzzle and leash on your dog before you start, if you have any concerns about aggression

How to do behavior modification for resource guarding of spaces
1. You are standing near the couch. Invite your dog on the couch. You can give him a few treats to keep him there, because now you will walk out of the room for a moment.

2. As you reenter the room, announce your approach in a calm, neutral tone. You can use natural language, like "Hey buddy, I'm coming in." This ultimately will be a cue to tell him not to worry or be startled by your approach.

3. When your dog perks up at your approach, cue "Place" and send or lure him to his mat on the floor.

4. Sit down and get yourself comfortable on the furniture. If your dog needs extra reinforcement, you can toss another few treats to him on his floor mat as you do this.

5. If you'd like, he can now join you on the couch (provided it is safe). Once you're ready for your dog to come up on the couch again, release him with "OK" and instruct him to go to a specific spot or "Place" on the couch.

   Remember! If your dog is not responsible enough to safely be on the furniture with you, he should not be invited up. Instead, follow the management instructions to make a cozy dog-only spot for him.

6. If another person approaches, be ready to tell your dog, for example, "Dad's coming in," and send him to his place on the floor again. Repeat this for every incoming person.

Video: https://www.
bklnmanners.com/
chapter8.html

Leveling up

Practice this sequence every time you approach, so your dog understands that "I'm coming in" is a friendly cue to get off the furniture and wait for you to get settled. You'll start to notice your pup get up and happily move away on his own, which is a much healthier pattern than hunkering down and guarding. I recommend practicing at this level for at least one month (and potentially much longer), to make a very clear new pattern.

Stealing and guarding items

In many ways, your little dog knows you, your habits, and your preferences better than you know them yourself. When you yawn a certain way, he jumps up because this means it's time for a nap. When you clear your throat around 5pm, he has already perked up, anticipating the next words, "Do you want dinner?"

Your dog also knows what holds value to you, and how to use these valuable items to get your attention. To a young dog, pretty much anything is a toy. A toy is most fun when someone wants to play with you. Therefore, once Winston the Cockapoo learns that stealing your sock gets you to "play" chase-me, socks have significantly increased in value. Compare this to a boring old rope toy; when Winston picks it up and gives you that mischievous side-eye invitation to play, you brush him off. Inadvertently, these patterns teach Winston that his dog toys have little value and do not get him any attention, whereas socks are the most valuable toys in the house.

What starts as a game can sometimes, over time, lead to resource guarding. Again and again, I see this pattern: tiny puppy Winston steals your sock playfully, you chase him around to get it, but once you corner him, tension has escalated, and he now feels trapped. He may hover, cower, lunge, growl, snap, or even bite when he feels that you are about to take his prized item. As Winston grows older, the pattern becomes more ingrained and the guarding behavior escalates, having lost all traces of its playful, attention-seeking origin.

This pattern is entirely preventable by following the guidelines in Chapters 3 through 6 to ensure your dog trusts you and communicates his needs politely. If your dog is already stealing and guarding objects, you can use the following protocols to work through this unpleasant and sometimes scary behavior.

Set the stage for success

As with so many of the behavioral concerns we've addressed, management is essential to success. Without managing your environment, you will not be able to implement the behavior modification properly. Make sure you've got these points down pat.

- Do not leave valued items in the dog's reach. This could refer to shoes, socks, remote controls, tissues, pens, or any other object your dog deems worth stealing. The way you do this depends on your home environment. In some cases, it's easiest to simply elevate all treasured belongings out of a little dog's reach. Things that cannot be elevated should be kept in secure boxes, bins, or cabinets. Or as I joke with clients, "Don't crate your dog, crate your stuff." In other cases, you can use gates, fences, and doors to prevent the dog from entering rooms that contain forbidden objects. Children's rooms will remain off-limits, that bathroom with the flimsy trash lid will have the door shut, the mud room with its shoes and backpacks is fenced off, and so on.

- If your dog does manage to grab a forbidden item, act cool. Do not gasp, jump up, scold, or show any other reaction that indicates your dog has something valuable in his mouth. Drama will only increase his arousal and intensify his desire to guard.

- On the flip side, when your dog picks up an appropriate toy, you should make a big deal. This can involve cheering or even encouraging him to come over to play tug or fetch. Do not chase him or react in a way that can trigger guarding, but rather use words and make gestures that indicate "how fun, wanna come here and play?" If he prefers to play on his own, that's fine. You can simply act as a commentator, encouraging him with "yeah, you got it" and other silly observations.

Behavior modification for stealing and guarding items

This "Drop It" protocol is designed for dogs who already have an aversion to letting go of valuable items. Follow the instructions and watch the accompanying video carefully. Because possessive aggression can be directed toward you, it's essential to put safety first with the following protocol. At first, you'll be practicing the steps with a neutral, "legal" object to help your dog get comfortable with the process before introducing anything guard-worthy. Consider a low-value dog toy, empty box, uninteresting article of clothing, or other boring object in your dog's mind. Have the item and a lot of small, super tasty treats in a treat pouch. This protocol is inspired by the "drop" training by Chirag Patel of Domesticated Manners, which I highly recommend checking out.

How to do behavior modification for stealing and guarding items

1. Put the neutral item on the floor. You are standing or sitting nearby.

2. When your dog goes to investigate the item, say "Drop It" and immediately toss at least four treats on the floor, several feet away. Your dog's mouth doesn't need to be on the item and in the beginning, it's actually better if he is only sniffing it or looking at it. So the order is: (1) dog briefly investigates the item; (2) you say "Drop It" even if he's not holding it; and (3) a split second later you toss a handful of treats away from the item.

3. As your dog eats the treats, help him out. If you see a treat that he hasn't found, point it out to him.

   This step has two functions. The first is to teach a dog that the words "Drop It" mean "treat party ... all the way over there!" You're encouraging your dog not just to drop an item, but also to move far away from it. Secondly, your hand is now helping him find the treats. This is important for little dogs who have a negative association with hands—in many cases, hands moving toward the dog mean you are about to take some valued item away. But now, your hand is actually helping the dog get more goodies, no strings attached.

4. About 50% of the time, do not touch or remove the item as your dog eats the treats. You want to build your dog's trust that "Drop It" is not simply an elaborate trick to take something away from him. The other 50% of the time, you can touch or pick up the item, then put it back down. This helps your dog see that, even when you pick up the item, you are not taking it away forever.

5. Watch your dog's body language carefully as he eats the treats. If the dog is watching your hands, ignoring the treats, eating the treats faster than before, or rushing toward the item, you are pushing him too far. Back away from the item and build more trust first by not picking it up.

6. Practice this game in any location where stealing might occur, indoors or outside.

7. Repeat this with other neutral objects. Your dog should hear the words "Drop It" and automatically start to move away from the item before you can even toss the treats. Once your dog is a B student over several sessions, you can go to the next step.

8. Repeat this process with a slightly more coveted toy. This should not be a toy that your dog guards. Keep a careful eye on your dog's body language as you repeat the above steps. With a slightly higher value toy, your dog is more likely to put his mouth on the toy. That's fine! Let him put it in his mouth for one to three seconds and then cue "Drop It."

9. Eventually, you can introduce an item your dog is known to steal. Choose the least valuable item. Repeat the process. If you have any concerns about your dog stealing this item, place the item on the other side of a fence or gate. So, at first, he is only looking at the item (and can't actually grab it) when you cue "Drop It." If the behind-a-fence method goes well, you can upgrade to tying a rope around the item, which you can hold. This will prevent your dog from stealing it and running off.

10. As the sessions continue, you will practice with increasingly valuable items. However, ensure these items are always safe. If for some reason your dog becomes possessive, it's better to walk away, leaving the item on the floor. By practicing with a number of items, both low and high value, your dog will be able to generalize the "Drop It" cue and will even be able to drop items that you haven't specifically practiced with.

Video: https://www.bklnmanners.com/chapter8.html

Leveling up

This cue works best when you practice it on a maintenance level, long-term. At least three times a week, incorporate a drop-it into your routine. This can happen naturally when your dog has a toy or chew in his mouth. Or you can set it up by placing an item on the floor for your dog to check out. As the video shows, I do this with paper towels and tissues—my dogs' favorite snack. The practices shouldn't always be challenging, as easy wins remind your dog how fun it is to drop things.

Phew, you've completed Chapter 8! Pat yourself on the back and pat your dog (but not on the top of the head!). As you work through your dog's behavior quirks, celebrate the small victories as they accumulate over time. I've found that guardians who approach their dogs' behavior modification methodically and with compassion develop a uniquely strong bond with their pups. By overcoming your dog's obstacles together, you two have the potential to become an unstoppable team.

Moving on to Chapter 9, what better way to celebrate your teamwork than to learn some fun skills and games together? You can practice the exercises in the following chapter on the same days and weeks as doing behavior work. In fact, the more fun you have with your dog, the stronger the bond and the higher your chances for success overall.

Chapter 9

Canine Sports and Games for Your Little Athlete

You've laid a solid training foundation for your pup, and you're working to address any behavioral concerns. Great job—now let's have some fun! This chapter introduces several ways to take your training to the next level using canine sports and brain games. Every dog is unique, so as you read through this chapter, think about your dog's personality, physicality, and interests. Which of the following activities would appeal most to your little sidekick?

The suggestions in this chapter are not simply ways to tire your dog out. By regularly engaging your dog's body and brain, you're doing your part to keep her healthy and satisfied for years to come. A study among laboratory Beagles found that the dogs provided with behavioral enrichment performed better on cognitive tests than the dogs that did not and they showed fewer signs of cognitive aging over a two-year span. "The behavioral enrichment intervention included three components: increased exercise, environmental enrichment, and possibly most important, a program of cognitive enrichment" (Milgram et al., 2005). This is only one of many studies, spanning many species, that confirm the importance of enrichment in daily life.

Since some small dogs have a complicated relationship with the outdoors, all of the activities here can be done indoors in a relatively small space. On the next rainy day, try some of these activities out for size.

Recreational scent work

If your dog has a nose, chances are she'll love scent work. This is the game of finding a hidden odor, which all dogs are naturally good at. Scent work has a number of benefits.

- It is a naturally relaxing activity that requires focus, similar to doing a crossword puzzle. In fact, I often use scent work games to calm dogs when they are stressed and it works like a charm! When dogs are happily seeking out something, they aren't worrying about the construction outside your window or getting overly aroused at the doorbell that just rang. In the most extreme example, one of my clients lived in an embattled part of Ukraine, enduring years of bombing. Her German Shorthaired Pointer's mental health drastically declined during this time. The one activity that could reset her dog's mindset and calm her nerves was this scent game.

- Scent work provides physical activity, but at a low intensity. It is suitable for dogs of all ages and abilities, including elderly dogs and those who cannot participate in more rigorous activities like agility and parkour. Inevitably, after I teach a scent work class, the participants say that their dogs slept better than ever.

- It's easy to teach and involves very little participation on your part. Your dog knows how to find an odor better than you do, so once you've set up the search area, you can mostly sit back and enjoy watching your pup play.

Try this scent work inspired "Find It" game with your dog. If your dog enjoys it, consider trying an in-person or online course, such as Scent Work University (www.scentworku.com) to learn the sport more seriously.

How to teach Find It

1. To prepare, have some stinky treats and also an exercise pen or tether as a stationing area for your dog. (If your dog has a solid "Stay" or "Place" cue, you do not need the pen or tether.)

2. Choose a stationing area where your dog can see what you're doing from several feet away. Put your dog in the ex-pen or on the tether. Alternatively, if your dog can do "Stay" or "Place," cue it.

3. Take one treat and place it on the floor in plain sight. Do not hide it. Your dog should be watching you do this.

4. Return to your dog. Say "Find It" as you unclip the gate or tether. Let her go find the treat.

5. While your dog is searching, avoid staring at the treat, pointing to it, or giving any other clues to help her Find It. If your dog looks up to you for help, just gently encourage her to "Find It" again and then look away. Wait for her to catch a whiff of the treat and find it herself.

6. When she finds the treat, cheer for her! Tell her "All Done."

7. Repeat this game until your dog clearly understands what to do. You can place the treat in different spots each time but continue leaving them in plain sight.

   Don't overplay this game; five reps or so is plenty per session, and then you can play again tomorrow. It's best to keep the game fresh and fun, leaving your dog wanting more.

8. After a few sessions, you can place up to three treats each time. The treats will all be on the floor, at least a few feet from each other. They are still in plain sight.

Your cue of "Find It" will remain the same, to start the game. After she finds the first treat, encourage with "keep going," which will tell her that there are more to find. At the end, tell her "All Done," same as before.

9. Once your dog understands the game, you'll move her stationing area, so she can't see the game area anymore. She doesn't have to go far, just around the corner or behind the couch will be fine. Now you'll repeat the game, with the treat(s) easily noticeable on the floor. Practice in short sessions until she is playing the game like a pro.

Video: https://www.bklnmanners.com/chapter9.html

Leveling up

As you play the game more and more, you'll be able to increase the challenge. You can do this a few ways:

- Place one or two of the treats slightly out of sight, such as behind a piece of furniture. The treats should still be easily accessible to the dog, meaning that she should be able to walk to the treat without having to jump, crawl, climb, or balance on anything to get it.

- Elevate one or two treats. Elevation should be no higher than the dog's chin, so that she can find and eat it without your help. If your dogs are as short as mine, you can use things like books or foot stools (but not coffee tables, chairs, or shelves). Make sure that, if you elevate a treat, it is on a stable, safe surface. Your dog should never be put in danger during this game.

- Expand the search area. You can place a treat or two in farther areas of the room, in an adjacent hallway or other room.

- Add more treats.

Only add difficulty one increment at a time. Remember the goal is for your dog to relax and have fun, not to get frustrated or give up.

Dog parkour

When I mention dog parkour to my clients, I'm often met with a blank stare, furrowed brow, or my favorite, the dog-esque head tilt. "Dog parkour? What's that?" You may be familiar with the human version, which involves daredevil tricks and stunts, such as jumping from the top of one building to another or flipping in the air over a flight of stairs. The dog version, when done properly, is far safer but no less enjoyable. Dog parkour activities focus on objects in an indoor or outdoor environment with which your dog can interact. Something as simple as a stool has numerous parkour applications: jumping over it, running around it, balancing on top of it, crawling under it, or backing up onto it with the rear paws. It can be done anywhere, and for some dogs, parkour is exclusively an indoor activity. If your dog prefers the indoors, then this is a fantastic sport for enrichment and exercise. If your dog loves going outside, then take a field trip to find some cool outdoor obstacles, either natural or manmade.

Parkour is a sport with many activities and creative applications and we could dedicate a whole book to it. (Actually, I already did! My book *Play Your Way to Good Manners* utilizes lots of parkour behaviors. I also created a Udemy online course to learn all the basics of parkour.) You can also see demo videos of numerous exercises at all-dogsparkour.com to get some ideas. Here is one exercise to get you started, which you can use both indoors and out. It's called Two Feet On and it teaches the dog to place her front two paws on any elevated object. The object could be stationary, like a book or a box; or it could move, like a pillow. Check out the accompanying video to see the steps in action.

How to teach Two Feet On

To start Two Feet On, use a very low, stable, and large object. It must not be slippery. A large folded towel is a good starting point. Have a lot of small treats in your pocket or treat pouch. Get started with these steps.

1. Drop a few treats on and around the object. Let your dog interact with it at her own pace. Avoid luring or pressuring your dog to interact with it. As your dog eats the treats, watch her body language. Is she confidently getting on and off the surface? If so, proceed. If not, stay at this level until she's relaxed.

2. Use a treat to encourage your dog to put her front two paws on the object. Hold the treat where her head would need to be. As soon as she has both front paws on the object, mark and reward with the treat. Give another few treats while your dog is in that position. Then release with "OK" to let your dog move off it.

3. Hold the treat still, so you are not teasing your dog with the treat. If you hold the treat to the dog's nose and try to lure her onto the object, this can come across as teasing. (Imagine if someone were about to hand you a $100 bill, but every time you grab for it, they move the bill slightly farther away. It doesn't feel good, does it?)

4. Repeat this sequence until your dog is comfortably putting her front paws on the object to eat the treats.

5. Add a visual and/or verbal cue. I say "Two Paws" and tap the object right before positioning the treat as before. Practice until your dog is a B student.

6. Now you can start to ask for more duration on the object. Once your dog has her paws on it, pause two seconds, then mark and reward. Pause two seconds, mark and reward. Pause two seconds, mark and reward. Then release with "OK." Practice until your dog is a B student.

7. Over time, continue adding one more second before marking and rewarding. Work up to five seconds.

8. Practice this pattern, starting from step 1, with a new object. It should still be low, safe, and stable.

Leveling up

Here are some suggestions to increase the level.

Video: https://www.bklnmanners.com/chapter9.html

- Switch the timing of the reward until after your release. You'll cue "Two Paws" and tap the object, let your dog put her paws on it, count to five, and then release with "Get It." Once your dog is back on ground level, reward with a treat.

- You can cue "Two Paws" from a distance, meaning you will stand a few inches away from the object as you say "Two Paws" and point toward it. With every correct rep, you can stand an inch or two farther for the next repetition. Go slowly; proceed in inches, not feet!

- You can get creative about the objects on which your dog puts her paws. Taller objects, less spacious objects, slanted objects, or moving objects are all options. If there is any chance your dog can slip or fall, always have her in a secure back clip harness and leash; hold the leash above her, so that if she slips or needs support getting off the object, you can provide it.

Indoor agility

While a typical agility course requires a large space, for small dogs you can recreate some of the best parts of agility in your home for rainy day recreational fun. Agility allows dogs to move their bodies, running and jumping and turning, in a focused and controlled way. It's part of my daily indoor play routine with my dogs, as I can set up a few jumps, a child's play tunnel, six weave poles, and a small teeter-totter in our basement, arranged differently every day. For small dogs playing indoors, you can find low-cost equipment from online retailers or get creative and make your own.

For safety, your dog will need cushioning on the takeoff and landing of any obstacle, as well as a non-slip surface for running and turning. This could be:

- A carpet with sufficient padding underneath, covering the whole training floor.

- Interlocking mats, typically used in gym flooring, covering the whole area.

- Yoga mats placed at the takeoff and landing. (This is suitable if you are only doing jumps in a straight line.)

Another important safety consideration relates to dogs under 18 months old. Until a dog's growth plates have fully formed, it's critical to avoid repeated jumping. Keep the jump bars on the ground, not elevated. For dogs over 18 months, it's still important to keep the jump height safe. Use the guidelines set by AKC Agility (or another venue) to find the maximum jump height appropriate for your dog. I highly recommend practicing with jump bars about four inches lower than the competition height, since you are doing this recreationally, not competitively, and you likely have a smaller space and less absorbent cushioning than a typical agility training space. So for my little Margaret, who would jump eight inches in a competition, we practice at four inches in our basement.

We'll focus on a basic form of teaching jumps and tunnels here, but if you'd like to go further, online programs such as One Mind Dogs (https://www.oneminddogs.com) offer comprehensive courses for at-home practice. Watch the accompanying video after reading the steps below.

How to teach agility jumping

1. Set up the jump standards, without the bar. You'll stand to the side of the jump standard.

2. Toss treats back and forth, from one side of the standard to the other. You're essentially asking your dog to go through the jump, without the bar. When you toss a treat, toss it several feet from the jump. This gives your dog a few strides of running on either side of the jump, which provides enough space to take off and land safely. Practice until your dog is comfortable running back and forth.

3. Add the bar, at ground level. Toss treats back and forth, as before. Your dog now has to hop a little over the bar to get the treats. Practice until comfortable.

4. Increase the bar height, setting it to at least four inches below the competition height for your dog. Now your dog is jumping over the bar to get the treat.

5. Do this in very short sessions, just a minute or two in total. If your dog is hesitating to jump or getting tired, stop for the day. Practice over many short sessions.

Video: https://www.bklnmanners.com/chapter9.html

Leveling up

For a more advanced version, try this. Put your dog's "Place" mat several feet from the jump, on the takeoff side. Cue your dog to her "Place" and ask her to stay there. Now you walk toward the jump, while your dog stays on her place. As soon as you reach the jump standard, release with "Get It!" and toss a treat ahead of the dog, toward the landing side of the jump.

As time goes on, you can walk farther and farther from your dog before releasing with "Get It!" This means that you can ultimately set up a second jump in a straight line and walk to the far side of the jumps before releasing.

How to teach tunnel

You can also teach your dog to run through a tunnel by following these steps, using a child's play tunnel. This is also demonstrated in the Indoor Agility video.

1. Fold up the play tunnel and fasten the Velcro loops, so it won't pop open. It will look like a hoop. Hold the tunnel upright and sprinkle treats all around it. The bottom of the loop is at ground level, so your dog may choose to walk through the hoop while looking for the treats. That's great! Sprinkle treats like this until your dog is confidently walking around and through the hoop.

2. Play the treat-tossing game with the hoop, just as you did with jumps. You'll hold the hoop upright, with the bottom of the hoop touching the ground. Toss treats from one side to the other, so your dog is running through the hoop to fetch the treat.

3. Now expand the tunnel. If it's a play tunnel, the design requires you to expand it all the way. This might scare your dog at first, so play the treat sprinkling game here, too. Some of the treats are outside the tunnel, some are right at the mouth of it, and some are inside the tunnel. Let your dog investigate at her own pace.

   Play tunnels are flimsy, so you should gently hold it in place, or roll up a towel on either side of it. This will prevent the tunnel from swaying and scaring your dog.

4. With time, focus more on tossing treats deep into the tunnel until your dog is comfortable walking back and forth through it.

5. Now, set up your dog's place mat at the opening of the tunnel. Cue "Place," so your dog is on her mat, facing the tunnel. Walk to the tunnel exit and crouch down, so you can see your dog through the tunnel. Call your dog with "Come" and cheer for her as she comes to you through the tunnel. Big rewards when she reaches you!

6. Once your dog understands the game, you can switch the cue to "Tunnel."

Leveling up

Here are some suggestions for increasing the challenge. Take your time and have fun with this. These are games you and your dog can play every day for years, so there is no rush to kick up the difficulty quickly!

- As time goes on, put the Place mat farther from the tunnel opening and you can step farther back from the exit. When you then cue "Tunnel," your dog should choose to go through the tunnel, not around it.

- With time, you can cue "Tunnel" from different positions. For instance, you and your dog are walking or jogging together toward the tunnel, and as you cue "Tunnel," you keep moving alongside your dog.

- Once your dog can comfortably do both jumps and tunnels, you can combine them in a line. You'll be on your way to your own agility mini-course!

Ring It, Don't Sing It: Use bells to communicate

As we've already discussed in the House Rules chapter, little dogs are experts at getting your attention. What if your dog could tell you, in English, that he'd like to go potty, play with you, have a meal, or get some cuddles? In fact, he can. Let's teach your dog to push a button near the front door that announces, "Take me outside." Or, if you prefer, you could use a button near the toy box that says "Let's Play" when pushed, as shown in the photo.

Tenrec uses a board with over a hundred Fluent Pet talking buttons on it! (Photo Credit: Alexis Devine)

As far as bells, you have a variety of options:

- Jingle bells that hang from your doorknob
- A "talking" button on the floor, onto which you record your voice
- A "smart" button that, when pushed, communicates wirelessly to a receiver that rings throughout your home, like a doorbell (Fluent Pet, see Resources)

Once you've gotten a bell or button, you're ready to start training. You'll also need some sticky notes and a bit of patience. The first few steps of training do not involve the button or bell, but during this time, you should leave it out on the floor. Your dog can investigate this funny new object at his own pace and get comfortable with its presence before we incorporate it into the training.

How to teach Pushing a Button

These steps teach the dog to hit a button or bells using a paw target. Both pushbuttons and jingle bells can be used this way, although the steps here focus on pushbuttons. Watch the video to see the steps in action.

1. Hold a sticky note to the floor, with a treat hidden behind it.

2. Your dog may try to eat the note or push it away with his nose. Ignore that.

3. The moment your dog moves his paw toward the note, mark "Yes" and reward with the treat behind the note. If your dog slaps the note with his paw, great! Skip to step 6. Your dog doesn't have to fully touch the note at first; any paw movement toward the note earns him a treat.

4. With more repetitions, your dog will start to offer an extended paw near the note, which always earns a "Yes" and treat. This is when you can start **shaping** the behavior, meaning, you mark and reward him only for paw extensions that get closer and closer to the note.

5. Continue shaping this until your dog is squarely hitting the note with his paw to get the treat. Make sure he is a solid B student before proceeding.

6. Now, remove the treat from behind the note. You are holding the note in the same position as before, close to the ground, but now there is no treat behind it. Your dog will hit the note, and you will still mark "Yes," but then reward from a treat in your pocket or treat pouch. Practice until he is a B student.

7. Add a verbal cue, "Hit It," at this point. You will say "Hit It," then present the note, let him hit it, mark "Yes," and reward with a treat from your pocket. Practice until he is a B student.

8. Your dog will ultimately need to hit the button hard enough to make it go off. If your dog is touching the note too delicately, then toss the reward treat a few feet away from him. This causes him to run away to get the treat. As he runs back to you, cue the next "Hit It" while he has momentum from running.

9. Now put the button in your hand and attach the sticky note on top of the button. The button should not have the sound turned on yet. Your hand should be as close to the floor as possible. Cue "Hit It," wait for him to hit it, then mark "Yes" and give a big reward. For some dogs, this is a startling sensation and noise, so make it fun!

10. Once your dog is a solid B student at hitting the button in your hand, then put the button on the floor and practice "Hit It."

11. With each successful repetition, peel a thin strip of the sticky note away. It should take about ten reps, maybe more, to slowly peel the sticky note off. Now your dog has learned to hit the button, not just the note.

12. Bring the button to the spot where it will permanently live. See below for suggestions. Practice "Hit It" there.

13. Once your dog is loving this game, turn on the sound of your button. If it has a volume control, keep the volume as low as possible at first and with subsequent reps, gradually turn up the volume one bar at a time. Always make sure your dog is a B student over several repetitions before proceeding to any future step.

14. Now you're ready to use it in real life. When your dog is showing that he wants something—let's say, to go potty outside—you will cue "Hit It," give a treat (yes, still give a treat at this stage) and then immediately bring him outside.

   Take note: If you normally have to put a leash or harness on your dog, it needs to be done quickly and without drama, so the reward of going outside happens with a few seconds of hitting the button. Your dog needs to understand that hitting the button gets him a treat and outside time, not the "punishment" of being chased around the house to get the harness on. He will never ring it on his own if he finds the consequence unpleasant. If you can't put your dog's equipment on quickly, I recommend leaving the collar or harness on your dog for now, as long as he is supervised.

15. Continue to practice this sequence right before all potty breaks, but not for long walks (unless you want him to ask for those by hitting the button, too). The sequence is to cue "Hit It," mark and reward, leash up quickly, and go outside. Practice until your dog is a B student over numerous sessions. We want this part to be well practiced before proceeding.

16. Now you can finally remove the treat reward. The sequence is cue "Hit It," leash up quickly, and go outside.

17. If your dog is not hitting the button on his own for potty breaks after a few weeks, add this step. When he needs to go potty, cue "Hit It" several feet before you reach the door. Your dog has to walk himself to the door and hit the button. This starts giving him the idea that he can ring the button without you being right there at the door next to him.

Video: https://www.
bklnmanners.com/
chapter9.html

18. Continue at this level until your dog has a "light-bulb moment," where he realizes that he can ring to go outside.

For small dogs, I recommend buttons placed on the floor rather than the wall. They need as much force as possible to hit the button hard enough to ring it. Once you have decided on placement, don't relocate or remove the button. Since the goal is to let your dog freely communicate with you, you have to keep the button accessible at all times, in its original location. Furthermore, once we have given them a communication tool like this, it will stay there for life. Removing an individual's ability to communicate would be stressful and unfair.

How to teach Ringing Jingle Bells

Does your dog prefer to use his nose instead of his paw? If your dog is more 'nosey' than 'pawsy,' use jingle bells that hang from a doorknob. This is primarily used for potty needs, but you can teach your dog to jingle the bells to communicate other needs, as well.

1. Rub a stinky treat or piece of meat or cheese on the bell, to make it tempting to sniff. Get comfy on the floor with your dog and have treats ready in your pocket or treat pouch.

2. Hold the bell firmly in your hand. Make sure it won't jingle or swing near your dog, as this can be scary at first.

3. Present the bell in your hand at your dog's nose level. The moment your dog moves his nose toward the bell, mark "Yes" and reward with a treat. If your dog touches the bell with his nose, great! Skip to step 6. Your dog doesn't have to fully touch the bell at first; any nose movement toward the bell earns him a treat.

4. With more reps, your dog will start to offer more intentional nose stretches near the bell, which always earns a "Yes" and treat. This is when you can start shaping the behavior, meaning, you mark and reward him only for nose extensions that get closer and closer to the bell.

5. Continue shaping this until your dog is squarely hitting the bell with his nose to get the treat. Make sure he is a solid B student before proceeding.

6. Now, loosen your grip on the bell, holding the strap an inch above the bell, rather than the bell itself. This means the bell will make a little noise when touched. Your dog will hit the bell, and you will mark "Yes" and reward. Practice until he is a B student.

7. Add a verbal cue, "Target" at this point. So you will say "Target," then present the bell, let him touch the bell, mark "Yes," and reward with a treat. Practice until he is a B student.

8. Hold the bell (or string of bells) from the top of the strap, letting the bell dangle. Practice "Target" like this, until he is a B student.

9. Loop the strap on your doorknob and practice "Target." Choose the door that the dog generally uses to go out to potty. Practice until a B student.

   You may need to hold the strap a few inches away from the door at first, so the bell dangles as in the previous step. Eventually, though, your dog should be comfortable targeting the bell even as it lies against the door.

10. Now you're ready to use it in real life. When your dog is showing that he wants to go potty outside, you will cue "Target," give a treat (yes, still give a treat at this stage) and then immediately bring him outside.

    If you normally have to put a leash or harness on your dog, it needs to be done quickly and without drama. If you can't put your dog's equipment on quickly, I recommend leaving the collar or harness on your dog for now, as long as he is supervised.

11. Continue this sequence right before all potty breaks. The sequence is to cue "Target," mark and reward, leash up quickly, and go outside. Practice until your dog is a B student over numerous sessions.

12. Now you can finally remove the treat reward. The sequence is to cue "Target," leash up quickly, and go outside.

    Your dog may already be hitting the bells himself now, in which case you can cheer and hustle to the door!

13. If your dog is not hitting the bell on his own for potty breaks after a few weeks, add this step. When he needs to go potty, cue "Target" several feet before you reach the door. Your dog has to walk himself to the door and hit the bell. This starts giving him the idea that he can ring the bell without you being right there at the door next to him.

14. Continue at this level until your dog has a "lightbulb moment," where he realizes that he can ring the bell to go outside.

Concept training

If your little dog is more of a brainiac than an athlete, don't worry. There are a number of games you can play with your dog to burn tons of mental energy. **Concept training** is an umbrella term referring to doggie brain games, no athletic ability required. At the advanced levels, dogs can learn to discriminate among different objects, colors, and shapes. Some dogs can even learn to count numbers on a board or understand relative terms like choosing the smaller of two objects. Yes, they are that smart! Watching dogs participate in concept learning gives you a deep appreciation of how intelligent and enthusiastic our furry companions are.

This game teaches the names of different items. Once your dog knows the names of items, she can search for them, fetch them, or choose one particular object among others. But, first things first; here are the steps to teach object names and discrimination.

Your dog will need to know a nose target, paw target, or bring it (as in, fetch the item) cue. If your dog doesn't know any of these, start here:

Video: https://www.bklnmanners.com/chapter9.html

- Nose target: teaching the dog to touch her nose to an object. Steps for this are outlined in the previous section, Ring It, Don't Sing It. In the example video, it is a hand.

- Paw target: teaching the dog to touch her paw to an object, as in Ring It, Don't Sing It. In the example video, it is a button.

How to teach object names

The accompanying video uses a "Bring It" cue, but a nose or paw target will be an easier starting point for concept training newbies.

1. Choose an item. It can be a particular toy, or a household object. Your dog shouldn't be scared of this item or have a past negative history with it. Let's say it's a banana stuffed toy.

2. Present the item in your hand and say its name, "Banana."

3. Then immediately cue your dog to physically interact with the banana toy. So the sequence is: For a nose target: present banana—say "Banana"—say "Target." For a paw target: present banana—say "Banana"—say "Hit It." For a bring it/fetch: present banana—say "Banana"—say "Bring it."

4. The moment your dog touches the banana toy, mark and reward. Repeat this sequence until your dog is a B student. Make sure your dog doesn't jump the gun. She shouldn't touch the toy until you cue "Target" or a similar cue. If she tries to touch it before you say "Target," simply remove the toy, take a deep breath, and start over.

5. Have the item in different positions. Sometimes you present it in your hand, sometimes it's on the floor in front of you, to your left, and to your right. Make sure your dog is a B student in these scenarios, able to touch or pick up the banana even when it's not in your hand or not directly in front of you.

6. Avoid using your hand, head, eyes, or body to point out the banana. Your dog should be able to find the banana without you giving body language tips. (Imagine if you lost the banana and then cued your dog to "Find It." If your dog relied on your body language for information, she wouldn't be able to problem-solve it herself.)

7. Have the item on the floor near you, with a few other items around it. The banana should be the most prominent item in front of the dog. Cue "Banana, Target" as before. If your dog chooses the banana and not the other items, mark and reward!

8. As time goes on, you can bring the other items next to the banana, and eventually, even in front of it. When your dog chooses the banana, mark and reward.

9. You can repeat this sequence with other object names as well. Start from the first step for every new object you introduce.

Video: https://www.bklnmanners.com/chapter9.html

When teaching a sport, playing a game, or practicing your dog's manners, remember that you and your dog are teammates. Overall, you should both be having fun learning together. Practice these activities in small doses to keep your dog wanting more and be kind to both your dog and yourself as you build skills and learn together.

Conclusion

This book may have come to a close, but the training journey with your dog never really ends. That's the best part! As you and your little sidekick overcome obstacles and learn new skills, don't forget to enjoy the ride. With time, you may find that the best outcome of all your training isn't a perfect recall or an A+ leash walk past other dogs. Rather, it's the relationship that you have fostered with your dog over the weeks, months, and years of learning and training together. Being small dog savvy, you can now appreciate your little one for who she is, and you'll know how to meet her needs when she's asking for help. She can look to you for security and guidance, fully trusting that you've got her back. Isn't that what teamwork is all about?

Cited Works

"Aggression toward owners is always problematic, but when is it pathologic?" (2019, April 2). The College of Veterinary Medicine at Michigan State University. https://cvm.msu.edu/vetschool-tails/aggression-toward-owners-is-always-problematic-but-when-is-it-pathologic

Bender, A., & Strong, E. (2019). *Canine enrichment for the real world: making it a part of your dog's daily life*. Dogwise Publishing.

Boros, M., Magyari, L., Boglárka Morvai, Raúl Hernández-Pérez, Dror, S., & Attila Andics. (2024). "Neural evidence for referential understanding of object words in dogs." *Current Biology*. https://www.cell.com/current-biology/fulltext/S0960-9822(24)00171-4

Englund, M. D., & Cronin, K. A. (2023). "Choice, control, and animal welfare: definitions and essential inquiries to advance animal welfare science." *Frontiers in Veterinary Science*, 10. https://doi.org/10.3389/fvets.2023.1250251

Fugazza, C., Moesta, A., Pogány, Á., & Miklósi, Á. (2018). "Presence and lasting effect of social referencing in dog puppies." *Animal Behaviour*, 141, 67–75. https://doi.org/10.1016/j.anbehav.2018.05.007

Guy, N. C., Luescher, U. A., Dohoo, S. E., Spangler, E., Miller, J. B., Dohoo, I. R., & Bate, L. A. (2001). Demographic and aggressive characteristics of dogs in a general veterinary caseload. *Applied Animal Behaviour Science*, 74(1), 15–28. https://doi.org/10.1016/s0168-1591(01)00153-8

Hargrave, C. (2017). Canine stress in a nutshell— why does it occur, how can it be recognised, and what can be done to alleviate it? *The Veterinary Nurse*, 8(3), 140–147. https://doi.org/10.12968/vetn.2017.8.3.140

Huang, M., Li, D., Cheng, X., Pei, Q., Xie, Z., Gu, H., Zhang, X., Chen, Z., Liu, A., Wang, Y., Sun, F., Li, Y., Zhang, J., He, M., Xie, Y., Zhang, F., Qi, X., Shang, C., & Cao, P. (2021). The tectonigral pathway regulates appetitive locomotion in predatory hunting in mice. Nature Communications, 12(1). https://doi.org/10.1038/s41467-021-24696-3

Jensen, G. D. (1963). Preference for bar pressing over "freeloading" as a function of number of rewarded presses.. Journal of Experimental Psychology, 65(5), 451–454. https://doi.org/10.1037/h0049174

Juster, R.-P., McEwen, B. S., & Lupien, S. J. (2010). Allostatic load biomarkers of chronic stress and impact on health and cognition. Neuroscience & Biobehavioral Reviews, 35(1), 2–16. https://doi.org/10.1016/j.neubiorev.2009.10.002

Kiyokawa, Y., Kikusui, T., Takeuchi, Y., & Mori, Y. (2004). Partner's stress status influences social buffering effects in rats. Behavioral neuroscience, 118(4), 798–804. https://doi.org/10.1037/0735-7044.118.4.798

Kurtycz, L. (2015). Choice and control for animals in captivity - The British Psychological Society. www.bps.org.uk. https://www.bps.org.uk/psychologist/choice-and-control-animals-captivity

Landsberg, G. (2018). Behavior Problems in Dogs - Dog Owners. Merck Veterinary Manual. https://www.merckvetmanual.com/dog-owners/behavior-of-dogs/behavior-problems-in-dogs

Martin, K., & Martin, D. (n.d.). Resource Guarding in Dogs: A Fear Free Approach. Fear Free Pets. Retrieved March 12, 2024, from https://fearfreepets.com/courses/resource-guarding-in-dogs

McGowan, R. T. S., Bolte, C., Barnett, H. R., Perez-Camargo, G., & Martin, F. (2018). Can you spare 15 min? The measurable positive impact of a 15-min petting session on shelter dog well-being. Applied Animal Behaviour Science, 203, 42–54. https://doi.org/10.1016/j.applanim.2018.02.011

Merola, I., Prato-Previde, E., & Marshall-Pescini, S. (2012). Dogs' Social Referencing towards Owners and Strangers. PLoS ONE, 7(10), e47653. https://doi.org/10.1371/journal.pone.0047653

Milgram, N. W., Head, E., Zicker, S. C., Ikeda-Douglas, C. J., Murphey, H., Muggenburg, B., Siwak, C., Tapp, D., & Cotman, C. W. (2005). Learning ability in aged beagle dogs is preserved by behavioral enrichment and dietary fortification: a two-year longitudinal study. Neurobiology of Aging, 26(1), 77–90. https://doi.org/10.1016/j.neurobiolaging.2004.02.014

Mills, D. S., Demontigny-Bédard, I., Gruen, M., Klinck, M. P., McPeake, K. J., Barcelos, A. M., Hewison, L., Van Haevermaet, H., Denenberg, S., Hauser, H., Koch, C.,

Ballantyne, K., Wilson, C., Mathkari, C. V., Pounder, J., Garcia, E., Darder, P., Fatjó, J., & Levine, E. (2020). Pain and Problem Behavior in Cats and Dogs. Animals, 10(2), 318. https://doi.org/10.3390/ani10020318

Mills, D. S., Maya Braem Dube, & Zulch, H. (2013). Stress and pheromonatherapy in small animal clinical behaviour. Wiley-Blackwell.

Owen, M. A., Swaisgood, R. R., Czekala, N. M., & Lindburg, D. G. (2005). Enclosure choice and well-being in giant pandas: is it all about control? Zoo Biology, 24(5), 475–481. https://doi.org/10.1002/zoo.20064

Ross, S. R. (2006). Issues of choice and control in the behaviour of a pair of captive polar bears (Ursus maritimus). Behavioural Processes, 73(1), 117–120. https://doi.org/10.1016/j.beproc.2006.04.003

Schilder, M. B. H., & van der Borg, J. A. M. (2004). Training dogs with help of the shock collar: Short and long term behavioural effects. *Applied Animal Behaviour Science*, Vol. 85, No. 3-4, pp. 319–334.

Shryock, J. (2021, November 24). Is it a kiss or a dismiss?. Aggressive Dog. https://aggressivedog.com/2021/11/23/is-it-a-kiss-or-a-dismiss/

Singh, D. (1970). Preference for bar pressing to obtain reward over freeloading in rats and children. Journal of Comparative and Physiological Psychology, 73(2), 320–327. https://doi.org/10.1037/h0030222

Spaulding, K. (2022). *The Stress Factor in Dogs*. Dogwise Publishing.

Udell, M. A. R., Ewald, M., Dorey, N. R., & Wynne, C. D. L. (2014). Exploring breed differences in dogs (Canis familiaris): does exaggeration or inhibition of predatory response predict performance on human-guided tasks? Animal Behaviour, 89, 99–105. https://doi.org/10.1016/j.anbehav.2013.12.012

Resources & Recommended Reading

Books

A Dog's Fabulous Sense of Smell, Anne Lill Kvam, 2022. Clear step-by-step instructions for training your dog to find everything from hidden treats to lost keys.

Behavior Adjustment Training 2.0: New Practical Techniques for Fear, Frustration, and Aggression in Dogs, Grisha Stewart, 2016. A book with protocols for reducing reactivity, aggression, frustration, and fear.

Brain Games for Your Dog, Kyla Denault, 2021. 50+ enriching games you can play with your dog, which will engage their senses, cater to their natural instincts, hone their problem-solving abilities and give them lots of confidence all the while having lots of fun!

Canine Enrichment for the Real World, Allie Bender and Emily Strong, 2019. A deep dive into enrichment and how to use it to directly improve your dog's quality of life.

Canine Enrichment for the Real World Workbook, Allie Bender and Emily Strong, 2022. A companion workbook with blank worksheets to ensure your dog's needs are being met which reduces undesirable behaviors.

Cooperative Care: Seven Steps to Stress-Free Husbandry, Deb Jones, 2018. A guide for building your dog's confidence with husbandry procedures.

Dog Grooming: An Owner's Handbook, Agnes Murphy 2024. Learn the basics of grooming your dog.

Doggie Language: A Dog Lover's Guide to Understanding Your Best Friend, Lili Chin, 2020. This easy-to-digest picture book explains how to understand dog body language.

Gentle Hands Off Dog Training, Sarah Whitehead, 2011. Step-by-step instructions for training basic behaviors and cues.

On Talking Terms with Dogs: Calming Signals, Turid Rugaas, 2005. This book will show you how to recognize the body language that dogs use to communicate with each other and with us.

Play Your Way to Good Manners, Kate Natio, 2019. A unique approach to your dog's manners training as a collection of cool tricks, exciting sports moves, and interactive games.

Plenty in Life Is Free: Reflections on Dogs, Training and Finding Grace, Kathy Sdao, 2012 .This book will help you rethink your relationship with your dog and what it means to have a partnership rather than fight for control.

Rocket Recall: Unleash Your Dog's Desire to Return to You through Motivation-Based Training, Second Edition, Simone Mueller, 2023. A step-by-step guide to building a joyful and reliable recall with your dog.

Separation Anxiety in Dogs: Next Generation Treatment Protocols and Practice, Malena DeMartini-Price, 2020. New and improved book filled with data-driven advice about how to treat separation anxiety.

The Stress Factor in Dogs: Unlocking Resiliency and Enhancing Well-Being, Kristina Spaulding, 2022. A deep dive into the impact stress has on dogs, and how understanding that can improve your dog's quality of life.

Veterinary Cooperative Care: Enhancing Animal Health Through Collaboration with Veterinarians, Pet Owners, and Animal Trainers, Pat Miller and Dr. Leslie Sinn, 2023. A compilation of experts in the training and veterinary field explaining how to make vet visits and care less stressful.

Websites

Fear Free website for pet guardians: fearfreehappyhomes.com

Fluent Pet: fluent.pet

The Muzzle Up Project: muzzleupproject.com

One Mind Dogs: oneminddogs.com

Scent Work University: scentworku.com

Index

About the Author

Kate Naito, CDBC, CPDT-KA, FFCP, ADP-CI, MS is the owner of High Ten Dog Training in Stamford, CT. She's the author of two previous books, *BKLN Manners*™ and *Play Your Way to Good Manners*, the latter of which won the DWAA Training and Sports book award in 2019.

Kate is certified as a dog behavior consultant through IAABC, dog trainer through CCPDT, Fear Free® professional trainer, and All Dogs Parkour instructor. Kate's blog, bklnmanners.com, includes numerous articles, videos, and other resources related to canine manners and behavior.

Did you enjoy this book?

WRITE A REVIEW!

REVIEWS HELP OTHER READERS DECIDE ON THEIR NEXT BOOK! GO TO WWW.DOGWISE.COM AND SELECT A STAR RATING (1-5) THEN LEAVE SOME COMMENTS DESCRIBING WHAT YOU ENJOYED OR SOMETHING YOU LEARNED WHILE READING THIS BOOK!

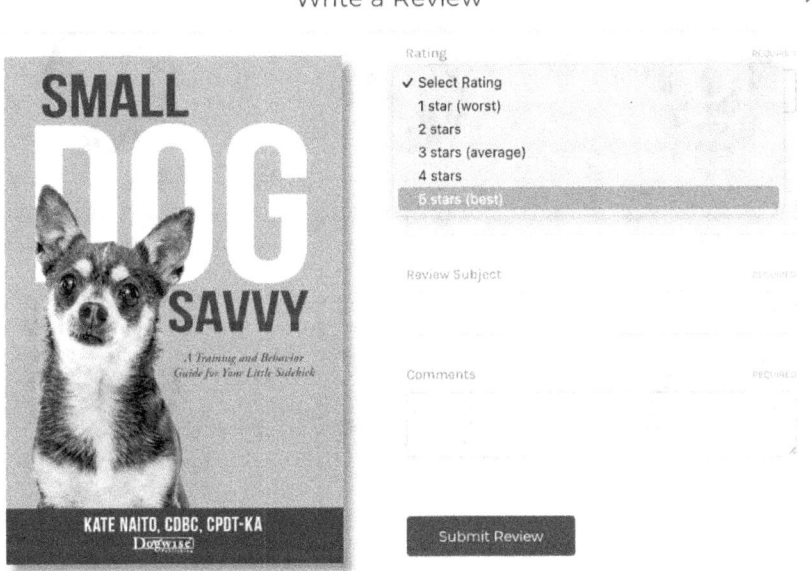

Connect with us

FOLLOW, LIKE, AND TAG US ON SOCIAL MEDIA TO STAY CONNECTED

SCAN THE QR CODES BELOW WITH YOUR PHONE'S CAMERA APP TO GO DIRECTLY TO OUR SOCIAL MEDIA PROFILES

instagram
@dogwise.books

facebook
/dogwise

youtube
@dogwiseclips

www.ingramcontent.com/pod-product-compliance
Lightning Source LLC
Chambersburg PA
CBHW081207280526
45787CB00006B/2366